Aileen Day

the JOY of SEX

Aileen Day

the

JOY of

SCEHX

the casual hook up to
understanding Customer,
Employee, and Human
eXperience

First published in 2025 by Dean Publishing
PO Box 119
Mt. Macedon, Victoria, 3441
Australia
deanpublishing.com

**DEAN
PUBLISHING**

Cataloguing-in-Publication Data
National Library of Australia
Title: The Joy of CEHX
ISBN: 978-0-6487580-9-9
Category: Business/customer experience

The views and opinions expressed in this book are those of the author and do not necessarily reflect the official policy or position of any other agency, publisher, organisation, employer, or company. Assumptions made in the analysis are not reflective of the position of any entity other than the author(s) — and, these views are always subject to change, revision, and rethinking at any time.

The author, publisher or organisations are not to be held responsible for misuse, reuse, recycled and cited and/or uncited copies of content within this book by others.

The ideas within this book are inspired ideas and observations by the author; ideas expressed and are not intended to replace any professional advice or offer business or career advice. The reader is advised to always seek professional advice according to their specific needs in this ever-changing world.

The stories and ideas in this book stem from the author's personal experiences and are created from memory. Although some details in this book are based on the author's life experiences and unique worldview, some names and identifying details of others have been changed to protect the privacy of individuals.

The landscape of business and customer/human experience is continual and always dynamic, therefore information within this book should be treated as such. Personal decisions or business decisions are the responsibility of each individual and should not be taken on the basis of their own situation.

Typesetting: Working Type Books
Illustrations: NailZ Van Diggele
Author photo: Nik Epifanidis

AILEEN DAY

USE AILEEN DAY AS A GUEST SPEAKER FOR YOUR NEXT CONFERENCE OR SEMINAR

AILEEN DAY ADVISORY

Telephone: +61 1800 (VALUED) 825 833
Email: aileen@aileenday.com.au
Website: aileenday.com.au

Aileen (pronounced Aye-leen) works with organisations and event organisers as Australia's premium speaker, customer experience advisor, mentor, and therapist, helping audiences learn how to deliver experiences worthy of their customers' trust and loyalty.

A UNIQUE PERSPECTIVE

Aileen is known for her rawness, her candid points of view, and her unique business background. Having worked in some of Australia's largest trusted brands, she knows what it takes to be the *best* in show.

Aileen also uses her unique toolkit of public relations, marketing, communications, and customer and employee experience and therapeutic skills to create a truly engaging perspective on what it means to be in business among all of the hype, challenges, and expectations. She helps business owners, leaders, and entrepreneurs understand how to alleviate the scary bits and amplify the best bits.

Whether for business advisory or as a fresh face ready to speak and create momentum at your next event, engaging Aileen is how, together, we transform from the old rules of doing business into the new way of creating purposefully designed futures. Now, how CEHX-y is that?

STOP! DON'T BUY
THIS BOOK YET

Before you buy this book, read this section. As the author, I'm quite adamant that I only want this book in the hands of humans who want to do the work. I'm guessing your next thought is, *Well, it depends on what 'the work' entails.* If I was close, then let me tell you a little about the work and, for that matter, me, the teacher and guide to the joy of CEHX (pronounced se-hx).

The work revolves around deeply understanding your customers and – if you have them – your employees. It's about realising we're in a business landscape where we're more likely to fail than succeed, but with the right teacher, you can indeed be on the flip side of those horrendous statistics.

However, I, your teacher, am not for everyone. I'm candid; I'm assertive; I challenge people to stretch themselves and push through their limiting beliefs. I like humans who do what they set out to do, who do life with integrity in their soul and a commitment to leaving a positive legacy for the people they care about. If that's you, we're absolutely made for each other, and the work in this book is by no means beyond your capabilities. In case you're still unsure, just know I'm in your corner and here to step you through what it takes to go from an everyday business to a trusted and value-driven brand where, in time, the advocates you create on this journey do the marketing and sales for you.

In saying that, know that this *is not* a marketing book. There are many amazing marketing books and resources available for businesses of every size in every market. However, the reality is that before you concern yourself with marketing, you must firstly concern yourself with the experience you deliver to your customers and your employees. This is the common error made in businesses all over the world. We're led to believe that just a few more leads will save us, just a few more products sold will keep us afloat, but that type of thinking is the beginning of our ultimate undoing. I promise you, unless you've strategically understood who your customer is, what they value as human beings, and how your business can become an imperative part of their lives, leading you to transform from a business to a trusted and value-driven brand, your marketing efforts will fall by the wayside. You'll end up overpromising and underdelivering, unaware of your customers' needs, expectations, jobs to be done, and what they personally value from a brand. *The Joy of CEHX* is the education every leader, business owner, and entrepreneur must undergo and implement to ensure the opposite occurs.

I also wrote this book to teach you how to take back time for yourself, not only by creating a value-driven brand, but also by taking these lessons and applying them to obtain a value-driven life.

The Joy of CEHX is strategic. It's tactical. It's candid. It's the education every leader, business owner, and entrepreneur needs but isn't getting. Until now. I'm here to provide those who want to feel the joy of CEHX with the pragmatic steps to get started. CEHX is more than just how we serve, how we market, and how we support customers and employees. It's also about how we become a destination brand and employer. The one thing I truly believe so many organisations have the opportunity to amplify is their human experience. At the end of the day, it's what sets us apart.

In writing this book, I've made it intuitive, relevant, industry and business size agnostic (because the joy of CEHX is for everyone, at any stage of business, in every industry and market) and above all, engagingly tactile. By completing the activities strategically placed throughout, with me by your side, you have the capacity to deliver, step by step, the joy of CEHX.

I've kept this book as true to my personality as I can because, to me, authenticity matters. That means I've added annotations, some important information, and some witty banter (because seriously, not another boring fucking business book, please). I recognise that many of you will still be looking for short cuts, so in each chapter I've added TL;CBF (too long; can't be fucked) sections because let's just be honest with ourselves and tell it how it is.

As a clinical psychotherapist, my first piece of advice is, if we're going to do this, at the very least we must be honest with ourselves. Throughout this book, we'll frequently be holding a mirror up to our challenges and opportunities, so we best acknowledge our vulnerabilities now.

Regarding the activities, I encourage you to write within the pages of this book, both within the spaces provided and outside of them. Get messy with it. I don't want to see any pristine versions of this book post achieving great CEHX. Instead, I want to receive pictures of cliff notes, dog ears, completed activities, pages thumbed – books dripping with passion.

If you're still reading, I reckon the decision has been made. Let's do this. Let's journey together. Let's take a deep breath and put our best foot forward. *The Joy of CEHX* awaits.

CONTENTS

PART ONE

GREAT CEHX BEGINS WITH THE BASICS

CHAPTER 1:
AN INTRODUCTION
TO CEHX

IT ALL BEGAN IN A BIG GREEN SHED

Years ago, in a big green shed in the south-eastern suburbs of Melbourne, Australia, a young woman by the name of Aileen (then Portarianos) came to be employed by one of Australia's largest retailers, known as Bunnings Warehouse. Now Aileen, new to the concept of hardware, lifestyle products, and building materials, was placed in charge of the thingamabobs and whatchamacallits – otherwise known as the special orders desk.

The special orders desk was a magical place where, on a daily basis, I had the opportunity to change the lives of regular humans and turn them into DIY superheroes. How did I do this? By deciphering their individual thingamabobs and working my fingers to the bone, not sleeping or eating until I discovered, for example, that a particular thingamabob was actually the brush off a 20-year-old Metabo drill the owner now needed to replace after deciding to pull his drill apart for the fun of it.

Every day, the thingamabobs and whatchamacallits piled in – some weird, some wonderful, none available off the shelf. That was the point. They came to my desk with a last lingering look of hope in their eyes after being disappointed over and over again, as no retailer stocked or sold their specific whatchamacallit. So, I would find it for them. Often, I would find it at a competitor, and I would purchase it on a customer's behalf. Sometimes I would receive a box of spare parts via courier, and the supplier would dare me to search through the box for the same-looking thingamabob, as they felt they had better things to do. My persistence likely either annoyed or amused, maybe even bemused them, as I would accept their dare and start digging for my prize.

Through these experiences, however, I learnt a great many things. I came to learn more about the joy of customer service. I came to learn more about systems. I came to learn more about humans. I learnt not only about my fellow employees who wavered between thinking I was either crazy or delusional but also about those from other businesses, whom I naively assumed were there to help me. However, I soon realised that not everyone loved their job as much as I did.

Over time, I started to get my head around customer service. I loved it. I was good at it, great even. A short time after I joined the company, Bunnings implemented what was known as customer service pins, a reward for receiving highly commendable feedback from customers. First, we received bronze pins. Once we had five bronze pins, we could hand them in for a silver. Once we had five silver pins, we could hand them in for a gold. So we needed 25 pieces of glowing feedback to receive one gold pin.

I was the first alongside my favourite Bunnings plumber George (may he rest in peace) to receive a gold pin, and we were both asked to write a statement explaining why we were the recipients of so much glowing feedback. I took great offence to the request and proceeded to lose my shit (not highly commendable behaviour, I know). Had they not read those 25 pieces of feedback? Why did we have to justify our gold pins to the boffins in head office? George especially shouldn't have had to justify his worthiness. He was a God among green aprons and red polos.

Seeing how offended I was – and I'm *not* easy to offend – George quietly said to me, "Aileen, let us have the last laugh. The joke's on them." I didn't really get it, but he was so wise. Who was I to question the great man? He calmly sat down and wrote a statement explaining why he had received so much glowing feedback, without a care or a stroke of ego in sight. I took a deep breath and followed his lead. We made our statements, handed them to our operations manager, and said not a word. The next day, we were presented with our gold pins in front of the team without any further discussion.

A MIND-BLOWING REALISATION

I knew I was good at customer service. In fact, I was one of the best ... in the company. So imagine my surprise when my manager Tracey said, "Aileen, I need you to leave special orders." Okay, I did that for dramatic effect. In truth, I was vying for a position in leadership. However, to move up in the company, I needed to be in a department with a bit more complexity past thingamabobs and whatchamacallits. So I was transferred to the paint department. I had never painted in my life. I had never used silicones. Maybe I sanded something for my dad once (he probably yelled at me for doing it wrong). I was going in green. I soon realised the inside joke was "which green" after learning there were over 300 recognised shades of green, and likely way more nowadays.

My teachers, Matt and Leisha, taught me everything they possibly could about painting and decorating. I was a thirsty learner, and I loved the experience, but I soon realised there was a little bit more going on than just customer service in the paint department. See, in comparison to the quite transactional special orders desk, the paint department was where relationships were built and, in turn, could crumble. If I had a dollar for every marital argument resulting in one half being walked out on or verbally abused at the colour selection wall, I'd be making a motza!

> What I learnt, apart from how to colour match by eye (the equivalent in difficulty of taking an order for 15 without writing it down and not fucking it up) was, at the paint desk, we didn't just deliver a service – we created an experience.

It was like coming in for dinner and a show, except it was a Bunnings snag and a paint mixer, and of course my shining per-

LAUGH → sonality. Customers loved it so much (except when they
HERE   had to wait), but even that could be made entertaining.

We built relationships. We learnt about customers' projects. We learnt about the human element of what they wanted to achieve.

We learnt about emotions and colour psychology. ←———

A favourite topic of mine even 20 years later

We learnt why customers wanted shiny walls when we suggested a more matte look. We learnt about what they'd seen on television and how they were now inspired to do it themselves (hopefully not inspired by Dexter and his need for easy-to-clean surfaces). We learnt about new technology in the industry that would help us deliver a better service to our customers, especially those in the painting and decorating trade who kept coming back (even though trade centres gave them better prices on paints and accessories). I learnt that we were indeed not just in the game of customer service but also customer loyalty. For a 21-year-old, that realisation was some mind-blowing shit!

THE BEST AND WORST OF HUMANITY ... A LOT OF THE WORST!

Let's fast forward a couple of years. I was now a fully-fledged department manager, and, as luck would have it (not really luck), my first managerial appointment was in the same store, in the same paint department where I'd previously been a team member. Ever become the boss of the people whom you used to serve alongside? The people who got you where you are today? Well, if you have, you'd know I was in for a fun uphill ride. For those who haven't experienced this, I suggest only doing it if you're interested in a long period of self-development and learning how to set new boundaries, over and over and over again. A good analogy is ... imagine if your children wake up one day and now they're the parents and you're the child. It's a confusing experience for everyone involved and one that confounded me regularly. But hey, what doesn't kill you, right? So now I was in charge. I was in charge of customer service. I was in charge of the experience my team delivered. I was in charge of their employee experience. As their new leader and an old friend, their welfare was my highest concern. That came with an even higher set of expectations from many of them. I had a lot to live up to.

After my team's welfare came the welfare of our customers. I took a lot of shit from some of them. One near took my head off when she threw a 1-litre can of paint at my head, missing me by millimetres, the paint can exploding on impact against the tinting machines (a horrendous mess to clean up). What triggered such an over-the-top reaction? She asked for 'heritage red', so I made her heritage red, but she didn't like heritage red. I insisted that she take the can, and I placed it in her trolley. She proceeded to pick it up and throw it at the back of my head as I was walking back to the paint desk. You might be thinking, *Wow, that's some crazy shit, but so what?* Well, *so what* is that, over the years, I got to observe, bear witness to, and personally experience the absolute worst and the best of humanity. I got to see customers crying, recalling the fact that they were picking colours for their new baby's room after 12 rounds of IVF, at one time being on the edge of suicide and entertaining thoughts of divorce. I got to see a customer have an epileptic seizure in the indoor plants section, then abuse the team the next day due to her ambulance bill, claiming the company was liable for her health issues.

Now, at the time, I was adamant these people were another level of special or opportunistic, but as I grew older and wiser, I learnt that this is humanity. It has both good free-range eggs and bad should-stay-caged-eggs, and everybody has problems those around them don't know about. When life happens, often we look outside of our world to seek blame. A senior citizen caught stealing in the tool shop told me he had to steal because he had no job, no income, and it was big retailers' fault for squeezing out small businesses. I learnt that humanity does a lot of justifying. Nonetheless, this was where I started to grasp the concept of a human experience or HX, as I like to call it these days.

THE ROLE THAT CHANGED EVERYTHING

Let's fast forward 6 more years to the point where I landed the role that brought me here – where I am today. If I thought I'd seen customer experiences, employee experiences, and human experiences in my career before, I was about to get knocked off my seat! I became the customer insights manager for all Australian Bunnings Warehouses and small-format stores. Over time, my role extended to New Zealand as well. My amazing, human-centred team would individually read, categorise, and record an average of 1,500 pieces of customer feedback every week. Towards the end of my tenure in the role, Bunnings Trade Centres and many new warehouse locations were coming online, leading to the amount of feedback we received getting larger each month.

Not only did my team handle all the customer feedback, but another part of the team was solely responsible for data entry and seeking insights from customers who had used specific services, such as carpet installation or kitchen installation. A major component of my role was to support all functions of the company with actionable insights to help meet customer expectations and deliver the best possible service. Not just meh service – we wanted to be the *very best* (tell me you're not humming the Pokémon theme song right now). Not just, "Yeah, I got my shade cloth" but, "Wow, I got my shade cloth, and they helped me understand how to install it, and they cut it straight, and I didn't get home to find out I'm missing the right tools to put it up." You get my drift?

It was known as a one-stop shop

We didn't have a label for it back then because the terms CX, and EX for that matter, were uncommon in Australian business in 2010, but the essence of my role was to influence the customer experience and, in turn, the employee experience to create infallible loyalty from both parties. I also broke the myth that our team was one party and our customers were another.

> The reality was that our team were our customers, and without their loyalty, we didn't have a brand – we only had a business.

This understanding changed the way I did business. From that role forward, I was so passionate (possibly to a fault) about the idea that *every* single store would understand what it meant to deliver a loyalty-driven *best-in-show* customer experience. Each day, I spent much of my time on the phone, speaking with store after store, manager after manager, walking them through systems, explaining the *why* (long before Simon Sinek did, but thanks to him, more get it).[1] My managers would tell me to revert the stores back to the training manual, but the training manual didn't have the passion, tenacity, motivation, and invigoration I had (in some cases, a training manual didn't exist).

I had many conversations with store managers and area managers who were frustrated and angry at their mystery shopping results, another area of the customer experience I managed. The most common argument was around the new metric I put in place stating that every customer must be acknowledged within 30 seconds of entering the "space" of a team member (I did this at both Bunnings and Officeworks). Humans don't like change at the best of times, but this really, really pissed them off. Why, you ask? Well, because a team member might be busy up a ladder; a team member might be on the phone; a team member might already be serving a number of customers, or even just one – or maybe they're just plainly ignoring the customer. Sure, that last one's a stretch, but maybe, just maybe that was a customer's reality. For example, a team member, while on break, might walk past a customer, knowing that if they acknowledge them, they could get stopped and miss their break. To me, these were behavioural justifications that proved there was more work to be done before we could truly be considered *the best*.

The reality was, I enjoyed getting out to stores and speaking at conferences because this nugget of a complaint *always* came up. I needed managers to understand the customer experience, so I created a little skit for upset managers to take part in. It consisted of them pretending to be a customer and me pretending to be a team member. They would walk into my "space," about 2 to 3 metres away, and I would pretend to be either stacking a shelf or talking to a customer, ignoring the manager. I would refuse to look at them; I would refuse to acknowledge their existence, and I would do this for 30 seconds. Now, 30 seconds doesn't sound long, does it? But ... in reality, when you *know* you're in someone's field of vision, when you *know* you're being ignored, when you *know* you're the customer and you have the choice to shop elsewhere – why the fuck would you put up with such crap behaviour? So what happened, you ask? Well, a variety of things ... but 100 percent of the time, the manager got annoyed during the skit. One manager exasperatingly exclaimed, "I know you can see me!"

In response, I would say, "Yes, but you can see I'm busy." They would get so frustrated. Usually, by this stage, a crowd had gathered, intrigued by the upset 'customer', wondering ← *Thank you Grant Nichol, best drama teacher ever!* what the theatrics were all about.

Then we would run the skit again, but this time, despite me being 'busy', I would acknowledge the customer. It might be a nod to say, "Hey, mate, I see you, I'll catch you after this customer," or a hand wave to say, "Hi" followed by a wave of the index finger to say, "As soon as I'm off this call, I'm all yours." There was a mountain of non-verbal and verbal methods that could count as acknowledgement, all capable of being achieved within 30 seconds, which, if you're being ignored, is a long bloody time. For context, it was previously 60 seconds before I changed it to 30, and even when it was 60, acknowledgement was abysmal!

After the two skits, we would debrief, and I would ask the

manager, "So, which situation would you prefer to experience as a customer?" They and the crowds would unanimously agree, skit two – *every time*. Of course they would, because they had just received an education on not just the customer experience but also the employee experience, and, in turn, they learnt empathy, which helped them develop their own emotional intelligence (EQ), further supporting the human experience.

Change can be hard, and sometimes it takes a bit of insight and persistence to see the *why*. With this in mind, many managers performed the same skit with their team members, and within 6 months of making the change, positive customer feedback soared, as customers felt a noticeable shift and started to feel welcome again. Average basket spends increased; theft decreased, and team members and managers reported considerable drops in customer complaints, all directly correlating to how the whole store team felt about their work. Positive change was in the air, and everyone was reaping the rewards.

> Never underestimate the difference 30 seconds and a smile can make.

TL; CBF (too long; can't be fucked)

* Change makes people anxious. Accept it and determine how to create insights and calm. We'll talk more about change management in part three of this book.

---

* Thirty seconds can feel like forever, unless you're in the bedroom ... in which case, you may need to reassess your performance metrics.

---

* People fucking hate being ignored, and, with unlimited competitor options, they don't need to stand for it.

---

* Start thinking about body language and how you can implement it to develop stronger, more positive relationships. I love the book *Body Language* by Australian author Allan Pease. He makes the topic easy to digest and fascinating to put into practice.

AN EDUCATION IN HUMANITY LIKE NO OTHER

For years, focusing on the customer experience continued to be my modus operandi (MO). I talked, walked, and worked constantly to become the 'go to' for all things customer experience, leveraging my way into the marketing team, HR, and learning and development. As I write this, I'm giggling as I recall how many pots of honey I had my fingers in. You name it – if it had anything to do with our in-store teams or customers, I wanted in. Even the mail room. I would often be found helping the gents sort mail just to, well, be helpful and chew the fat, all the while observing mail quantities and the types of communications stores were receiving. There were constant complaints in stores about wasting so much time on unnecessary mail, so I put it on the list of problems to address. It became the precursor for discussions on how we (store support) communicated with the team and how we could streamline the process and communicate more meaningfully, with less negative impact to the team and the environment. This thought stream was, in reality, ahead of its time (yes, I want a badge and an award, ha-ha!). Nowadays, we take for granted all the online systems used for internal communication within organisations, but back in 2011, they were practically unheard of. Oh, how times have changed.

Over the next 5 years, I worked on understanding how to listen to people and what they really needed – difficult for someone like me who loves to talk! I learnt that sometimes silence can tell you more than words. I learnt so much more about human behaviour, reactions versus responses, personal values, and emotions and what drives them. I learnt so much more about business, what it takes to ethically influence and motivate people, what it takes to get shit done, what it takes to keep people coming back – ultimately, what it takes to create a trusted and value-driven brand.

My career became an education in humanity like no other. To this day, whenever I feel a tinge of impostor syndrome, I remind myself: fewer than five people in Bunnings have held a position like mine, fewer than three in Officeworks, and I'm the only one in the world who's had my experiences, my opportunities, my losses, my gains, and learnt my lessons. In this book, I'm sharing it all with you. To help you extract your brand purpose, for which you get the fuck out of bed with vigour and enthusiasm. To help you be strategic in your business activities. To help you create meaningful change that supports you in delivering a value-driven brand so, in turn, you can live a value-driven life.

TL; CBF

- I worked for several of Australia's most trusted brands and know some good shit.

- I've been doing this for years – I urge you to keep reading, learning, and doing.

- I'm hilarious, and I want you to have a laugh while also feeding your brain and taking your business and turning it, step by step, into a trusted and value-driven brand.

CHAPTER 2:
THE DEFINITION
OF CEHX

WHAT DO I EVEN DO?

It was early 2020, before the spicy cough era, and Australia
was burning while the then prime minister enjoyed his second
or third holiday in months, sipping a cold beer at a private
Hawaiian resort, embodying the, "She'll be right, mate" motto
at a time when things were anything but.

I was now a business owner, no longer hanging with the corporate peeps but helping as many businesses as I could with
their own customer, employee, and human experiences. One
night, I was at home entertaining some friends who were also
local business owners. As we ate an amazing dinner (I mean, I
cooked it, so I could be biased), the conversation revealed that
neither my friend Josh nor Mailese quite knew what I did in my
own business. Now, this was a common source of frustration
for me. You can imagine the confusion I caused potential customers who also didn't know why they needed me. In the realm
of accountability, that was my bad, and it was something I was
continually working on (and potentially always will be) to create
clarity around what I did.

Even as I write this circa 2025, customer experience is still a largely unknown or misunderstood business discipline. It's time to change that.

LET'S HANG A DEFINITION ON IT

Firstly, let's get clear on the definition of customer experience, or CX (pronounced see-ex). According to TechTarget …

> Customer experience (CX) is the sum total of customers' perceptions and feelings resulting from interactions with a brand's products and services. CX spans the lifetime of a customers' relationships with a brand, starting before a purchase is made, continuing through active use and to renewal or repeat purchase.[2]

When I explain this in layman's terms, I love to use a home furnishing retailer as an example.

If you're like me, at this point, your eyes are probably getting tired. So scan the QR code to hear me read the example. You're welcome!

Imagine you have some wasted space in your laundry. One day, you realise you could maximise the space by installing some storage systems. You sit on your couch and think about what could work, and there on the coffee table is an absolutely stunning, nearly fashion magazine quality catalogue from a nearby home furnishing store. You pick it up, realising it has been sitting there for weeks and you've just been moving it around the house, unable to bring yourself to throw it out because it would be like throwing out a book. There's a visceral incongruence that occurs. You can't bring yourself to do it, knowing the effort that must have gone into producing such a piece of, dare I say, art. You think, *Huh, oh yeah, lucky I held on to that!* You flick through the pages, now fantasising about remodelling every room in your home. Finally, you get to storage systems. You find the perfect piece. It's priced appropriately, so you convince yourself their products surely can't be that hard to assemble before heading out the door, catalogue in hand.

Once you arrive at your destination, you park the car, walk inside, stop, take a deep breath, compose yourself, and venture onward into the furniture jungle. After battling other shoppers and a confusing store layout, you finally come face to face with the storage cabinet of your dreams. Leaving the store, you now have your cabinet, but you've lost your car. You find your car. You attempt to load the unwieldy box onto the back seat, playing a seemingly unwinnable game of Tetris, finally getting it to fit when it really shouldn't.

Back at home, despite the near-indecipherable instructions, you successfully assemble the cabinet, deciding that the three leftover screws are spares. ← *There's that human justification at work again* Finally, you install the cabinet in the laundry and ... *Aaahhh.* It was all worth it! The cabinet looks just like it did in the catalogue, minus the herringbone tiling, sunken marble sink, and clean grout. While your laundry isn't a catalogue-worthy work of art, you're happy with the result.

The cabinet lasts the test of time, but eventually the time comes for a complete laundry renovation. The cabinet has to go. You summon your inner Marie Kondo and thank it for its diligent service to you and your family, and remove it to make way for those herringbone tiles and a custom-built storage solution. You've used the life out of it, and there's no repurposing this old soul. The cabinet must be disposed of. But that's okay. Assembled, it doesn't fit in your car, and you can't bring yourself to smash it down – you've seen *Toy Story*, and you know inanimate objects have feelings – so you hire a trailer. Still, no stress.

You heft the cabinet into the trailer and drive it to your local disposal (landfill) centre. You drive up to the window, and they inspect your load. The attendant announces that you can't dispose of your cabinet in their landfill. Confused, you ask, "Why not?" They declare that your cabinet is made of carcinogenic materials that cause damage when leached into the Earth, and you now need to track down a disposal centre that accepts dangerous goods.

Now flustered, annoyed, and still confused, you drive around, looking for a location where you can dispose of the cabinet without damaging the Earth. After plenty of googling, driving to a suburb across town (much farther than the drive to buy the cabinet in the first place), you find a suitable burial site. Being a "dangerous good," they charge you a fistful of cash for the privilege of ruining the Earth on your behalf. Finally, you say goodbye to that trusty ol' cabinet for good.

On the long drive home, all you can do is curse the home furnishing store where you bought the cabinet. *Who the fuck still uses carcinogenic materials?* (Actually, heaps of companies do). *Why do they make it so hard? Maybe I should have kept the cabinet and revamped it. But I couldn't have done that – it wasn't real timber. Gahhhh! Fuck that company.*

The thoughts and feelings of aggravation continue for some time, but eventually they dissipate ... *until* the time comes to decide where your new cabinetry is coming from for that laundry makeover. The scene plays out again. Of course, the home furnishing retailer's catalogue is sitting on your coffee table. You consider flicking through it, but you're still traumatised from the cabinet disposal experience. You forget about the 12 years of loyal service the cabinet provided. You can't see past the last few hours of your experience. You decide unashamedly to throw the catalogue in the bin and head to Google, seeking options that won't have you reliving the nuisance cabinet experience in the future.

To really cement the example, fast forward 2 years, and your friend is telling you they're looking to revamp their storage solutions. You vehemently warn them, "Stay away from that company!" So, long after the cabinet is gone and buried, and the company likely isn't using carcinogenic materials anymore, you're still micro-influencing others, steering them away from the retailer, all due to your one negative experience. Of course, the reverse could be true if you'd had a completely positive experience, but humans are more inclined to discuss negative events over positive. Negative experiences simply hit harder.[3]

What I've just so eloquently described is *customer experience.*

From the day the customer has a need (laundry storage), to finding you, to purchasing and using your product or service, to the day they no longer use that product or service, and even beyond. It's the front-end that customers face at every touch point at the beginning, middle, and end of the journey, with the back end being the processes, systems, technologies, equipment, policies, operations, service, support, manufacturing, supply chain and logistics, positioning, recruiting, products, services, partnerships, marketing, governance, and so much more. While customers may not see all the back-end action, it still directly influences the customer experience.

TL;CBF

- Customer experience starts earlier than you might think and, in reality, never really ends.

- CX is more than just how you serve customers.

- CX refers to the sum of all the touchpoints a customer experiences while interacting with a business, and their perceptions and feelings throughout the customer journey.

NEVER AIM TO BE THE SMARTEST PERSON IN THE ROOM

As I explained CX to Josh and Mailese, their eyes widened with a sense of clarity, and Mailese excitedly exclaimed that Josh had just purchased a raft of books about customer experience. He had accidentally purchased his wish list in full – a meagre 26 books. "I hope you enjoy reading," I said, and we all had a laugh. One book Josh discussed was Jason Bradshaw's *It's All About CEX!* Now, what came out of my mouth next was another example of why people tell me I'm the dumbest smart person they know. "Oh ..." I replied. "Yeah, my parents had that book."

CEX = ↗ pronounced sex

Looking at me puzzled, Josh said, "No, not *The Joy of Sex*," which is a book Alex Comfort authored in the 70s to help people in their heyday make the most of their sex lives. Josh repeated, "*It's All About CEX!* like **C**ustomer, **E**mployee e**X**perience."

Now, in all of my years working in customer experience (CX), and even though I was certainly passionate about the employee experience (EX), never in my normally dirty mind had I considered the effect of placing C and E together to imply the word sex. My tiny mind exploded that night. ←——— *Yes, I love me some self-deprecation* We all had a good laugh, and I received an unexpected education. Never believe you know it all. You don't.

As the conversation continued and we delved into the concepts of customer and employee experience, I realised I had stumbled onto something that might help me create clarity and engagement around what I did as a business advisor. However, as I said to Josh and Mailese that night, "There's something missing from the acronym. I'm not sure what it is, but I'll eventually put my finger on it. I'm certain of it."

COULDN'T STOP THINKING ABOUT CEX

A few days, possibly weeks went by, and, like when I obsessed about wanting a second child, ← *Which took me 11 years and a new husband to achieve* I couldn't stop thinking about CEX. I spent hours reflecting on what was missing from CEX. Not just for me, but also for those whom I helped create great CEX. The concept certainly wasn't new to me, as for years I had been offering a consulting program where I focused on the customer, the employees, and the business, stating that I delivered business solutions from the outside in. The statement was also bemusing, as there's a book about CX (another one I didn't know about at the time) called *Outside In*, written by Harley Manning and Kerry Bodine from Forrester (a big fuck-off consulting group in the US).

I couldn't shake the feeling that the CEX acronym wasn't complete. What was something consistent in my experiences with customers and employees? What was something relatable to every situation, every challenge, every opportunity, every achievement? What was something I knew a thing or two about and that I could uniquely advocate? By George, I finally had it. ← *And thankfully much quicker than getting that second child!* It was the human experience (HX). That was the answer.

Barely 18 months earlier, I had been standing in front of an audience, speaking at a TEDx Casey Fireside Chat about 'Experiencing Human'. It was raw. It was real. It was hard, and it was beyond emotional. After the event, I received so many compliments and messages from people thanking me for being vulnerable and helping them reframe their own human experience.

> A human experience is an experience we all have in common, whether we're customers or employees – but not enough businesses understand this.

After my revelation, I wrote down the acronym CHEX. I put it into Google and instantly received a search page full of American cereal brands. *Okay, so not CHEX. Maybe, I can try to be a bit edgy like those before me* (for example, Jason Bradshaw with *It's All About CEX* and global speaker Bernadette McClelland with her aptly named 'Let's Talk About CEX, Baby' content series).[4] I realised I was likely late to the CEX acronym party and figured some smart cookie had surely already proliferated the addition of the humble 'H' to create CEHX all over the interwebs. Once I saw it, it felt like such an obvious addition. But lo and behold, there were *Pronounced se-hx* two, yes, only two search results that had the term CEHX in them, and neither were related to customer, employee, and human experience. In fact, they were the Instagram pages of two students in Asia, and, for the life of me, I couldn't fathom what CEHX was referring to. So, by golly gosh, I was certain I had just found my edge, my unique message. By proliferating the term CEHX, which without me even trying is literally pronounced *sex*, I would not only get people's attention, but I could also help more businesses create a next-level customer, employee, and human experience. The fun part? We would turn heads and raise eyebrows doing it.

TL;CBF

* I created and now proliferate the acronym CEHX (pronounced se-hx), meaning the Customer, Employee, and Human eXperience.

---

* As business leaders, we need to remember that the common denominator, for the love of robots, is we're all just fucking humans. It's time we started doing business with this understanding at the centre of everything we do.

CHAPTER 3:
THE TRAPS WE SET

THE STATS PAINT A GRIM PICTURE

Data shows that many businesses ultimately crumble within a short-lived cycle of trading. Research from the Australian Bureau of Statistics (ABS) shows that within 4 years of beginning operation, around 50 percent of new businesses fail, and fewer than 60 percent of survivors are profitable.[5] In the US and EU, the numbers are also grim. In the US, around 50 percent of new small and medium-sized enterprises (SMEs) fail within the first 5 years of operation (keeping in mind that an SME in the US is any business with 500 or fewer employees).[6] In the EU, around 20 percent of businesses fail within their first year of operation.[7]

TL;CBF

+ Building a business is hard.

+ Staying in business and being profitable is even harder.

+ This is a worldwide predicament.

WHY SO MUCH FAILURE?

Now, the reason so many businesses fail is multifaceted. Data from Failory shows that marketing problems (56 percent) are the biggest startup killer, especially a lack of product-market fit. Team and resource problems (18 percent) are the second highest contributor to business failure, and finance problems (16 percent) come in third.[8]

However, out of all the contributing factors, of which there are so many more, there's one common and underlying problem that, if it had been addressed, could have gone a long way towards saving those businesses from doom.

> One reason businesses don't succeed is because SME owners often don't adequately understand the need to implement a business model that clearly and accurately details the customer experience. This one fundamental piece of knowledge can, in fact, change the trajectory of your business.

Many of us, when we wake up one day and decide, "Gosh darn it, I'm going to quit my job and be my own boss," only consider what we'll sell, where we'll sell it, and how much we'll sell it for. We consider the commodification elements (the bits that anybody can copy and compete on), and from there we convince ourselves we're all Kevin Costner in our own version of *Field of Dreams*. So, we build it, and we wait for the crowds to come, and we know that when they do, we'll smile, and we'll greet them and be helpful, and they'll love what we built, and we'll spend our days hitting home runs. But this isn't a business reality. The reality is, while we instinctively understand good customer service (well, most of us, some people should stay out the back), simply being friendly and helpful isn't enough. No one will come just because you have good service if everything before and after isn't equally considered, valued, and experienced positively. This is where the concept of a 'customer experience' comes into play. You want to make a home run? You want the crowds? You want the adoration and legacy beyond four years of struggle town? Then you need to dust off your kit and get ready to hit some balls into the CX park.

CX = MORE THAN CUSTOMER SERVICE

At its core, customer experience is the sum of all customer experiences (internally and externally) that result from interacting with your business. Remember the home furnishing retailer analogy in chapter two? Let me summarise it for you. A customer's experience starts before they even know they need you to the moment they find you, choose you, spend with you, and even beyond, possibly never using you again. CX details the front-end experience, as well as the systems, the processes, the policies, the platforms, the marketing, the operations – it's all-encompassing. Customer service plays only one part in your rendition of *Field of Dreams*. An important part? Yes, but only one part.

> The fantasies we allow ourselves to believe around just being good to customers can ultimately lead to our undoing, landing us on the wrong side of those global statistics.

We set ourselves a trap by not implicitly understanding the journey we're embarking on. We must educate ourselves on what it takes to deliver a rigorous, value-driven, trustworthy customer experience from the outside in. "What does that even mean?" I hear you say ...

TARGETING THE RIGHT HUMANS (AUDIENCE)

Always start with your target audience. Ask them what *they* want. Ask them *how* and *when* and *why* and *where* they want it. Then build your field of dreams from there. In reality though, sometimes the customer will say something that doesn't match their behaviour. So, where possible, observe behaviours to give you a more congruent insight into what your customers want and need.

The 'jobs to be done' or 'JTBD' framework is a great tool to help create insights into customer needs without the latency, helping you proactively deliver a unique customer experience. What are your customers trying to achieve? What are the jobs to be done? With a JTBD mindset, you don't simply dive into creating a product or service; you first consider what your customers need and act based on those insights. What's the problem you're going to solve? From there, you can create a product or service that delivers value. To run a successful business, you *must* know how you're going to deliver value. Now, value is highly subjective, but if you first work to understand who your target audience is, gaining insight into what they value is much easier.

While many business owners know about demographics, ethnographics, and psychographics, there's also a new realm of data that helps businesses learn more about their target audience – *valuegraphics*. The concept was created by Canadian David Allison (connect with him on LinkedIn to get all the most up-to-date insights. Tell him Aileen sent you.). David and his research team have learnt that your target audience may be wider than you think, based on what people personally value. For example, through valuegraphics, a brand selling insurance to aged pensioners might find that their biggest customers aren't actually aged pensioners. When they go to market, they might instead need to target the children of aged pensioners, as they share their parents' values of being protected and cared for. Now, if you don't gain the right insights and just go to market targeting who you *think* your buyers are, you may inadvertently cut out a whole subsection of customers, resulting in lower profits and potentially putting you at risk of being the next business on the chopping block when your competitors figure it out first.

TL;CBF

- Take a moment to understand valuegraphics and how it opens up whole subsections of buyers you may never have considered.

- Demographics isn't the only way to understand your customer.

- Observation of your target audience is one of the best ways to learn about your customers.

CREATE A SEAMLESS JOURNEY

Consider the journey you want your customers to take. Map it out. When I say 'map it out', I don't mean go all Marco Polo, but, in saying that, you bet your bottom dollar even Marco had a semblance of a map to help him on his travels. However, mapping your customers' CX journey looks slightly different to a ye olde treasure map.

Your CX journey map is basically a visual aid that allows you, as a business owner, to define the activities and customer touch-points you wish your customers to experience when they engage with you. As mentioned, the journey starts before they know they need you and continues to the point of loyalty and advocacy. It details what's happening in the front end and the back end with systems and processes. It helps you consider the customer's thoughts and feelings (those human experiences) ensuring your business model accounts for and mitigates any potential challenges. Being a visual aid, it helps you understand the gaps in your customers' experience, opportunities to improve it, and your unique touchpoints, which can help you dominate the competition. It's the road map for how to best move your customer from not knowing your business to loyal and advocating for your trusted, value-driven brand. Ultimately, the experience should seamlessly and frictionlessly advance them through each stage of their customer experience.

We'll cover customer journey mapping in full in chapter six.

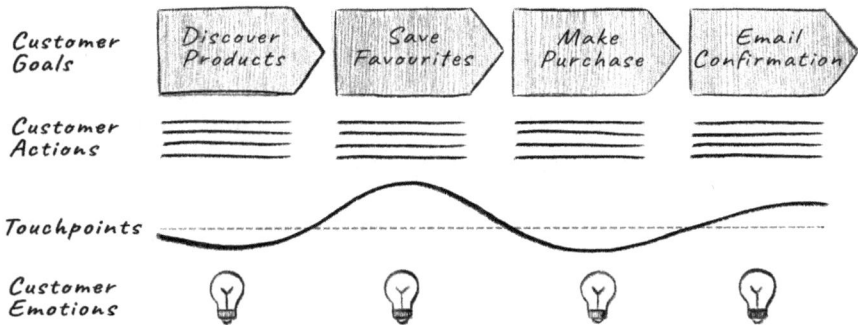

High-level CX journey map.

YOUR TEAM, YOUR ADVOCATES

Once you've started from the outside (your external customers), it's time to listen to your team (the 'inside' component) and also your internal customers. Ask them the same questions. You want your employee experience (EX) to match your outstanding and values-driven customer experience. Your team is literally the face of your business. They're your front-line advocates. If they hate working for your business – maybe hate is too strong a descriptor – let's go with if they're impartial, neutral, or feel 'meh' about working in your business, this attitude shines through to your customers. Your customers may feel that if your team can't be excited to be there, why would they?

It's the vibe and ah, no that's it. It's the vibe."

– *The Castle*

Now, that's not to say team members have to always be "on" like coked-up Energizer bunnies, but they do have to exude a level of personality that shows those on the outside looking in they're not just there for survival. They're there because they share your organisation's purpose and vision. They're there because the employee experience helps them improve their skills, maybe offers them the opportunity to challenge themselves and develop their careers, or simply helps them live a value-driven life. As important as it is to understand what your customers value, *Not everyone wants to be a CEO* it's equally as important to understand what your team, and prospective team members, personally value. Work with them to build an experience that also makes them loyal to your brand and sees them advocating for your workplace.

I always use the analogy of the barbecue. At any barbecue, in the name of small talk, it's guaranteed that someone's going to ask, "How's work?" likely more than once as you do the rounds. Now, as a business leader, what do you want the next words that come out of your employee's mouth to be? If it were me, I certainly wouldn't want it to be anything but, "Bloody awesome,

I just got to [insert cool thing that adds personal and professional value to their life]. I'm so lucky I get to do something I love." Could your employees say that? If you think there's any chance they would say anything different, it's time to transform the experience to transform the conversation.

EMOTIONS AND RELEVANCE MATTER

What do you want your customers to *feel* when they hear your name? Illicit those feelings. The reality is that when we go into business, we're often bombarded with technology and the chance to automate and digitise the way we operate, but in doing that, we get further and further away from what I call the human experience (HX).

Now, don't get me wrong – I love technology (as long as I don't have to set it up), but I implore you, when you're setting out to deliver your magic thingamabob or super awesome whatchamacallit, to deeply consider the emotions you want your customers to feel when they engage with you. This is a very underrated part of mapping out your CX journey.

> It's well-known that humans become attached to brands for the intrinsic feelings and emotions they elicit.

Let's take Nike, for example. I hate running but when I see Nike advertisements, there's something inside me that believes I can run a marathon. I have feelings of inspiration and self-belief, no matter how misplaced they may be.

Another example – when I engage with the Australian Surf Life Saving charity and donate money, I instantly feel like I may as well have been the lifesaver pulling a vulnerable swimmer from the choppy seas of Bass Strait (one of the hardest and cruellest oceans to sail). My act of giving elicits such strong emotions that I'm likely to continue giving due to the surge of dopamine I receive in return. ←———— *I'm still waiting to win the dream home or gold bullion*

Even when I had to return a broken pair of earrings, a potentially negative experience became a positive, resulting in me crying with appreciation. When I returned to the jeweller, I was sure the team would make returning the earrings difficult, maybe even accuse me of being careless and breaking them. As it turned out, the beautiful team at Simon Curwood Jewellers were nothing short of empathetic, humane, amiable to my needs, and genuinely apologetic that their product didn't stand the test of time. I received an immediate replacement, with no bombastic side eye retailer guilt. What a breath of fresh air!

Compare that experience to dealing with a certain telecommunications retailer here in Australia that leaves me feeling the wrong emotions with *every single* engagement. I get angry, frustrated, confused, exacerbated at the level at which they can't perform simple requests, resulting in very low levels of serotonin, dopamine, and, as there's never any love gained, oxytocin. Never fear, I fucked them off years ago, but I'm sure to continue telling anybody who will listen all about my experiences with them and why they should steer clear.

No one wants to feel sad and depressed after engaging with your business. The ability to be relatable and elicit positive emotions from your customers is a prized asset your competitors may struggle to replicate.

TL;CBF

+ Work with your team to understand the experience they need to become loyal and engaged advocates in your business.

+ Emotions are a good thing. ⟵ Positive ones
  You want people to cry with   anyway
  happiness, not frustration.

YOUR KISS TECH STACK

What platforms, programs, and systems do you need to implement to keep you on top of your business and keep your customers coming back? Prioritise them. You may be reading this thinking, *Yeah, that's nice, but with what money?* If, as a startup, you're still working to stabilise your cash flow, buying into new programs and systems can feel daunting. However, that doesn't mean you can't at least be aware of the programs and systems you can eventually acquire as you improve your cash flow and reinvest a portion of your revenue back into your business. Until then, it's just a matter of doing the research to identify the programs that will allow you to operate as effectively and efficiently as possible within your current budget.

Let's also note that we're in a golden age of digitisation, AI, and open-source programs and systems, many of which are available for *free* and, in so many cases, are full of amazing functionality. Often, you can avoid having to buy into mega-pricey programs or systems (check out the website theresanaiforthat.com).

For example, when I first started my business and cash flow was irregular, I couldn't reinvest my revenue into anything to do with my business, as my household bills exceeded my income ... *but* I wanted to start podcasting. And so, my podcast, the Value Driven Brand was born.

For the first 12 months of podcasting, I used no less than seven different programs to record and produce each episode. However, I knew through research that with a particular recording and editing product, those seven different programs could eventually become *one* system. So, I determined what I needed to do to accumulate money to invest in the program, and over time I slowly but surely saved the coin. With the new system, I saved myself 6 hours per week, which was time and energy I could redeploy elsewhere in my business to make more money, to make more investments. However, had I not understood my customer experience journey, and the systems and processes needed to deliver it, I may have just continued to suffer through the situation,

Scan the QR code to check out the Value Driven Brand podcast

without doing anything to improve, innovate, or streamline the process, ultimately undoing any return on investment.

Let's normalise working smarter, not harder. No matter what stage of business you're at, your tech stack must be aligned to that seamless and frictionless customer journey. Your tech needs to integrate smoothly. Keep it simple, stupid ... you know – KISS.

AI GOT A NEW PR AGENT

Let's chat about artificial intelligence (AI). AI has been around for about as long as I have (40-something years). Like Lindsay Lohan's and Donatella Versace's faces, AI just experienced a glow-up and a new PR agent. While AI isn't new, it *has* had some work done and is now getting much more attention. Positive or otherwise, AI is this era's must-have thing. Therein lies the problem.

AI is more than Chat-GPT and Anthropic, otherwise known as generative AI. In the realm of CX, we're becoming big consumers of natural language processing (NLP) AI, which helps organisations interpret qualitative data in real time. With this technology, teams can determine the sentiment and assess patterns in feedback based on common words. It's even possible to train NLP AI in the natural language of the area from which it captures data. For example, an Australian may comment that a product is "sick," and NLP AI would be trained to know that Aussies use the word 'sick' interchangeably to mean the negative 'unwell' or the positive 'absolutely fantastic'. When we were trialling the technology in Officeworks, the minor language differences were a headache for my American NLP provider mates. However, technology has certainly come a long way since then.

To that point, implementing any type of AI, or tech for that matter, must be done with consideration for the customer, the employee, and the human experience.

DON'T LET GROWING PAINS BECOME A SERIOUS PROBLEM

If you're no longer a startup and cash flow isn't your biggest concern as you lay your head on your pillow at night, you may be in the boat of businesses that, in my experience, are working through a period of growth but still seem to be spending their days putting out fires. Coming home and having to continue answering emails, taking calls, anticipating more bullshit rolling down the proverbial hill, sprinting down the path to burnout – hey, you're making the dough, right? So you suffer through it. Well, I'm here to tell you: *"No! No! No! Bloody no!"* What I just described isn't a value-driven brand, and it certainly isn't a value-driven life.

Just because you're on trajectory to become a brand, it doesn't mean you have to suffer day and night to make it a reality. In reality, that tells me that you, my friend, are playing a small business game in a big business ballpark and you're about to strike out, to use another baseball analogy (hilariously, I don't even like baseball, but it makes for an excellent business analogy). You're swinging the bat, going for the hit, but you're gonna miss.

Instead, I want you to consider a more evolved version of the customer experience, employee experience, and overall human experience you can deliver and even personally experience. I mean, how is causing yourself and your team emotional and physical burnout for the sake of money creating a value-driven human experience? Yes, people may share your vision and want to be there with you through thick and thin, but eventually, if you don't lead them to calmer waters, their loyalty will be tested. The same goes for customers. While it's great that you're growing, scaling, making yourself a necessary commodity in people's lives, even your most intense advocates will be tested if you start taking on more than you can chew for too long and the experience you once delivered, the one that made your customers loyal to your business in the first place, isn't sustained.

Rapid growth without detailed insight and an executable plan for the CEHX you're delivering is, in no uncertain terms, the fast track to business failure and emotional damage. The world is littered with examples of businesses that showed promise in the market but, for many compounding reasons, found themselves kicked to the curb. Starbucks in Australia, half the Australian building industry, Shoes of Prey, and so many more. You need to stop yourself from falling into the growth trap. In reality, business is often the same, no matter which part of your journey you're at.

> From startup to expansion to maturity, all businesses must work consistently on their resources, their procedures, their policies, their systems, their experiences, their operations, their culture.

Like many things in life, it's all relative to where you are on the journey. Don't fall into the trap of thinking that, just because you've made it to the next phase in business, that's it. No more research, no more innovation, no more change, no more streamlining. You should be eager to step into each phase with a mindset of continual growth but with the frame of being purposeful.. Otherwise, why be in business?

CULTURE IS KING

According to businessculture.org, "Culture illustrates the accepted norms and values and traditional behaviour of a group."[9] In simpler terms, you might have heard it described as "the way we do things around here." Researchers Robert E Quinn and Kim S Cameron from the University of Michigan identified that every organisation operates with a blend of four distinct culture styles, though one typically dominates.[10] The four styles are:

1. **Clan culture:** Think of this as a workplace that feels like a big, close-knit family. Collaboration is key, and everyone is encouraged to work together. Leaders act as mentors rather than bosses, and the company thrives on shared values, teamwork, and open communication. Traditions and a strong sense of community keep things running smoothly.

2. **Adhocracy culture:** This culture is all about innovation, creativity, and taking risks. Employees are given the freedom to experiment, and leadership is dynamic, often filled with visionary entrepreneurs. The focus is on new ideas and pushing boundaries rather than rigid processes.

3. **Market culture:** Here, success is measured by results. It's a competitive and goal-driven environment where high performance is expected. Leaders set ambitious targets, and the organisation is united by a drive to win, outperform competitors, and achieve measurable success.

4. **Hierarchy culture:** This is the structured, process-driven style. Stability, efficiency, and order are the priorities. There are clear rules, procedures, and chains of command, and leaders focus on organisation, coordination, and consistency to maintain control and predictability.

After reading the culture type definitions, can you see which mode of organisational culture your business fits into? Answer the following questions:

1. What's the dominant culture mode in your business?

----

2. Is it the mode you want to be known for? If so, why so? If not, why not?

----

3. Does this particular culture mode allow you to reach your brand vision?

---

4. What are your top five attributes from any of the four styles that resonate with you?

---

5. What are the top five attributes from any of the four styles that make you screw up your face?

In all fairness, you might be scratching your head at those questions. So, let's back the truck up. To have a successful, value-driven brand, you need a brand vision. You need to be able to articulate why you're in business and what you want to achieve by doing what you do.

> My brand vision is to influence 10 million business owners, leaders, and entrepreneurs to create value-driven brands so they can live value-driven lives.

It gets me out of bed every day. ← *whether I get 10k a day or not*
It helps me sleep knowing I've spent my energy fulfilling that vision. It helps me engage like-minded employees who intrinsically feel and engage with the meaning and passion behind this vision. It helps them strive to achieve it. It helps us deliver a culture that envelopes elements from all four of the aforementioned organisational culture modes in a healthy and meaningful way. If you're unclear on your brand vision – don't stress. I'll cover the topic in full in chapter five.

Alongside a strong brand vision, you need to step away from the trap that says having a vision and values is so 1995. At a CX webinar I was speaking at, I was asked by the host to comment on an attendee's scenario in which she faced disengaged employees who were masters at lip service (telling her what she wanted to hear) but had little to no integrity and ultimately didn't do what they said they would do, risking her brand and everyone's ongoing employment. I was asked if I had experienced this during my tenure at Bunnings, as it grew to become one of Australia's most trusted brands, and if I did, how did I manage the situation? The answer was very straightforward. I explained that Bunnings lives by its brand values. Now, I say brand values, but the cincher is that every store created their *own* list of values *they* decreed were best for them and their diverse and inclusive group of team members. Now don't go all, "Gahhh, woke shit, I'm out of here!" on me. The reality was, and is, that diversity and inclusion are part of the great success story that is Bunnings, and Officeworks too, for that matter.

I mean, sure it wasn't perfect by any means. I once sat in a group recruitment drive with a department coordinator who instantly shortlisted all the hot young high-school chicks for the register jobs. But that was truly the exception to the unwritten recruitment rule, which was: merit matters, but organisational compatibility sits above all else. In layman's terms – first and foremost, did they fit our brand culture? Next, did their merits, experiences, and skills suit our needs? After that, did they demonstrate the will to use their skills and learn new ones.

Give me will over skill every day ←

Due to this approach, stores all over the country are made up of as many women as they are men. It's why there are females working in the trades department (put a MIG welder or drop saw in front of me, and I'll blow you out of the water with my skills) and men in the plant nursery. Without making a blanket statement – because I'm sure someone will come at me with the intent of proving me wrong – *in my experience*, gender ain't shit in a green or blue shed. No one really cared (except sometimes the customers, who refused to let me serve them paint because I was a chick ... *deep sigh* – their loss). For the most part, all anyone cares about is that you're not a dickhead and you live up to the store's and business' values, which ultimately are shared values. These values are created collaboratively; they're created candidly, and they don't just suit the business but also the humans working in the business. They're the team's personal values displayed through 'the way they do things around here'.

Due to the nature of these values, it became much easier to hold the team to account, no matter where in the hierarchy they sat. Team members had a clear and concise understanding of how we (they) did things around here. When the values weren't demonstrated – maybe someone walked past another team member trying to lift something heavy and awkward, therefore, not displaying teamwork; or maybe a manager said they would update a team member's roster but didn't do it by the deadline, therefore, not displaying integrity – the team understood it went against the agreed upon culture. So, with a candid conversation and a referral back to the vision and unlived values, it became a teachable moment. There was very little room for lip service. There was no place for personal politics. Because we were all accountable to the same vision and values, we created an employee experience worthy of their loyalty. We were all responsible for creating a destination culture – a culture employees wanted to be a part of.

As additional context, the recruitment process for these trusted brands is layered, systemised, and replicable. Imagine each layer as a sieve, shaking out what doesn't fit the culture until you're left with the finest humans. Now, it's not perfect, but I can attest to seeing more success and a broader range of humans than in any other organisation.

Now, as a CEHX advisor out on my own, I don't dare let a customer slip through my hands without having them apply these integral and foundational elements to what is to become a value-driven culture in every sense of the phrase. Without laying these foundations for your brand culture, you're inviting anarchy and chaos. You're inviting bullshit and politics. You're inviting self-indulgent management and over-entitled employees. You're inviting the creation of a road map to shutdown town. Your organisation's culture can and certainly will evolve as you grow because what you needed as a solopreneur will inevitably change as you start to incorporate other individuals, teams, products, systems, procedures, and so on, so don't be scared if you're currently sitting there thinking, *Hmmm, that's not great.* You're exactly where you need to be. Exploring and innovating ways to make culture king in your organisation is how you'll create the drive to motivate and influence those around you to achieve.

You see – building the field of your dreams means more than just being friendly and helpful. It means creating a business that's considered, valued, and in the economy of experiences. With those experiences, you deliver a business worthy of your customers' loyalty, and with your customers' loyalty, your business stays on the right side of the statistics. You steer clear of the trappings, and you get to have your real-life field of dreams.

TL;CBF

- When you get it right, culture is a loyalty driver for your employees and your customers.

- To get it right, you need a mix of culture styles (stop CBFing and go read page 42 to figure it out).

- Even if you're a solopreneur right now, document your brand vision (what you want to achieve in your business, for whom, how, maybe even when), and make it measurable.

- Then write down the values that align to your brand's vision and your soul to attract the right humans to your universe.

- Make all future business decisions based on whether they'll enable you to succeed in your brand vision by living your brand values.

- Decision-making then becomes quite simply either a "fuck **yes**" or a "fuck **no**."

CHAPTER 4:
THE MODERN CX

THE EVOLUTION OF CX

Customer experience, or CX, is still in its relative infancy in many parts of business and the world. Back in the day, circa 2000, CX was near unheard of, and if noted, usually referred to the customer's electronic marketing journey, during front-end service interactions, and for a short period thereafter, if such services extended to, say, customer support.

Twenty odd years on, customer experience is now one of the fastest-growing business disciplines out there. Even the definition of customer experience has evolved, moving away from its vague and short-lived predecessor. As it now stands, customer experience is the sum of every experience customers have while interacting with your brand, from the moment they didn't know they needed you to long after you last heard from them.

With its growing popularity comes some weird and wonderful job roles aligned to its implementation, such as customer success manager, customer experience manager, customer happiness manager, customer loyalty officer – and many more, should you feel the need to be bemused and investigate. The key similarity is that all of these leaders are put into an organisation to help their teams work together to create a seamless, consistent, friction-free experience for customers, whether they be customer-facing or in the background. In 2023, LinkedIn's 'jobs on the rise report' found that the role of 'customer success manager' was among the fastest-growing in Europe.[11] It's only a matter of time before it becomes a global trend.

Gone are the days when customer experience was one metric (usually NPS [net promoter score]) on a business dashboard, helping CEOs and executives alike believe that a post-engagement score from one piece of the journey was enough to understand the inner workings of customer loyalty and future business. Now, however, customer experience is being understood holistically.

> Everyone in an organisation, be it a business of 1 or 1000s, must intrinsically understand the important role one another plays in the customer journey.

This understanding is becoming the difference between the approximately 50 percent of organisations that shut down within their first 5 years and the other half that make it through. But it's not just about survival; it's also about becoming a trusted and value-driven brand, then becoming a legacy.

IN TECH WE TRUST

Technology, as expected, has played a major role in the development and implementation of customer experience strategies within organisations all over the world. By the end of the 1970s, there was a thirst for knowledge – organisations wanted to better understand their customers. This incited the boom of agency-led customer research firms, the disciples of CX. Businesses such as Gallup, Roy Morgan, and Oxford Economics all became industry leaders in delineating consumer insights to better understand the satisfaction levels, motivators, and performance indicators of customers from different economic backgrounds, for all sorts of businesses in all manner of industries.

By the 1990s, there was even more change afoot, and with the introduction of new technology came the need to re-engineer processes and operations. Businesses wanted more data and insights, and they wanted it at their fingertips rather than being at the mercy of expensive research agencies. Let's remember, it was the 90s that brought us the internet. Yes, there was a time before the internet. It's okay – my son doesn't believe me either, but it's true. With the introduction of the internet also came the introduction of online portals, with businesses diving in headfirst to email their customer base (we see you Amazon). It was a turning point for what had previously been a world of pen, paper, and landline telephone communication.

In the early 2000s (my personal introduction to CX), many businesses were still acquiring their customer insights traditionally through paper-based surveys or direct telephone calls. However, with new players, such as Survey Monkey (1999) and Qualtrics (2002) joining the customer experience market, that all started to shift. These digital-based platforms started doing for businesses what the Gallups and Roy Morgans of the world were doing, but quicker, more customisable, certainly more affordable, and, above all, at scales never seen before.

You see, prior to these new players entering the field, much of the data was captured on paper. You had to get customers to answer your questions on the spot, leaving minimal room for actual consideration and forethought. Other avenues included the dreaded telephone survey where, once you were hooked, who knew how long you would be stuck answering questions only deemed important by some marketing team in some conglomerate, pretending to care about what you think (likely to never actually use your feedback)?

As more and more people acquired personal computers and email became more popular (we all remember our very first Hotmail address #cringe), learning about customer experiences through digital surveys became more practical. Because personal email was still a fresh concept, the novelty of receiving a survey hadn't worn off. Many people didn't mind opening those emails, filling out the surveys, and hitting send. Oh, how things have changed.

Nowadays, 95 percent of my email goes straight to the trash. We get emails we never asked for, choking up our already full mailboxes. We have no care for strangers blatantly begging for our time and attention without doing anything to deserve it. If you're reading this thinking, *Huh, my business uses digital surveys*, I implore you to make your own executive order and hit pause on them until you can clarify the following:

1. What's the purpose of your survey?

2. Who is it serving, you or the customer?

....

....

3. Have you implemented a closed feedback loop to ensure customer confidence?

....

....

4. Are surveys returning quantitative and qualitative data that can be transformed into actionable insights?

....

....

5. Do you have a road map that publicly shows the impacts or changes you'll deliver based on these survey activities?

....

....

Later in the 2000s, we saw call centres take a new avenue to understanding the customer experience, albeit for what was just one aspect of the whole customer journey. At this point, businesses hadn't quite had the realisation that customer experience is actually a considerably broader canvas to be understood and admired.

Call centres all got on board with measuring customer satisfaction using the newcomer to the field, NPS. This measure was the easy go-to to give organisations a snapshot of a customer's likelihood of advocating for the business after a specific interaction, in this instance contact with an organisation's support or call centre.

In short, the call centre operator would request that the customer stay on the line post their conversation to answer a survey. Depending on the metric the organisation used, which at this stage was nearly always NPS, the customer could usually just respond with a number that correlated to the experience, and that was it. By no means was this the be all and end all of customer experience metrics (even if we thought it was back in the 2000s). It was great for its time, but as the definition of customer experience evolved, so did the ways in which organisations took to measuring it, via touchpoints and as a whole.

CX BECOMES A VOCATION

In 2011, with the concept of customer experience on the rise, the pioneers of CX realised they needed a specialised academic organisation for those interested in its disciplines. And so, the Customer Experience Professionals Association (CXPA) was born.

With the founding of CXPA, it was now possible to become certified for one of the most sought-after job roles in modern business. Those with the prerequisite skills and aptitude could now become a Certified Customer Experience Professional (CCXP), a globally recognised credential.

The founders of CXPA, Jeanne Bliss (founder of Customer Bliss) and her colleague Bruce Temkin (head of Qualtrics at the time), came to realise that customer experience was more than just one piece of the business puzzle. It was more than collecting feedback here and there. Customer experience was a journey, and that journey was about to become more detailed and purposeful than ever before.

CLEARING THE MUDDY WATERS

As we move into the modern day of customer experience, you could say we've come a long way, but still *every day* I find myself explaining customer experience to business owners at all levels, running businesses of all sizes in a wide range of industries. Years ago, at one business event, I was part of a pitching exercise, and nearly all 30 business owners asked me if I was pitching them customer service consulting. Well, not much has changed. At least not here in Australia anyway.

To make matters worse, we're also dealing with the ongoing and ever-evolving understanding of what customer experience really means to those in the business and consumer worlds. Enter the latest addition to the CX mix ... BX. Yes, now we have big agencies in the consulting world claiming that CX is no longer adequate to describe what it means to holistically deliver customer experiences and we now require a higher-level acronym to help us compute the concept. Those pushing the BX (business experience) agenda are working to define what we in the modern CX industry already understand (inside and out). What's the point of rebranding a concept people in many industries were already struggling to grasp? Well, it makes the people pushing the new and unnecessary term *look* like thought leaders, regardless of the facts. They often claim CX isn't an accurate description for modern times. In my opinion, the redefinition just muddies the waters and dilutes the very serious and passionate work of those practising in the customer experience realm. The new definition simply repeats what we've been saying for years.

> You can dress it up and strip it down however you like, but ultimately, as a leader, you should want your whole business to create and deliver the best CX possible.

If you need a new acronym to help your organisation understand that CX is a whole business responsibility, fine. But remember – your goal in business is to create and deliver experiences worthy of your customer's trust and loyalty. That's it.

TL;CBF

- The business disciplines of customer experience management (CMX) have come a long way in a relatively short time.
- CX roles are still some of the most sought-after in organisations of all sizes around the world.
- However, many organisations still don't get it. There's definitely wiggle room to get our collective shit together in business.
- Tech and AI are some of the biggest priorities for organisations of all sizes, but do your due diligence. Know who you're serving, what their jobs to be done are, and how any tech stack can securely help and deliver a ROI.

WHAT DO THE BIG DOGS SAY?

According to Forrester Research (a big global research company that knows good shit), creating a great customer experience requires six key elements:

1. Strategy

2. Customer understanding

3. Design

4. Measurement

5. Governance

6. Culture.[12]

Similarly, the global governing body for CX, the CXPA, states the framework for high-quality CX includes:

1. Customer insights and understanding

2. Customer experience strategy

3. Metrics, measurements, and ROI

4. Design, implementation, and innovation

5. Culture and accountability.[13]

Interestingly, research from Bain and Company found that from 362 surveyed organisations 80 percent believed they were delivering experiences worthy of their customer's loyalty, but, adversely, only 8 percent of customers agreed with that sentiment.[14] Now, if we were standing together in real life having this conversation, you might hear me remark … "What the actual fuck?" in shock and disbelief. You might assume I couldn't believe that only 8 percent of customers agreed, but that's not the surprising part. In actual fact, the astonishing part of that statement is that 80 percent of businesses believe they're delivering experiences worthy of their customer's loyalty. I mean, let's be honest, if that were true, I wouldn't have needed to write this book. I wouldn't be faced every day with business owners trying to correct me, thinking I'm specifically talking about customer service. I wouldn't be seeing organisations of all sizes closing down at the rate of knots. I wouldn't see families breaking up because there's no balance in their lives – business owners are constantly drowning in work, putting out fires, making poor decisions, working without a baseline, always trying to fix things that shouldn't have broken in the first place. I wouldn't be consoling and counselling grown men in tears and on the brink of suicide as they struggle to keep their businesses, their families, their lives together, hanging on by a thread (this has actually happened more than I like to recall). If that 80 percent were true, I wouldn't be encouraging business owners with so much to give but so little self-worth to stop playing small. I wouldn't need to be helping them understand how much humanity needs them and what they have to give. I wouldn't need to convince them they have the right to grow, to be wealthy, to be leaders, to build a value-driven brand and get that value-driven life. Now do you see why the 80 percent figure shocks me? And that's just the tip of the iceberg.

Now, by no means am I the be all and end all in the world of customer experience. Not today, likely not ever. Doesn't mean I don't aim to be one of the best, but what I *am* right now is an advocate of the highest order. I *am* qualified, and I *am* experienced. Based on my qualifications and experience, I *am* able to share some well-defined, tried and true strategies for practising high-level customer experience management consistently, helping your business transform from a daily grind into a lifelong legacy.

THE THREE DEES OF CX

If you're struggling to wrap your head around the customer experience concept, Bain and Company's "three Ds" model provides a succinct and straightforward approach to CX, focusing on three key elements:

1. **Design** the correct incentive for the correctly identified consumer and offer it in an enticing environment.

2. **Deliver** the proposed experience by focusing the entire team across various functions.

3. **Develop** consistency in execution to ensure success.

If we were to break these down and apply them tactically, we could consider the following:

1. DESIGN

Design the correct incentive for the correctly identified consumer and offer it in an enticing environment.

While it's nice to get into business for you (remember the field of dreams?), to stay in business, to build a trusted and value-driven brand, to obtain that value-driven life, you need to be in business for the service of others. When you're in business for the service of others, you tend to understand that designing experiences, services, offers, and products means considering your customers and *their* needs first.

This is my favourite service to humanity quote.

> The best way to find yourself is to lose yourself in the service of others."
>
> *– Mahatma Gandhi*

In their book, *The Experience Economy*, authors B Joseph Pine ll and James H Gilmore provide further details on the design principle. With the 4 Realms of Experience model, they help organisations create further clarity around designing memorable and loyalty-inspiring customer experiences. In short, designing experiences can be broken into four realms:

1. Entertainment

2. Escapist

3. Esthetic

4. Educational

Pine and Gilmore state that designing great service is about time well saved; however, designing great experiences is about time well spent. Now that's a statement worth remembering.[15]

As per Joseph Pine II and James Gilmore, experiences under the Experience Economy encompass 4 realms or dimensions.

The 4 Realms of Experience - Overview

Joseph Pine and James Gilmore Identify 4 distinct realms of experience based on the 2 dimensions of customer participation (Active vs. Passive) and connection (Absorption vs. Immersion)

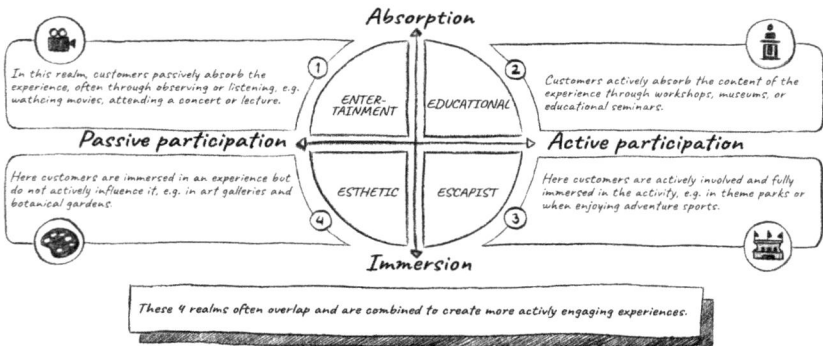

In this realm, customers passively absorb the experience, often through observing or listening, e.g. watching movies, attending a concert or lecture.

Customers actively absorb the content of the experience through workshops, museums, or educational seminars.

Here customers are immersed in an experience but do not actively influence it, e.g. in art galleries and botanical gardens.

Here customers are actively involved and fully immersed in the activity, e.g. in theme parks or when enjoying adventure sports.

These 4 realms often overlap and are combined to create more actively engaging experiences.

The Experience Economy 4 Realms of Experience.

2. DELIVER

Deliver the proposed experience by focusing the entire team across various functions.

Delivery is where good intentions go to die. What I mean is, I see so many organisations directly and indirectly work out what they can do to support their customer and grow their market, and they have great insights and the drive to do the right thing, but without the stability and foundations of a solid and strategic design, they struggle to execute their intentions consistently. In the game of consumerism, capitalism, and competition, consistency in your delivery can be a game changer.

The key is to get clear as fuck on your vision, your customer segments, their needs, their jobs to be done, and design and innovate to deliver a consistent standard. Remember, shit in, shit out. Delivery starts at the beginning.

3. DEVELOP

Develop consistency in execution to ensure success.

As mentioned, developing consistency in execution is critical. Development also includes the modes, methods, and strategies you apply to facilitate the consistent development of your employees, your customers (don't underestimate this part), and the human element of CX.

As a business working to become a brand, you have a wide

berth when it comes to innovating and disrupting the way we experience you. Through the consistent delivery of utility information (helpful information), gamification, and intelligent innovations, you can grow your audience's knowledge and capacity to take in, hold, and utilise useful information. They'll then credit you for their new knowledge and, in turn, advocate for your brand, helping develop your scalability.

Development is your opportunity to take your brand and crank it up to a legacy. To grow your raving fans and your offers, you must develop systems that help your employees focus on the customer and are easily replicable and scalable to allow success in not just one location or business, but many.

One thing is for certain: the modern customer experience has continued, and will continue, to evolve. Not just in its definition but also in its proven capacity to skyrocket profits to the realm of 95 percent for businesses that care about the customer experience. As far as I'm concerned, that's a damn good return on investment.

In the current age of customer experience management, we must design our businesses to engage the customer's emotions, meet their needs consistently and, where viable, exceed them to obtain the customer's elusive loyalty and advocacy.

↑
Use storytelling to create engagement

THE HIERARCHY OF ADVOCATE NEEDS

I really like an excerpt I found on the difference between customer loyalty and customer advocacy while researching to write this book:

> Loyalty is a purchasing behaviour. Loyal customers will return to your brand, make repeat purchases and continue to choose your business over competitors.
>
> On the other hand, advocacy is an emotional connection, as an advocate will promote your brand on your behalf and generate word-of-mouth referrals for your business.
>
> Advocacy comes after customer loyalty. This means loyal customers might purchase many upgrades, but they don't always become advocates. Whereas advocates need to become loyal customers first.[16]

Now that we're clear on the differences between loyalty and advocacy, it's time to convert that knowledge into action.

> Loyalty is a purchasing behaviour ... advocacy is an emotional connection."
>
> *Userpilot Team*

ACTIVITY: UNDERSTAND BRAND ADVOCACY

Using the three columns provided, complete the 'understand brand advocacy' activity. As tempting as it may be, don't skip it! Understanding **why** some customers become brand advocates is a critical step in cultivating your own raving fans. ←——— *Another name for advocates*

In column one, write down 4 to 6 brands you've been a loyal customer of. In column two, write down 4 to 6 brands you're an advocate for. In the third column, perform a gap analysis. Ask yourself, what makes you an advocate beyond loyalty? What steps have brands taken that have compelled you to advocate for them? Which of these tactics, activities, or behaviours can you establish in your own business to create brand advocates? Bullet point your answers.

Brand (Loyal Customer)	Brand (Advocate)	Gap Analysis

When it comes to brand advocacy, potential advocates have certain needs. The key is to meet those needs at every level.

Heirarchy of Advocate Needs

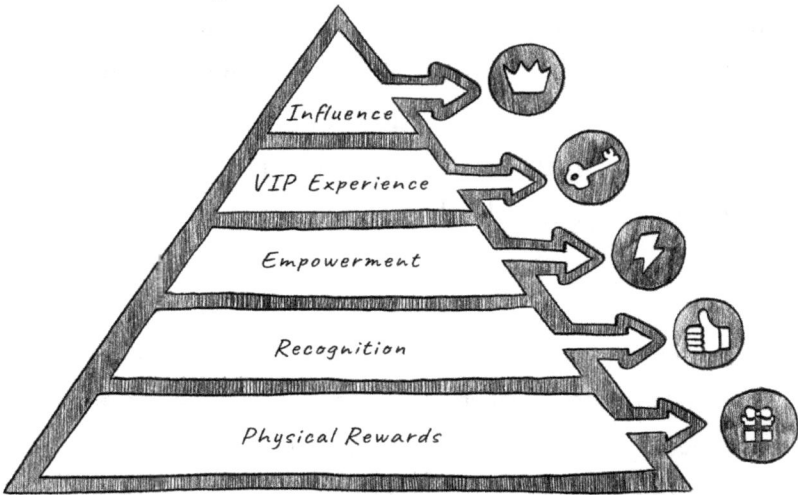

Influence

VIP Experience

Empowerment

Recognition

Physical Rewards

BE THEIR 'ROCK', NOT THEIR 'HART'

In your research on CX and CXM, you may come across advice that states your customer experience must *always* be about exceeding expectations. The reality is that this isn't actually what most customers, employees, or humans want. According to research firm Gartner, the average consumer unequivocally wants brands to be dependable.[17] That's right – above all else, consumers want stable, reliable brands. They want *consistency*. Yes, the occasional nice surprise does win extra points in the loyalty and advocacy game, but you know what they say – you really *can* have too much of a good thing.

Gartner has shown that providing an "effortless customer experience" creates more loyal customers than trying to "delight" every time (PS – establishing a new level of delight each time a customer interacts with your brand is exhausting AF).[18] Not only does constantly trying to delight consume time, energy, and other resources, but customers don't even want it, not even from luxury brands. All those resources are better spent on creating and maintaining dependability.

> In the modern business world, managing customer experience centres on designing, delivering, and developing a seamless, silo-free, frictionless experience ... **consistently**.

Here's a little reality checklist:

- ❑ You are easy to use or shop with via your customer's chosen mode, and the process of switching from one mode to another is seamless and intuitive.

- ❑ You are transparent in your dealings, including around pricing, services, products, and policies.

- ❑ Your teams clearly understand their and one another's roles in the customer journey and how their work can affect customer advocacy and, in turn, the success and longevity of the organisation.

- ❑ You are proactive in your approach, ensuring that you're always ready to communicate around and act upon issues affecting the customer or your organisation with the highest integrity and customer centricity.

- ❑ Your support mechanisms are exactly what your customers need, when they need them. While this can be hard in a global market and a world that never sleeps, you're in the big leagues now. No excuses!

- ❑ You exist to drive value into your customers' and your employees' lives, enriching their human experience.

TL;CBF

- Customer experience is built on key disciplines like strategy, customer understanding, design, measurement, governance, and culture. Despite 80 percent of businesses believing they offer great CX, only 8 percent of customers agree. Talk about a gap in perception vs. reality.

- Bain and Co's 'Three Ds' framework emphasises:

  - **Design:** Creating the right experience for the right customer.

  - **Delivery:** Ensuring company-wide execution of the intended experience.

  - **Development:** Consistently improving employee, customer, and brand growth.

- Loyal customers are repeat buyers, but true advocates have an emotional connection and spread positive word of mouth.

- Research suggests customers prioritise reliability over constant 'delight', meaning businesses should focus on being seamless, transparent, and proactive in their CX approach. This is a big one!

THE CUSTOMER EXPERIENCE PYRAMID

The model I so dearly love to use when educating new audiences on customer experience is derived from Dr Elizabeth BN Sanders' work, and it's one of the easiest models to grasp – the Customer Experience Pyramid. I first learnt of it while reading the wonderful *Outside In: The Power of Putting Customers at the Center of Your Business*. I now live for the simplicity of this model and how it speaks to organisations of all sizes and their consumers. Let's check it out.

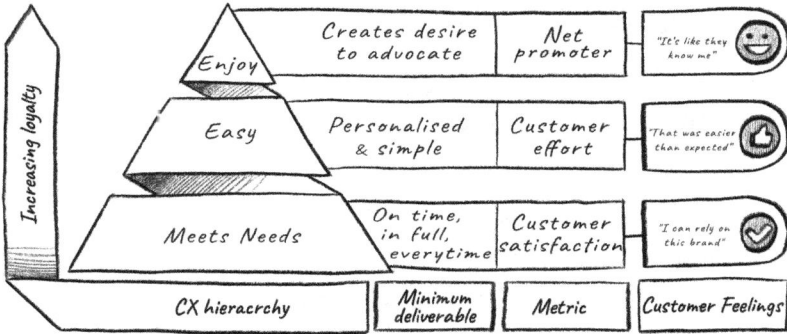

Dr Elizabeth BN Sanders' Customer Experience Pyramid.

The fundamentals of the pyramid, which, over time, have been adjusted to suit changing CX needs, comprise three core segments. As Neil DeGrasse Tyson would say, "Let's go deeper."

GREAT CEHX SHOULD BE ENJOYABLE

The first base level of the pyramid is 'meeting needs', which is similar to Maslow's Hierarchy of Needs.[19] It's the bare minimum we can do as business owners, leaders, and entrepreneurs before we can even consider ourselves worthy of our customer's energy. The disappointing reality is that many organisations don't even reach this level. That's why it's so easy to be seen as a great player in the game when all you deliver is the barest of bare minimum.

Before writing this, I watched a YouTube video of a gentleman bragging about how he only has to do the bare minimum to meet his wife's needs. He implied that doing the dishes after their evening meal is all his wife expects of him, and that alone is enough to keep her satiated. What a truly sad state of affairs for a scenario you should (in my opinion) only enter because you have a love and commitment to be there beyond the bare minimum, always working towards the pinnacle of the pyramid, an enjoyable and value-driven life. Now, I get it – no one particularly likes doing the dishes, but to gloat that all you need to do is the bare minimum to stay in your so-called loved one's good graces seems callous and danger- *Oh yeah, I forgot to mention that* ous. As a practising clinical therapist, I can tell you I had more questions than answers, and something tells me there are few to no CEHX-y times happening in that relationship.

The scenario mimics how countless businesses around the world believe they can do the bare minimum and still satiate their customers. *Remember, 80 percent think they're doing enough* But here's the hitch (and my message to them): you, my miserly friend (I'm acutely aware those businesses aren't reading this book) will soon find yourself no longer in business. Why? Let's turn our attention back to our YouTube friend, shall we? From the human experience (HX) perspective, more often than not we see, appreciate, and become loyal to those who fulfil our needs. Those who *show* us we're valued. Those whose actions (not words, they don't mean shit in this instance) make us *feel* valued. Now, what would happen if our YouTube friend's wife came across another human who recognised that her worth and loyalty deserved more than just the bare minimum effort? Would she be tempted to do some further research into this new option, ready and waiting to transform her current existence from mediocre and bare-minimum to engaged, aware, interdependent, innovative, and always value-adding? Well, of course she would. She's only human.

The reality is, if you sit around in front of your webcam, glorifying how little you need to or want to do for the so-called love of your life, you've made it easy for her to question her loyalty – there's certainly no advocacy in these situations – once she becomes aware of a brighter existence. If you become complacent and deluded thinking that your customers – your reason for being in business – will always remain loyal and all you have to do to obtain said loyalty is deliver the bare minimum, get ready to be the next Kodak, the next Blockbuster, or the next General Motors (Holden for my Aussie mates). If you're a smaller business and those examples are too big to resonate, take a walk to your local retail precinct and check out all the vacant retail spaces. Oh, you're online? Name five online brands you used to

At best, there are only shallow justifications for her staying

shop with 10 years ago and tell me if they're still around. The odds aren't in their favour.

All those businesses that are just dialling it in, I call them 'level four businesses'. They're hoping for the best while bringing nothing of value to the table, and they're the first to tell everyone the problem's not them – it's someone else. They're the most shook when they get left behind, scratching their heads, taking no accountability, and spending their days bitching about how they did all they could in this cold, hard world.

You are not the victim in this plotline

Your success in business ultimately depends on you wanting to be there, doing the shit jobs, listening even when you think you already know the answer, asking how someone's day has been, and learning how you can make it better. Essentially, it's about putting in the effort to provide more than the bare minimum to deservedly rise above the competition.

practise staying curious

Remember, COMPLACENCY KILLS ...

Now that leads us into the next level of my favourite pyramid ...

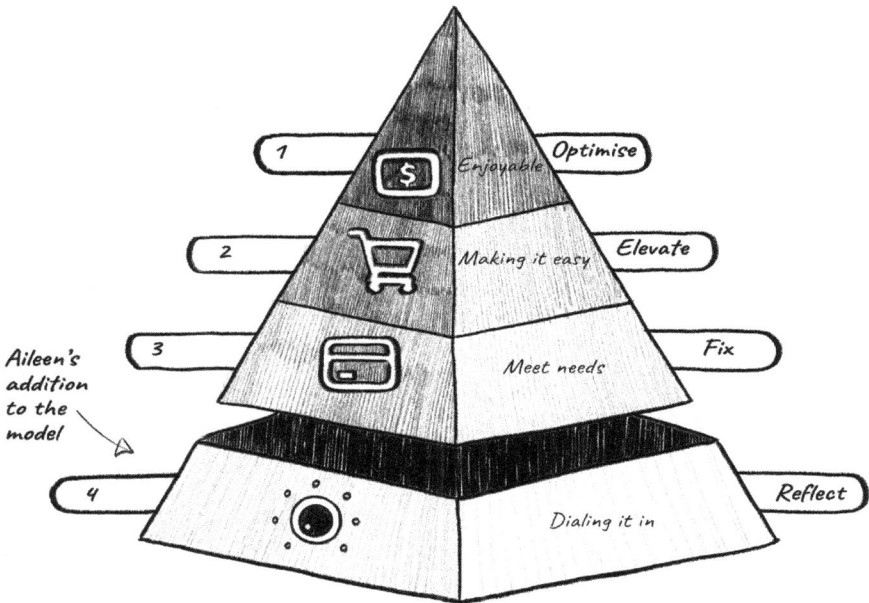

CX Pyramid by contrarian Aileen Day.

WHEN THE EFFORT IS REAL (EASY)

The next level focuses on how you're going to make your customers' lives and experiences easier. Even when you go from doing the bare minimum to meeting your lover's basic needs, it's still not enough to keep away Brian, the single dude who just moved in up the road and has shown an interest in your unsatiated, certainly not loyal given a better option, wife (yes, we're sticking with the YouTube guy analogy).

So, what would our YouTube guy have to deliver experience-wise for his wife to move past simply feeling neutral about their relationship and have a reason to reconsider her attraction to the shiny new option on the block, Brian? Because be certain – Brian has come to town having done his homework. He knows who's ready to walk. He keeps an ear to the ground and listens fervently to the feedback of the local wives. He hears the challenges they're experiencing. He has also done some intense self-development to ensure he can be the sustainable answer to those challenges, ← *YouTube's Green Flag Man, Dustin Poynter, would be so proud* whereas lowly YouTube husbands are creating wider and wider chasms in value. They deem it unnecessary to innovate or pursue additional value-adding activities that might help prevent their lovers' eyes from wandering, looking for something fresh and exciting.

In business, this is where new competitors come in to take over what *was* yours. They barely have to be better than the bare minimum for your customers to fall into the arms of a new lover. I mean, player. We see it every day in every industry in every market – from real estate agencies to car dealers to supermarkets to dog groomers to cafes. Hell, here in Australia, we even saw it in home improvement with one of our biggest brands, Bunnings, finding themselves in the path of some stiff competition following a joint venture between Lowes (US) and Woolworths Group (Australia). The partnership brought a new big-box player, Masters, to the home improvement and hardware industry. When Masters announced their entry into the game, I was the customer insights manager for Bunnings Australia. I was responsible for mystery shopping and customer experience, and while we mystery shopped our own stores, we also mystery shopped the new player.

Of course, our team members knew the metrics, and we made the strategic decision to measure the Masters locations using the same criteria. Well, blow me down when I got reports stating that, in some instances, Masters was outperforming the stores in our own network. Why, you ask? Well, for a long while, Bunnings didn't particularly have any natural predators. We didn't have any Brian's moving in down the road. We became a little bit like our YouTube husband. A bit indifferent to our customers. A bit full of ourselves. A bit lacking in motivation because, as long as we delivered the bare minimum, customers continued to turn up. I mean, where else were they going to go? Sure, there were, and continue to be, other players in the market, but none were the destination Bunnings was. None were that one-stop shop that Bunnings was. Like our friend on YouTube, we were evidently starting to feel a bit too comfortable in our lethargy when it came to delivering on our brand promise, our vows of sorts, and we had vowed to be the best. The reality was glaringly incongruent.

Masters entering the Australian home improvement market certainly would have made even YouTube husband sit up straight and start second-guessing all that bravado. During this period, I often received a statement posed as a question from people both within and outside of Bunnings: "Oh, I bet you hate Masters, hey?"

Every single time, I would reply, "No way. Masters is the best thing to ever happen to this organisation." They would look at me like I was dumb or start squinting at me and try to guess if I was a double agent (this literally happened, and more often than anyone anticipated). When I explained the reason behind my response, people were usually either offended by or in agreement with the insightful reframe placed before them. There was no middle road.

So, why was Masters the best thing, *in my opinion*, to happen to the big green shed? Well, until then, working in the organisation as a team member in store to looking after the customer experience for the country, I had never seen an outside influence shake an organisation up like Masters did to Bunnings. It was the Brian to our YouTuber husband. It was the metaphorical kick in the arse we needed to go from 'meeting needs' (or even embarrassingly, sometimes dialling it in) to that transformational next level, and if we were smart, we wouldn't stop there. It was time to hit the ground running and *earn* back what we had taken for granted for all those years. Yes, YouTube husband, I'm also looking at you.

> As a practising therapist, I now know that we tend to treat those we love dearest the worst. We have this innate belief that they'll always be there, which can create a chasm between us, and over time our poor behaviour negatively impacts much more than just our relationship.

Tactically, the way Bunnings served those they loved (their customers) had to change. The customer experience mattered more now than it ever did, and there was very little margin for error. Masters was watching every move, studying what we were doing, what we had done, and how it all worked, and they were hiring and headhunting from within the big green shed to get a better understanding of the organisation.

Initially, Bunnings went on a 'find and fix' mission. I started meeting with cross-functional leaders to help them better grasp the impacts they and their teams were having on the customer experience. ← *Something they'd never even considered* We aimed to determine how to strategically improve the journey and, in turn, earn back customer advocacy. The predicament was ... despite receiving more than 1,500 pieces of unsolicited feedback every week, much of it was either at one extreme or the other. For example, we would hear from those who absolutely *loved* the experience and those who absolutely *loathed* it but rarely from anyone in the middle. So, we had very few quantified or qualified insights into the everyday shopper, their needs, their expectations, and their feelings on their experiences. The solution to this potentially skewed feedback? Car park surveys.

Every few months, retail store managers would go to a buddy store and survey everyday customers, asking them six or fewer questions, depending on how reciprocal they felt. It was a great insight into what I call the 'minds of the neutral'. Neutral in the sense that they often weren't the same customers who had gone out of their way to express their feelings of advocacy or detraction. The lessons learnt were to become invaluable.

We learnt that, in some areas of the country, we were resented by customers for being the only choice in the market, so when it came to asking, "Would you recommend *I mean, more than once was too many* this store?" the question was too often met with dissonance and clammy responses, such as, "Well, who else am I going to recommend?" That, my friend, is not an advocate. On the flip side, we learnt that other locations had such tight bonds with their communities that the customers surveyed felt like they were part of the Bunnings family, often joking that they visited so often they may as well get their own Bunnings apron. One customer, a grown adult, explained that he had his birthday party at his local store where all of his friends came and did a DIY class and ate red and green cake. Now *that's* an advocate.

At the time, Bunnings knew that to stay number one in the hearts and minds of its teams and customers – any organisation's two most important assets – they needed to start digging deeper. To start looking within. To learn about the wants, needs, and aspirations of those assets. To get the organisation off the bottom of the pyramid. To gain momentum that would see a transformational shift into the middle of the customer experience pyramid, making them easy to engage with and, in turn, with persistence, resilience, consistency, strategy, and a customer-centric vision, hitting that top tier and surpassing every competitor in the market to become ... *easy* and *enjoyable*.

In reality, the modern customer experience has been somewhat of a roller-coaster for many an organisation attempting to execute the disciplines and stay the course without getting distracted by the low-hanging fruit or naysayers who aren't the right motivational fit for the vision (heard the term hire slow, fire fast?). Those who can steer the ship and influence change will continue to reap the rewards, disrupting markets and industries wherever they go. For those who try but can't keep the momentum, it can turn into one hell of a dumpster fire ... trust me, I've seen them metaphorically and in reality. They are putrid in both examples.

REACHING FOR THE SUMMIT

Are you willing to learn? Are you open to change? Are you seeking a brighter, more advocacy-driven future? If you answered 'yes' to all three questions, congratulations, you're ready to reach for the summit of the CX Pyramid. To get there, you'll need to innovate consistently and deliver and measure all aspects of the customer experience framework.

The summit is where we create customer experiences that become not just easy but also enjoyable. At this point, you're working with the CX framework and living by the pillars of the Customer, Employee, and Human eXperience. Your organisation is optimised, and, as its leader, you're in a position to work *on* the business, not just in it. ← Thanks Michael E Gerber

At the summit of the CX Pyramid, the experiences you deliver create fond, positive, emotive, and impactful memories. This is when customers become driven to advocate for you, sharing their experiences willingly and loyally.

Yet, how do we even know what CX involves? I often explain to business leaders that successful CX is more than just how you serve customers. Imagine that CX management is like a delicious and filling pie. Customer service (what most people hear when I say customer experience) is only a slither of that pie. An important slither, but a slither nonetheless. That very full pie also includes a slice of the systems you use and the governance, or policies and procedures, you live by. It has a slice that's full of tasty values that align to your brand vision. Another slice, which is quite big, is all about how you uphold your organisation's culture – how you and the humans you recruit show up for your organisation, for themselves, and especially for your customers. You see, the pie is big; it's full of premium fillings and when sliced up, you can really start to sink your teeth into the importance of having, at minimum, a casual understanding of how to bake it to place you ahead of your competition.

CX FRAMEWORK CASUAL HOOK-UP

As mentioned previously, according to the CXPA, the CX framework includes:

1. Customer insights and understanding

2. Customer experience strategy

3. Metrics, measurements, and ROI

4. Design, implementation, and innovation

5. Culture and accountability.[20]

Let me give you the casual hook-up on what the CX Framework involves.

CUSTOMER INSIGHTS AND UNDERSTANDING

- Let go of what you think you know – it's probably wrong. The loudest complaints aren't always the biggest problem. When I was doing CX at Officeworks, the company was ready to sink a fortune into fixing Print & Copy, assuming it was the main customer pain point in stores. But data showed otherwise. Tech was the real issue. While Print & Copy customers often yelled, causing the biggest scene, many tech customers simply walked out and bought elsewhere. Thankfully, having the data needed to analyse actual customer experiences helped us redirect funds and make strategic fixes where they mattered most.

- Do your research from the outside in. Once again, don't base change on what you *think* you know. Do the research. Observe customers in their natural setting (qualitative) and get data (quantitative) to support your findings. If you can't do this, speak to your team to get their take until you can implement a functioning program that helps customers inform you of their own experiences. ← *Known as a voice of customer or VoC program*

- Focus groups are usually full of shit. Don't bother. They're like toddlers who know how to manipulate you for the last cookie. Too often, they'll tell you what they think you want to hear. Find other more integrity-driven ethnographic

Long-term observation

and valuegraphic modes to learn the truth, such as immersive longitudinal studies and triangulated truth-seeking.

Use three models of research to cross-verify

- Ask your team what they see and hear and have them give examples. No bullshit motherhood statements like, "Oh, I reckon we could" or "should" or "would." Hard facts. They know more than you might realise. Let them tell you their stories.

No vague, feel-good platitudes

CUSTOMER EXPERIENCE STRATEGY

- Strategy, in its truest sense, is the conscious ability to be unique. To differentiate yourself from everyone and everything. In the context of CEHX, it's the same.

- Adopt the strategy that suits your audience. Don't cherrypick or randomly throw your strategy together, hoping for the best. This isn't a juice bar, and your customers aren't boba pearls (different on the outside, all the same on the inside).

- Your strategy should align to your organisation's vision. Not sure it does? Don't stress – I'll walk you through it in chapter five.

- Getting to the top of the pyramid doesn't happen by accident. It happens through executing activities that produce action-driven data that help inform value-driven strategies that drive loyalty-driven experiences. I'll explain more as we move through the chapters.

- Your customer experience must be memorable for the right reasons. Sometimes your strategy might be a bit off, so have plans in place to rectify challenges quickly, such as prototyping change rather than performing full rollouts with crossed fingers. Agility is key.

METRICS, MEASUREMENTS, AND ROI

- What gets measured gets done. But you should use metrics that positively drive the strategy, and use more than one metric. NPS isn't the be all and end all, and these days there are many other metrics that can be applied to different customer journey segments to better understand the experience and the customer's advocacy. We'll break these down further in chapter seven.

- Use a variety of CX, operational, and behavioural metrics to help drive better actionable insights, leading to better questions and resulting in smarter strategies.

- As tempting as it is to get stuck in the details (live, singular feedback), keep an eye out on the bigger picture (the stories data collection can tell you as opposed to once-off feedback). Otherwise, you could find yourself making mountains out of molehills and missing the point and the patterns.

- Before you apply any performance-based metrics to anyone in your organisation, go read *Drive: The Surprising Truth About What Motivates Us* by Dan Pink. Legitimately an excellent book that every leader should read.

- The three common CX metrics are descriptive (what happened), perception (what they thought), and outcome (what they will do). These can also be configured into 'leading metrics' (which predict future CX) and 'laggard metrics' (which explain past CX).

DESIGN, IMPLEMENTATION, AND INNOVATION

- Your customer touchpoints must be purposefully designed and not left to chance. There must be clarity in execution, purpose, and desired outcomes. You can't fluke it – which is why more and more organisations that get CEHX are upskilling and applying human-centred design, systems, and future thinking to CX and EX.

- Design is about your problem-solving process. It's not about brand attributes like logos and HEX codes. It's easy to get wrapped up in this stuff but if your customer's experience is shithouse, none of it matters. Prioritise the CEHX journey.

- Implementation must be frictionless, streamlined, easily anticipated, user-friendly, secure, replicable, optimised, innovative, scalable, and, to reach the summit of the CX Pyramid, downright enjoyable.

CULTURE AND ACCOUNTABILITY

- Accountability comes in the form of great governance. A fancy term for your systems, policies, and procedures. Essentially, the way you do things in your organisation. When everyone is aware of their responsibilities, it makes an organisation more accountable for its performance.

- Culture is where you can set yourself apart from the competition, as many organisations determine the journey, touchpoints, and experiences but let themselves down with team culture. Always remember that your team is your first line of advocates, but culture takes time, trust, and consistency to build.

- Customer experience should be the responsibility of every team member at every level within the organisation. This includes everyone from C-suite to the janitor. *Everybody* can and does impact the Customer, Employee, and Human eXperience, and holding everyone accountable helps align behaviours to the successful execution of the CX strategy.

- No longer allow projects and changes to occur without first having a solid and documented understanding of the CX impact and ensuring their alignment to the customer experience vision and strategy. Build CX into every aspect of your business – only then are you customer-centric.

Implementing these disciplines can be tough, ← *Especially if you're rolling back bad habits* time-consuming, exhausting, and challenging. Many try and fail. But for those who see the value, align ROI with existing efforts, and commit to building an experience economy, the effort pays off. Someone asked me recently if I think CX is a disruptor. My answer? "Yes ... if you're doing it right."

> This is a journey, not a project. It has a beginning but it doesn't have an end."
>
> — *Kevin Peters, former president Office Depot*

Like everything, customer experience will continue to evolve. But unlike most projects, it doesn't come with an end date, only a start date. So when are you going to start?

TL;CBF

- The Customer Experience (CX) Pyramid, inspired by Dr. Elizabeth B. N. Sanders, has three core levels: (1) Meeting Needs (bare minimum or dialling it in), (2) Making Life Easier (reducing friction in customer experience), and (3) Creating Enjoyable Experiences (optimising and driving customer advocacy). Many businesses fail at even the first level, leading to lost loyalty.

- Companies that only provide the bare minimum risk losing customers to competitors who listen, innovate, and add value. The analogy of a neglectful husband vs. an attentive new suitor illustrates how businesses can lose loyal customers when they fail to evolve. Examples like Blockbuster, Kodak, and Holden highlight the dangers of complacency.

- Businesses must proactively analyse customer feedback, remove friction, and optimise their customer journey. Measuring the right metrics (beyond just NPS), applying human-centered design, and continuously innovating are essential for long-term success. Companies that fail to adapt like Bunnings was before facing competition from Masters risk losing market relevance.

- Customer experience isn't just about external service; it's about internal culture too. Organisations must embed CEHX principles into their governance, leadership, and team behaviours to build a customer-first mindset. When executed well, businesses reach the CX Pyramid's peak, creating experiences that are not just easy but genuinely enjoyable.

- Stop surveying customers and not having a closed feedback loop in place. This includes potential employees in the recruitment process.

ACTIVITY: 3–2–1 REFLECTION

In the space provided, write:

- ◆ 3 key takeaways from the chapter that resonate with your business.
- ◆ 2 actions you can take this week to implement these ideas.
- ◆ 1 challenge you foresee and a possible solution.

3 Key Takeaways

----

2 Actions

----

1 Challenge (and Solution)

CHAPTER 5:
CREATING THE VISION

IT ALL STARTS WITH A VISION

In so many examples in business, many of the challenges and fires requiring attention can be traced back to misaligned or non-existent organisational visions. These misaligned visions lead to misaligned values that lead to misaligned activities that ultimately result in needing to put out spot fires or, in worst case scenarios, full blazing infernos. We affectionately call these 'dumpster fire organisations' (or is that just me?).

It would be easy for me to sit here and say creating an organisation that can exist without putting out fires is simple. Well, only people who have no lived experience in creating, developing, and growing a business could inaccurately claim that to be the case because, in reality, it's actually quite difficult. In every aspect of the business development journey, you're highly likely to encounter instances that require more than their fair share of your energy. The trick, however, is to have the discipline to navigate and the smarts to learn from each challenge. A wise person once said ...

The only real mistake is the one from which we learn nothing."

– Henry Ford

Now ain't that the truth. Another cool cat also proclaimed that the definition of insanity is doing the same thing over and over again and expecting a different result (Albert Einstein). Sadly though, this happens far more often than it should. We bang our heads against the proverbial wall and lie awake at night wondering why we can't sleep, confused as to why nothing seems to be going right in our world, ⟵ *Therapist Aileen asks if you've self-sabotaging* be it in the workplace or even at home. Well, let me break this down for you: there's no vision. And if there is, as the leader, you may not have been clear in painting that vision nor done enough to get your team and customers on board. ⟵ *Or family, for that matter*

Motivational speaker Zig Zigler, the consummate salesman, once said (and I agree): "If you can dream it, you can achieve it." However, to dream it, you must first envision it. Then go one step further and believe it to be real.

Next, consider the relationship between you and your team. Are there any shared values? If so, as a team, are you living them? Without a shared vision and values, a few spot fires caused by misaligned expectations can quickly grow to a full-blown dumpster fire where you're in the news and your family – at home and at work ⟵ *I also call my team my family; it's a whole thing* – is now torn about whether to continue supporting you or start blaming you, leaving you standing there looking for a scapegoat. Sounds extreme, but it's standard practice in politics and, disappointingly, all too often in business.

For inspiration on what not to do, check out the book *Rocky Road* written by Robert Wainwright. It's the true story of confectionary company Darrell Lea and a great blueprint for how to fuck shit up in just three generations.[21] A real chocolate-filled dumpster fire, which isn't as sweet as it sounds.

So how in the heck do you go about creating an organisation that doesn't result in you being publicly pantsed? Simple. Create a strong and engaging vision that not only drives you to get the hell out of bed every day but also drives those around you to do the same, and more.

We go into business for so many different reasons. Your reasons may, and likely will, be different from mine. You may have gone into business to be of service, to make a living on your terms, to make bank and run, or, if you're anything like me, because you're not a very subordinate employee and decided to become the leader of your own destiny. ← *Definitely a bottle of wine story*

Whatever the reason, what's the same for all of us is: we all have customers (well, hopefully, if not, you will by the end of all this). It's through this simple similarity that I can talk to you about what it takes to keep those customers and your team coming back for more, helping you to not just see yourself as a *business* but also as a trusted and value-driven *brand*.

What's the difference, you ask? Well, in short, your business is the operations, the nuts and bolts, if you will. Your brand, however, is your image, your reputation, and the identity that your team, your customers, and the public perceive. Your brand elicits emotions; it makes us *feel our feels*. Think Kmart, think Bondi Beach, think the completely non-functional but must-have Stanley Cup, think Australia Day lamb commercials with AFL legend Sam Kekovich. ← *If you're not an Aussie, go check them out* They all come with vivid imagery and spark emotions whenever you hear their names. How does an organisation reach this point? By living and breathing every aspect of their brand vision over many years.

DREAM THE DREAM TO ACHIEVE IT

If you're new to business – even if you're not – there are several activities you must complete to set yourself a strong and sustainable foundation for becoming a favourable brand. In my more than 20 years' experience, the first major activity is getting clear on your vision, then your values, then setting it all in motion. It sounds easy enough, but you must do it right. Luckily, there are several tactics you can use to create a strong brand vision and accompanying values.

Firstly, all great brands have a clear **vision** that unites the humans they serve. An aspirational view of their future that helps them to succinctly articulate why they get out of bed and what they want to achieve for the greater good. Secondly, they have a set of core **values** (the human attributes that hold the highest value in the organisation), which help lead and align their team's behaviours and activities to the organisation's goals, cementing a solid business and brand culture. Thirdly, many of the titans support their vision and values with an engaging **mission** statement.

> Your vision, values, and mission are your guiding light, leading you to achieve the brand you want by ensuring only activities that align to these three elements are prioritised.

It can be easy to make each element personal. However, ask yourself, "Can my vision and values be easily explained, easily lived, and a driving force for ongoing growth and achievement for the business and the individuals who work within it?"

Here are some well-known businesses and their vision statements, which have ultimately helped create some of the world's most value-driven and trusted brands:

Google

"To provide access to the world's information in one click."

Headspace

"All young Australians are supported to be mentally healthy and engaged in their communities."

Microsoft

"To empower every person and every organization on the planet to achieve more."

Apple

"To make the best products on earth and to leave the world better than we found it."

THE JOY OF CEHX

Now, in some of these organisations, maybe the vision came simply and was an instant hit among the team (or the founder, as they were the only one toiling away in their garage, biding their time, creating a multibillion-dollar conglomerate – we see you Bezos). However, for many of us in business, our vision requires some edits, and, like most good things, it continues to evolve until one day, by Jove, we've got it!

For example, my brand vision changed multiple times before I settled on what it is now. With it, my business model and purpose also changed as my business matured from the startup phase to the growth and establishment phase. There's absolutely nothing wrong with this. Why, you ask? Well, just having a vision in place means you're working towards an aligned position. You're always considering what's best for your organisation, for your customers, for your up-and-coming team.

Like with many organisations, mine included, you may find that the vision created back in your garage doesn't hit the same now as it did at its inception. That too is completely normal, and the great thing about creating a brand vision is it's not set in stone. That's not to say visions are fluid, but they can, in some circumstances, reach a point where they don't serve you the way they used to. If you do find that your brand vision is no longer serving you, don't ignore the situation, instead take the opportunity to:

1. **Regroup** and collect your thoughts, with the right people to help you.

2. **Reflect**, assess what you were, what you are now, and what you want to be.

3. **Recreate.** If Madonna can do it to stay relevant, so can you.

Look at me just creating a new 3 Rs ←

ACTIVITY: CREATE AND RATE YOUR BRAND VISION

In the space provided, draft three versions of a potential brand vision for your organisation. Then on a scale of 1 to 10 (where 1 is "this ain't it at all" and 10 is "it's so great I could cry") rate each version using the following criteria.

1. This vision paints a vivid image in my mind.

2. This vision feels aspirational and a little bit scary to achieve.

3. This vision is easily understood by those who don't know my business.

Brand Vision Draft

TRUSTED BRANDS HAVE GREAT CEHX!

Let me remind you of what great **CEHX** is ...

> Simply put, **CEHX** is the **C**ustomer, **E**mployee and **H**uman e**X**perience that all well-known and trusted brands map out in detail to understand every touchpoint of their business and how you, as a customer or employee, and certainly as a human, will be impacted by that experience.

Let's take IKEA, for example. Their customer experience is world-renowned. Every single IKEA is laid out the same, a racecourse track of sorts. You can only easily go forward. Turning back becomes a battle, as you spend your journey walking into oncoming traffic, so you're essentially forcibly encouraged to continue moving with the herd. As you bear witness to the KALLAX shelving units, the POÄNG armchair, and so many other unique and interesting pieces of furniture and home bric-a-brac, you begin to loathe the experience (maybe it's just me), but then you smell freedom.

That's right – IKEA understands that after that shopping experience, customers deserve a reward, ← *Love that dopamine hit* and what better reward is there than sitting in the Swedish-inspired cafeteria to wet your taste buds with some Swedish meatballs or a tumbler of fresh VINTERSAGA (Swedish festive drink). Personally, I'm going for the DRYCK BUBBEL

PÄRON (sparkling pear drink, the closest to a sparkling wine I'm getting).

Tell me you've been to IKEA a few times without telling me you've been to IKEA

Whatever takes your fancy, the point is, IKEA understands the assignment. To be perceived as a value-driven brand, they need to give their customers an *experience* beyond the rudimentary customer service many businesses focus on and keep you on their premises for as long as possible, leaving with a full belly and lots of serotonin rushing through your body. IKEA understands that their customers need a different value proposition.

Social media fights in the attention economy better than everyone

IKEA created a vision, "To create a better everyday life for the many people," and went to work building the business model that supported the experiences they wanted to deliver. This is great CEHX, as evidenced by IKEA's year-on-year profit growth in the billions, their ongoing commitment to their vision, and their ongoing developments and innovations to keep employees, or co-workers as they're called, loyal to their brand.

Swedish for thank you → IKEA's Tack! employee recognition program is a terrific example. Through the program, the company gives eligible co-workers a superannuation bonus (above and beyond the regulated payments), helping to increase what was already a higher-than-average employee retention rate.[22] For example, employees who stay with the company for 5 years receive a $2,000-plus bonus.[23] This feeds into the employee experience, as co-workers start to feel a greater sense of stability. They feel valued as humans and can tangibly experience the positive difference of being employed by IKEA.

Ultimately, IKEA comprehends the strong correlation between a positive employee experience and engaged, active, and innovative employees who want to serve their customers. In turn, those customers feel valued and, despite systems and automations, feel as if they're being treated like human beings. As a result, and despite the fact that they'll soon have a whole other experience assembling flat pack furniture, they'll revere the experience and come back again, and again, and again, telling anyone who'll listen how great the company is. Essentially, they become advocates of a trusted and value-driven brand.

IT'S THE JOURNEY, NOT THE CLIMB

When laying your brand's foundations, consider consciously understanding the touchpoints your customers and employees will experience, and build the bones around supporting those experiences in an exceptional and innovative way.

One great way to start is to perform a customer experience blueprint activity, or journey map, as it's often called. The good news? In chapter six, I'm going to help you map your customer experience. Performing a CX Journey Map is also a great opportunity to gain a clear comprehension of any opportunities for improvement in areas such as operations, customer service, technology, and more.

KNOW THINE CUSTOMER

All great brands have spent immeasurable amounts of energy on getting to know their customers. Now you may have heard of getting to know your audience with demographics (population-based facts such as age, gender, race, religion, marital status, education, and income). There's also a lesser-known measurement used by businesses called psychographics, which involves understanding and classifying humans based on their beliefs, attitudes towards certain subjects, aspirations, and many other psychological and social measures.

While these are great, I invite you to also consider the newcomer to the study and classification of brand-loving humans – valuegraphics (discussed in chapter three). Valuegraphics involves creating a random stratified statistical representation of the population and what it values. Why is this so important?

> When you learn what your customers truly **value** and how it influences their purchasing behaviours, you can gain an edge over your competitors.

Let's take the concept for a spin, shall we?

Consider a brand that's loved by humans of all creeds: Australian retailer, Rebel Sport. Rebel may have an archived document somewhere that breaks down how they'll market to all their different customer segments, and how they'll become a trusted sporting retailer for everyone from kids doing Auskick on Saturday mornings to professional athletes swimming the English Channel. The reality is, their target audience is *very* broad. While the people in that broad audience might come from different socio-economic backgrounds, drive different cars, and have different levels of fitness, they share some core values. In general, Rebel's customers hold the values of health, performance, quality, choice, integrity, and passion, leading them to choose Rebel as their sporting goods destination over any other brand or sporting retailer. These are the values, the emotions Rebel stirs deep within its customers nationwide.

So, as a business, if you understand what your customers and employees value in their heart of hearts, you have the edge to create a value-driven brand. One that can deliver experiences that create a visceral emotion every time they engage with you, keeping them loyal to your brand.

So many businesses in every industry aren't effectively working towards becoming a brand that elicits trust and loyalty from their customers. ← *Despite what they say* Therefore, only 27 percent of customers are loyal to a brand based on their overall shopping experience. That's an enormous opportunity to be better than your competitors at a time when a meagre 5 percent increase in customer loyalty can result in a profit increase of over 25 percent.[24]

Why wouldn't you want to become a market-leading, or for that matter, an industry-leading brand? It's certainly within every business's reach to deliver a customer experience worthy of loyalty. So let's go get 'em!

TL;CBF

- Many business challenges stem from a lack of clear, aligned vision, leading to misaligned values, inefficient activities, and ultimately constant firefighting. Remember, vision misalignment = business chaos, and nobody needs that in their life.

- A business is its operations, while a brand is its reputation, emotional impact, and identity. Trusted brands like IKEA, Google, and Microsoft have clear visions that guide their actions and customer perceptions.

- The power of CEHX (Customer, Employee, and Human eXperience) – brands that meticulously design customer and employee experiences create loyalty and long-term success. IKEA's seamless in-store experience and employee benefits exemplify this approach.

- It pays to know your customers deeply. Demographics, psychographics, and the emerging field of valuegraphics (focusing on what people truly value) help businesses build stronger emotional connections with their audience.

- Only 27 percent of customers are loyal due to customer experience, and even a 5 percent increase in loyalty can boost profits by over 25 percent. Prioritising experience and trust can set your brand apart. This is where brand loyalty = profitability!

CHAPTER 6:
MAPPING THE JOURNEY

A MURKY ORIGIN STORY

As a reminder, a customer journey map is a tool commonly used to achieve a deeper understanding of the touchpoints and milestones customers will experience using your business. In turn, it can help determine the likelihood of taking a customer from unknown to advocate.

In recent years, customer journey maps have grown in notoriety and popularity, with new SaaS (software as a service) platforms being developed and launched, often to help users create anything from simplified to complex customer journey maps. No matter who conceived the concept, it was clearly a worthwhile effort, as it has now helped millions – okay, maybe hundreds of thousands of organisations globally design customer experiences worthy of their customer's trust and loyalty.

KNOWLEDGE IS POWER

In essence, a CX journey map is one of many available tools used for gaining deeper insights into the experiences your business delivers to your customers, your employees (even if you don't have any yet), and the humans you serve. It's a visual representation of a specific aspect of the CX. Often, organisations map a service they're already delivering. However, I would like to see more organisations use the customer journey map earlier in the process to understand how to best bring their products and services to market. It's your strategy that shines in this activity. It's about your ability to know what best practice looks like, and be better. The other great thing about having a visual representation is that our mere human brains process images 6 to 600 times faster than text.[25]

Your chance to be unique →

Why limit yourself to being ← the same as everyone else?

When I think of a CX journey map, it reminds me of process mapping and the importance of creating a visual representation of the movements, decisions, and outcomes related to the execution of a process. The difference between a simple or even complex process map and a CX journey map is that, traditionally, a process map is the operations and mechanics of a service, whereas a CX journey map saddles operations beside the human experience. It's where human-centred, rather than process-driven, design begins (we'll talk more about human-centred design in coming chapters).

Essentially, a CX journey map utilises customer personas, demographic, psychographic, ethnographic, and, my favourite, valuegraphic information to form an engaging picture of what it's like to be your customer.

WHEN TO MAP THE CX JOURNEY, AND WHY

Organisations that want to truly create a customer-centric culture must be strategic (remember, strategy is your chance to be unique), on point with their customers' needs, wants, and JTBD (that is, jobs to be done), and conscious of the experience they're delivering. With all of this, a CX journey map can help.

We want purposeful wins

> Mapping the customer experience journey provides the opportunity to understand not just the journey itself but also the individual touchpoints, pain points, opportunities to do it differently, do it better, or, in some cases, stick to the plan if you can demonstrate you're on the right track.

But what if you didn't do the journey map? What if you didn't take the moment to learn that, in fact, you had some really great stuff happening, and you went off half-cocked and inadvertently changed it, therefore ruining your chance to achieve a loyalty-driven customer experience? Imagine!

Delivering experiences in a business willy-nilly is a recipe for certain disaster as you work your fingers to the bone delivering experiences your customers don't even appreciate and your employees (remember them, your front-line advocates?) grow to resent. *You* also become resentful of all the spot fires you have to put out and the lack of sleep you're getting as your bottom line falls out the arse of your less than strategic and mostly guess-timate-driven endeavours. You wonder if it's all worth it. You wonder if you should just fire everyone and go back to whatever job you had before entrepreneurship, before that burning desire to run your own ship took over. Remember those days, all care and no responsibility? Ahhhh, weren't they grand? No? Ohhh yeah, that's why you left.

Okay, so there's an easy way to turn the ship around and mitigate the fires, the pissed off customers, and the resentful team. Did I say easy? Actually, that's not true. It's tough, but it's effective, and it starts with working strategically, *[Purposeful activities that assist in achieving long-term goals]* becoming conscious, and becoming response-*able*. That's right – response-*able*. Once you reach the point of consciousness, you're becoming response-able. You're growing to respond more appropriately rather than react, like the aspirational leader you know you are, the one your team deserves. As I tell my therapy clients and as Australian business mentor the late Kerwin Rae taught me, think of life as a swinging pendulum in a clock. Nothing good comes of that clock when the pendulum swings too hard at either extreme. Learning to stay gently centred is the best possible way to make things tick along smoothly. But you have to put the ego away. You have to calm it down and go out and listen, and I mean really listen. Listen to your team without repercussion *[Honest but not rude]* because you're building a safe culture where candid communication is celebrated. Gather data and listen to your customers without bias, excuses, or defensiveness.[26] Read between the lines, read into

[Educate yourself about HX and bias to be a better human. check end notes for resource]

their silence, read into their requests, read into their behaviours. I know this business is your baby and some people might just need to tell you your baby is ugly, but at least you'll know, and you can give that baby the best glow-up anyone has seen! If Old Spice can come back and be deemed 'cool again', *I was personally a Brut 33 fan* then so can you.

As I mentioned before, great governance (processes and systems) dictates that no new program, service, product, or idea should be released into the ether until a fully fleshed-out CX journey map has been created, with associated personas determined. This activity needs to be business as usual, or BAU for those who froth over a good bit of corporate jargon. When it becomes the way you do business, it becomes every person's responsibility to cultivate a culture of customer centricity and alleviate bullshit politics, allowing cock-ups in experience design to be found quickly, *Because we love candid communication* causing as little impact as possible, which my PR *I'm also a qualified PR specialist* hat approves of immensely.

At the beginning of a new innovation is certainly the first point at which an organisation should complete the CX journey map; however, it's definitely not the last. Your customer experience isn't something you set and forget like that half-arsed business and marketing plan you made *There's no tick and flick here* 7 years ago that never saw the light of day. We'd need a whole other book to discuss why *that's* unhelpful, even detrimental – and maybe I'll write one – but unlike that business plan, customer experience is always changing. You may not be changing it, but outside factors, such as new competition or altered customer needs, can drive change in behaviours. Due to all the outside parameters, it's necessary to measure and remeasure the customer experience journey often – if not often, regularly enough to stay informed and agile to change where necessary.

You might learn that your organisation is on the precipice of change, which ← *Don't do a Kodak* can, in turn, affect the customer experience in ways you may not have considered. Take the epic example of Coca-Cola changing the Coke recipe in 1985 and creating 'New Coke'. There was worldwide upheaval. To many, the taste of Coca-Cola is a sacred cow, as demonstrated by the Pepsi-Coke war that has raged for decades. Within months, Coca-Cola conceded they'd innovated without understanding the impact of the change *Imagine how mad fans were when the cocaine was removed* and were scuttling to reinstate the old recipe back into circulation.

Now, consider the costs, damage to the brand, not to mention the distrust Coco-Cola earned from its customers. What a public relations nightmare, much of which could have been mitigated by understanding customer personas and creating a solid CX journey map from the start. It's also a timely reminder that just because a company is large, it doesn't mean they do everything well and you couldn't do a better job. I promise you, you can.

THE CASUAL HOOK-UP TO CREATING A CX JOURNEY MAP

Completing a customer persona and customer experience journey map is like skinning a cat. Did I mention I used that metaphor once and in the audience (virtual conference), there was in fact a lady sitting there on screen with her cat in her lap? She was utterly offended. I could have said snake, but I guess my subconscious brain saw a cat and decided that was the animal to use. I laugh now, but I'm also fascinated at how strongly imagery can influence the subconscious mind. Anyway, back on topic.

As with any mapping method, with the CX journey map, there's a foundational process. Over the years, many a 'thought leader' has come along and attempted to placard their name on the process and innovate it in some way, shape, or form. So, in reality, there's no wrong way to go about it as long as you cover the baseline disciplines of creating your customer personas and journey map.

CREATING A CUSTOMER PERSONA

First things first – you can't just make this shit up. I mean, you can, but it has to be based on some level of factual knowledge. So, you're going to need some data, and the best type to use is what's known as qualitative data – information *Remember, shit in, shit out* based on actual human behaviours, for example, comments. Quantitative data, on the other hand, focuses on the number of people who acted out those behaviours, that is, statistics.

If you don't have access to your own customers' feedback that discusses topics such as "I visited your store," "I used your services

XYZ," "We purchased product ABC and took it with us to Do-Re-Mi," you must put effort into obtaining such information to ensure you create an accurate persona. You can do this through customer surveys via platforms such as SurveySensum (not a paid ad, I just love their work) or asking for specific feedback through your socials. Before I even had customers, I would go to well-populated Facebook groups and ask members to tell me their stories of different experiences that I could then relate back to my buyer persona. But before you do this, try to find communities that have a relative alignment to your target audience; otherwise, again, you'll be just making shit up that won't work for the people you want to serve. The other option is to actually invite real customers of your brand to come in and perform the activities with you. Hear it from the horse's mouth.

Once you have some relevant insights, consider who those insights came from. Even if you only have their name, from their feedback you can still try to determine their age range and what they value (read between the lines on this one if you have to). If there's customer feedback stating they had to wait a long time to achieve something or receive something, they value their time. If there's feedback around how hard it is to find something, they also value their time. If there's feedback around how nice a team member was to their kids despite the child having a meltdown, they value kindness and respect. Put yourself in the shoes of that customer. If that was your kid losing their mind and someone was understanding and calm despite the ruckus, how would you feel? Would you value the experience more than you would have had they shuffled you out the door, rolling their eyes, unwilling to understand the situation you were in? If conscious empathy isn't your bag, you can use the empathy mapping tools in the upcoming activity to help kick it up a gear. I'm a firm believer that empathy can be taught if there's a will to learn. ← *Love that will over skill*

Now that you have some insights into what your customer is likely to value – for example, family, time, integrity, respect, kindness, helpfulness, positive engagements, stability – it's time to consider demographics. Remember, while demographics are helpful, they're certainly *more* helpful when used in conjunction with valuegraphics. If you're a retailer with multiple sites, please don't fall into the trap of believing you have only one customer persona to consider. In reality, you might have several just for one customer type alone. For example, you might have a location in the Melbourne CBD and one in Melbourne's western suburbs. Although only 20 kilometres apart, they may as well be different countries. ← *They probably are if you're in Europe* One is full of urbanites under 30 and corporate boomers over 50; the other is a melting pot of immigrants originating anywhere from New Zealand to South Sudan. Their values may only alter slightly, but their demographics could be miles apart. So you see why it's so important to take everything into consideration, not just demographics, like many of the resources on the subject narrow-mindedly instruct.

WIIFM

In spending time applying a deeper understanding to the customer experience, you're strategically creating a more aligned WIIFM proposition. What's WIIFM, you ask? Well, the casual hook-up to WIIFM is understanding consciously, *Consciously means purposefully* "What's in it for me?" and delivering on those key benefits. Who's the *me* in this scenario? Well, it's you. It's your customers. It's your team. It's even your indirect customers, like your suppliers, your consultants, your mentors, your family who have to deal with you at the end of a hard day. *But we're working to replace hard with smart* WIIFM keeps people involved. It makes them feel valued, and it makes them revere you enough to come back for more.

In knowing who your customer is (of which your organisation may have several, depending on what you put out to the universe) and documenting their personas, you can dive deeper into what the journey looks like from their point of view. Not just the operating experience, like a process map, but also the human experience (HX). A quality customer experience journey map considers the thoughts and feelings of each persona at each touchpoint of the journey.

> When we care for the human experience, we can create empathy for those we serve, which, simply put, means we're willing and able to put ourselves in their shoes.

Jobs to be done Their JTBD are at the core of our service and product design, and they, as customers, can sense and feel this. For example, imagine you're a community-owned bank and one of your customer personas hears a radio advertisement for your organisation. Now, a process map wouldn't tell you that, at this particular touchpoint of the customer's experience, they have major distrust for the banking industry and are thinking to themselves, *Ohhh, another fat cat preying on small communities.* So, before any new service or product release, ensure the completion of a CX journey map and consider your customer persona's emotions, behaviours, and intended outcomes. This allows you to identify and address potential negative triggers that could unwittingly harm your brand and go unnoticed until the damage is already done.

If you're familiar with the Johari Window (an old but reliable coaching and leadership tool), you'll have ascertained that your community bank is now in the 'open' window. You know, and others know. Because you now know what you know, you can understand that your customers highly value integrity, so you may introduce a report card that offers full transparency around your profits. You may also ensure it's plainly written (if you need help, call on Leslie O'Flahavan, founder of E-Write and the queen of plain writing) and engaging so it gets read, is easily understood, and works towards building your community bank as a trusted and value-driven brand. This is why we do customer experience journey maps and, just as importantly, why we seek to know who our customers are and what they value.

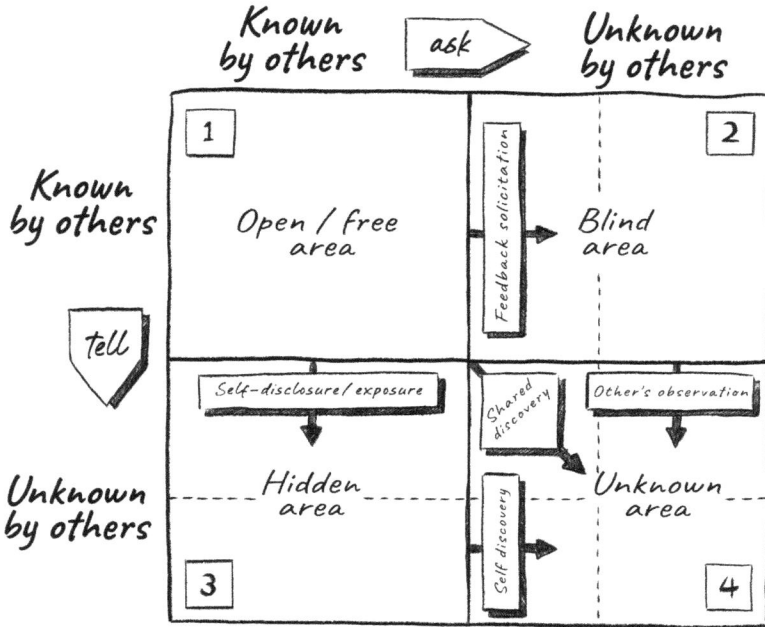

Known by others | ask | Unknown by others

1 — Open / free area — Feedback solicitation — Blind area — 2

Known by others

tell

Self-disclosure / exposure — Shared discovery — Other's observation

Unknown by others — 3 — Hidden area — Self discovery — Unknown area — 4

The Johari Window – a feedback model for self-awareness.

ACTIVITY: CREATE A CUSTOMER PERSONA

♦ Visit **aileenday.com.au/tjocehx-tools** to download a template to create your very own customer persona, starting with the main person you're in business for. Once you've completed a customer persona for at least one customer your business serves, ← known as a customer segment return to this activity.

* Return to the **TJoCEHX Tools section** of the website and download the 'empathy map' template. Using your completed customer persona template, follow the instructions on the empathy map template, taking the following into consideration:

* Based on your research or assumptions, brainstorm what your customer might express in each area when engaging with your brand.

* Identify pain points and motivations from this map to shape your upcoming customer experience journey map's key moments.

TL;CBF

* Tools such as customer personas, CX journey maps, and empathy maps can make an indelible impact on the way you deliver CEHX in your business.

* Using qualitative and quantitative customer feedback will help support your mapping experience, increasing its accuracy.

* Be open and ready to take accountability for any less than ideal customer and employee experiences you learn about. Candid communication creates clarity and promotes a solution-focused culture.

- CX journey maps help everyone in the organisation understand how they **all** play a role in the successful delivery of a customer-centric brand.

CREATING YOUR CX JOURNEY MAP

Like with customer personas, there are plenty of ways to skin this snake. Some people use emojis; others use charts; some overcomplicate it; others oversimplify it. However you do it, the purpose must be the same: your CX journey map must help you create clarity, transparency, and actionable insights into how you can deliver a customer experience worthy of your customer's loyalty and advocacy. Like the title of CX goddess Jeanne Bliss' book asks, "Would you do that to your mother?" An important question to keep in mind.

Now, I've completed many customer journey maps for myself and my clients, and when it came time to explain the process in writing, I was trying to work out, how do I hook a brother up, or sister or anyone in between, without overcomplicating the instructions? Well, I came up with what I would consider eight reasonably simple-to follow-steps.

For those who process information more visually, scan the QR code to watch me create a CX journey map (using Excel) and, if you like, create your own at the same time.

ACTIVITY: CX JOURNEY MAP

* Head over to **aileenday.com.au/tjocehx-tools** and download your Excel CX journey map template.

* Return to this activity to read the eight steps of customer experience journey mapping. Don't do anything yet! Just read and let it all soak in. As you read through the steps, refer to your download-able CX journey map to see where each piece of the puzzle fits.

Before you start mapping out your CX as it currently stands or, if it's not yet implemented, how you believe it would be best delivered, be clear on what part of the experience you would like to map. You may want to start with your most purchased product or service, as each offer requires its own journey map. For example, I offer an in-person and online group coaching program, and I also offer in-person clinical therapy. Those two services can't be put on the same CX journey map, as the journey is different for each service. However, if you sell a variety of consumable products from a bricks-and-mortar retailer, putting the experience on one journey map may be suitable. However, if you sell both in store and online, you'll need two journey maps. You feel me?

A typical CX journey map is broken down into five stages, or phases, of the buying process. These phases are listed horizontally (as rows) across your map. Your job in this mapping activity is to understand how you move your customers *That's the advocacy bit* from awareness to retention. The five stages are:

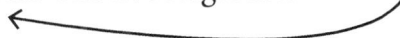

1. **Awareness:** The part of the journey where the customer has a need or a driver – a job to be done – yet they may not yet be aware of your business. What can you do to help them know you exist and are worthy of their consideration?

2. **Consideration:** Refers to the customer learning about your business. At this stage, you must be consciously aware of how you present yourself to potential buyers and help them understand that you're their best option.

3. **Acquisition or purchase:** Refers to the customer selecting you over any other potential competitors. They actively engage with your business. They buy your products or pay for your services. They are now officially a paying customer.

4. **Retention:** Ongoing engagement is the goal here. Have your cross-functional teams collaborate on how to *AKA loyal* meaningfully engage and keep customers buying through your brand. Work to alleviate the constant looking for a better option.

5. **Advocacy:** The pinnacle of the customer experience pyramid. We're looking for loyalty *and* advocacy, and customers in this part of the journey exhibit exactly that. They're steadfast in their commitment to your brand.

Remember that from chapter four?

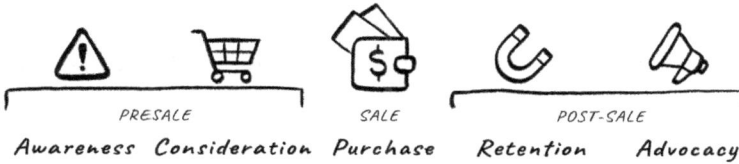

Horizontal axis of a standard CX journey map (phases).

The columns in Excel

On the vertical of the map, the headings can be slightly different depending on who you're learning from. The most common headings include:

1. **Customer goals:** In the true CX discipline,

   Visit unipro-solutions.com to learn more about JTBD

   we call these drivers or jobs to be done. What's driving the customer in this part of the experience? Throughout the different stages of the CX journey, the goals will evolve. For example, in the *awareness* phase, the customer goal might be to find a business that can fix their vehicle. As they move through the phases, this goal can evolve. For example, in the *acquisition* phase, the customer has acquired your services; however, their goal is to now get their vehicle serviced and returned in better condition and for a reasonable fee (not get ripped off).

2. **Customer actions:** Customer actions describe the specific behaviours and steps customers take during each phase of their journey. These are observable activities like researching online, asking for recommendations, comparing options, making purchases, or seeking support. Actions can span multiple channels and often reflect the customer's emotional state and level of intent at each stage.

3. **Touchpoints and channels:** In this section of the CX journey map, we list the touchpoints applicable to each section of the journey. We also document the channel we're using to produce and deliver that touchpoint.

    In the more advanced version of CX journey mapping, we have what's known as 'customer experience blueprinting', which creates transparency around the front and backstage touchpoints, including systems, processes, and policies that apply to that touchpoint. But let's crawl before we run.

    So, in this portion of the map, we simply need to document which touchpoint is relevant to each stage of the journey and which channel is being used to deliver that touchpoint. For example, in the *awareness* phase where the customer's goal is to find a mechanic and the customer action is to get on Facebook and ask for a recommendation, the touchpoint and channel are: customer learns of Jimbo's Auto Repairs through recommendations and visits the Facebook page for more information. In the next stage, *consideration*, the customer's goal is to learn more, and the customer's action is to visit Jimbo's Auto Repair website; therefore, the touchpoint and channel is visiting the online services page and bookings page.

4. **Customer questions and feels/thoughts:** This, for me, is one of the best parts of customer experience journey mapping. It's where empathy hits the road and we can take off with insights that, had we not done this activity, we most likely wouldn't have had. Sadly, many CX journey mapping resources don't include this piece on the map, but I believe it's where the gold is! ← *More wins for you!*

In this section, we get to put ourselves in our customers' shoes. If you're lucky enough to have a willing customer come in and work on the journey map with you, even better! Using our customer persona and understanding of the human experience, we can visualise exactly what the customer is experiencing. What do their concerns feel like? What thoughts are they having? What objections are coming up for them? How do past experiences or the opinions of others affect their decisions? In our case study of Jimbo's Auto Repair, it could be apprehension. Jimbo might not have any testimonials but seems like an affordable option, so a customer may be confused. They may be sceptical and concerned that they might get burnt on the quality of work for the sake of a good price. They may have questions about how long they'll be without their vehicle or what qualifications or experience Jimbo has relating to their specific vehicle. You can already see the array of opportunities Jimbo has to create a feeling of calm and confidence for his customers through content or copy ← *The words on your website, socials, and so on* that speaks to these questions, feelings, and thoughts.

5. **Overall CX:** In many CX journey map resources, there's a section that refers to the customer's overall emotion through each stage of the journey. Many like to use emoticons that show expressions such as dissatisfied, neutral, and satisfied ☹ 😐 🙂. I say get creative. It's your licence to show customer emotions in a way that resonates with you and your organisation. For example, I've seen emotions displayed as different weather types (clouds and lightning bolts, sunshine, rain, rainbows, and so on). Use whatever resonates with you, but ultimately it's your visual representation of your overall customer experience *Get your creative brain fired up* at each stage. For example, you could be all smiles from *awareness* to *acquisition* but because you spent so much energy attracting leads, your service delivery was less than anything worth writing home about, so customers begin to feel neutral and don't move to the retention stage, let alone become advocates. Overall, that stage would get a fiery sad face. Essentially, visualising emotions highlights all the overarching pain points in your CX journey.

6. **Pain points:** Once we have a clearer insight into our customer's experience, their goals, their thoughts and

feelings, and the touchpoints we're delivering through each stage, we should now have deeper insight into the pain points experienced by us, our customers, and our employees. ← *Remember, they are your first line of advocates*

For example, we now know that customers are sceptical of the quality of work from Jimbo because he's so affordable yet has no testimonials or social proof. In the pain points under consideration, we would state, "No testimonials, no social proof of quality." *Aim to obtain these in your own business*

When we get to the *service* stage, a customer may have taken the chance on Jimbo, but a lack of organisation in his automotive garage creates anxiety for that customer, creating the pain point of "untidy garage." This is customer experience at its finest. Everything matters. ← *It's more than just your service*

7. **Opportunities to improve:** At the bottom of the CX journey map, we can detail the opportunities to improve the customer experience at each stage based on our learnings. In the case of Jimbo and his automotive garage, to move customers to the retention stage and beyond, the *awareness, consideration,* and *acquisition* phases may need additional focus. More specifically, he may need to deliver a more consistent marketing strategy with curated content that provides a mix of utility and fun, aligning to Jimbo's vision and values for his business. In the *acquisition* and *service* stages, Jimbo may find that creating a more inviting workspace not only entices quality tradespeople to want to work there, thus improving the

employee experience, but also creates a sense of confidence and trust for the customer. In the *retention* stage, Jimbo might conclude that his competitors offer a discount on every fifth service. However, it doesn't appear that this has built loyalty or generated much additional revenue, so he decides to create a referral program instead, which also encourages his team to do high-quality work.

← And his customers to do the marketing for him!

8. **Priorities:** Once you have taken the time, energy, and effort, it's time to identify your organisation's priorities. To be frank, there are a shit ton of ways to break down your priorities. In reality, you won't have the capacity to focus on

I call out all three separately because that's what it takes to complete this activity with a genuine intention to do and be better for your customers, your team, and yourself

them all at the same time. However, some activities and opportunities might be what's considered low-hanging fruit, meaning they're reasonably simple to achieve and provide a decent return on investment. Some activities might need to be shelved temporarily when others must be completed first. Some opportunities might be blue-sky thinking – a type of creative thinking that typically sees grandiose ideas turned into viable solutions. They're big and can be impactful but often require solving other problems before they can become a focus.

FUCK OFF THE NOISE AND GET SHIT DONE

To help you prioritise your activities and opportunities, you can use a priority matrix. Using a priority matrix tool means you list priorities as either 'important and urgent', 'important but not urgent', 'not important but urgent', or 'not important and not urgent'.

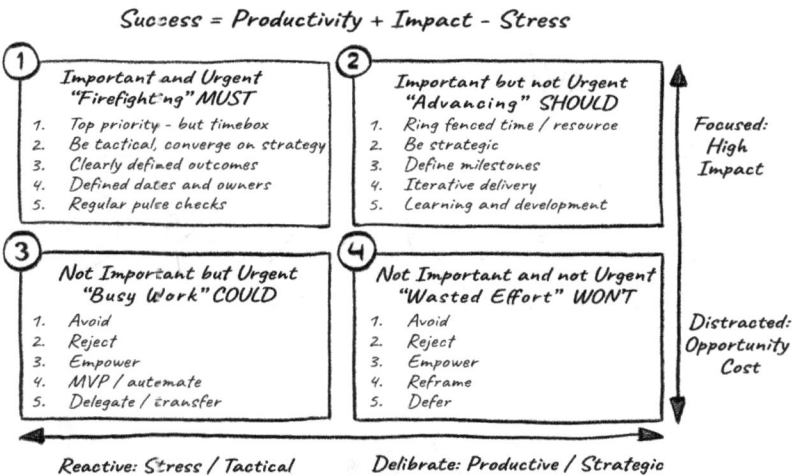

Success = Productivity + Impact - Stress

1	Important and Urgent "Firefighting" MUST	2	Important but not Urgent "Advancing" SHOULD	
1.	Top priority - but timebox	1.	Ring fenced time / resource	Focused:
2.	Be tactical, converge on strategy	2.	Be strategic	High
3.	Clearly defined outcomes	3.	Define milestones	Impact
4.	Defined dates and owners	4.	Iterative delivery	
5.	Regular pulse checks	5.	Learning and development	
3	Not Important but Urgent "Busy Work" COULD	4	Not Important and not Urgent "Wasted Effort" WON'T	
1.	Avoid	1.	Avoid	Distracted:
2.	Reject	2.	Reject	Opportunity
3.	Empower	3.	Empower	Cost
4.	MVP / automate	4.	Reframe	
5.	Delegate / transfer	5.	Defer	

Reactive: Stress / Tactical   Delibrate: Productive / Strategic

Example of a Priority Matrix.

Once you've established your priorities, it's time to set some goals and assign the activities to their rightful owners. Remember – *everyone* in your organisation is responsible for your customers' experience. However, as the leader, it's up to you to lead by example and hold yourself and your team accountable for their part.

Now, goal setting, like priority setting, is a snake that can be skinned a million different ways, and what works for the goose might not work for the gander. However, one goal setting model that works no matter how you crack the nut is SMART. Now, I could make an *ass* out of *u* and *me* (assume) that everyone reading this knows what SMART goals are, but just in case you don't or you struggle to remember it all, with the help of the wonderful business resource Mindtools and *Attitude Is Everything* author Paul J Meyer, let's break it down.[27]

SMART goals breakdown.

S – SPECIFIC: Your goal should be clear and specific. When drafting your goal, try to answer the five 'W' questions:

- What do I want to accomplish?
- Why is this goal important?
- Who is involved?

- Where is it located?

- Which resources or limits are involved?

M – MEASURABLE: So you can track your progress and stay motivated, a measurable goal should address questions such as:

- How much?

- How many?

- How will I know when it is accomplished?

A – ACHIEVABLE: Your goal should stretch your abilities but still be possible to achieve. An achievable goal will usually answer questions such as:

- How can I accomplish this goal?

- How realistic is the goal based on other constraints, such as financial factors?

R – RELEVANT: Your plans drive everyone forward. Having a relevant goal means answer 'yes' to these questions:

- Does this seem worthwhile?

- Is this the right time?

- Does this match our other efforts/needs?

- Am I the right person to reach this goal?

- Is it applicable in the current socio-economic environment?

T – TIMELY: It's imperative to set an end date for each goal, helping to ensure prioritisation among the day-to-day grind but also to ensure you achieve your goals in a timely manner. Having a time-bound goal usually means answering these questions:

- When?
- What can I do 6 months from now?
- What can I do 6 weeks from now?
- What can I do today?

Once you've planned your projects and activities using the SMART goals model, it's now up to you to hold yourself and your team accountable in delivering on your new customer experience. How you do this depends on your specific situation. However, remember … clear, candid, transparent, timely, targeted communication is key to overcoming any barriers that stand in your way. ← *We're building that trusted and value-driven culture brick by brick*

Once you understand your customer personas and have mapped out your CX journey, you can begin delivering a customer experience that positions you as a trusted, value-driven brand. We're on our way to feeling the joy of CEHX. But wait – that's not all folks.

TL;CBF

♦ There's gold in dem thar hills. Go pan for it. Get ready to make the CX journey a meaningful and properly considered piece of business development. You are now officially working **on** your business to alleviate forever working **in** it.

♦ Know that before diving into creating a CX journey map, you need to acquire data that helps you understand who your customers are and their opinions regarding their needs vs. what you deliver.

♦ Taking that data, you then need to assemble a customer persona – an image that helps you bring to life the customer segments for your business.

♦ Next, you need to create an empathy map to help you and your team put yourselves in your customers' shoes Learn to value what they value.

♦ With all that information, you're ready to put effort into creating your CX journey map.

COMPLETE YOUR CUSTOMER JOURNEY MAP

Visit **aileenday.com.au/tjocehx-tools** to download the customer experience journey map template. Remember, you can also follow along with me via the video if that suits your style.

CHAPTER 7:
MEASURING SUCCESS
IS CEHX-Y

THE MAGIC OF METRICS

Often, I see leaders champing at the bit to get customer experience disciplines implemented into their businesses – once they inherently understand why doing so is beneficial at least. They want to get on the survey bandwagon; they want to get on the creating pretty dashboards to give them real-time insights bandwagon, or many other fun bandwagons that come with CX. However, there's one bandwagon they rarely consider or want to put the energy into, and that's metrics. In my mind, metrics are undeniably necessary in any business activity. Otherwise, how do you know you're succeeding? How do you know you're not wasting your time, wasting your resources, or, even worse, pissing people off more than before? Good intentions won't save you.

Many organisations claim to "just know" when their customers are happy, but just knowing is as good as having all your policies and procedures in your head. It's not measurable. It's not shareable. It's not learnable. Worst of all, it's not consistently replicable; therefore, it's unscalable. You're essentially creating the grounds for disaster. So how do we move from just knowing shit to absolutely knowing and making strategic choices based on what's known,

Remember the Johari Window in chapter six?

not just assumed? Remember what it means to assume – it makes an *ass* out of *u* and *me*.

I know measuring things isn't the funnest activity in business, but I promise you if you're measuring the right things, at the right touchpoints, with the right metrics, you'll start to see that measuring success is CEHX-y. When you start to see the uptick from your efforts, results can become quite sexy and desirable. However, until that uptick occurs, I understand *Sexy, if you haven't yet caught on to the phonetics of the acronym* how these things can feel like a bit of a drag. Checking reports, filing through data, double-checking numbers, at a minimum, recruiting a great analytics talent who can do it all for you and reveal the story behind the numbers. *Please don't just throw AI at this haphazardly* Regrettably, you then need to converse with your accountant to see where the funds are moving and shaking. If you have a cool accountant like mine who's always a pleasure to chat with, maybe that's not so horrendous. Shout-out to Shehan!

So what must you do to put your best foot forward – *il migliore piede avanti.* (fun fact, I have this tattooed on my right foot) and be on top of the metrics to create that trusted, value-driven brand you know you want and your customers and team deserve? Let's find out.

PLAYING THE MATCHMAKER

When you created your brand vision (remember the activity from chapter five?), you would have ascertained that there were particular activities required and milestones to reach to make that vision a reality. For example, as mentioned, my brand vision is "to influence 10 million business owners, leaders, and entrepreneurs to create value-driven brands so they can live value-driven lives." With this vision, I've ascertained that to fulfil it, I will need to complete activities that allow me to be far-reaching. This book is just one of multiple strategic modes and methods to enable me to achieve that vision (that's why writing this book was a 'FUCK YES' activity). I will need to lead the way and show business owners what a trusted and value-driven brand looks and feels like. I will then need to perform activities that will help them take the characteristics and behaviours that allowed them to create their own value-driven brands and apply them more broadly, therefore, creating their own value-driven lives. Since starting to write this book, I've taken it a step further by becoming a qualified clinical hypnotherapist and psychotherapist, helping me help millions more business owners fulfil their destiny of becoming value-driven brands and living value-driven lives. Anyway, back to you.

Each activity you perform requires a set of metrics to understand whether it is working or is a flop. If it's a flop, you need to decide whether to stick at it or find another mechanism to help you achieve your vision. Essentially, you matchmake your activities to the fulfilment of your vision, and each one must be measured to understand its overall return on investment and capacity to help you achieve your brand vision.

INSTANT GRATIFICATION SYNDROME

Look, I'm technically a gen Y or an elder millennial according to one of my fave comedians, Iliza Shlesinger. I'm acutely aware of the yearning for instant gratification. I would go as far as to say my generation invented it. However, as I age and my wisdom grows, I see how this syndrome has become its own pandemic, and knowing what the world went through during COVID, I don't use the word pandemic lightly. I would be shocked if you or anyone could sit there and say in all seriousness that you've never performed an activity expecting an instant, gratifying response. For example, you put up a thought-provoking post and instantly want 100 likes, but you only get four, so you figure, *Fuck it* or, *Fuck them, they wouldn't know awesome if it bit them on the arse.* You complete a major project that saw you nearly burn out, and, in return, you get a single champagne flute as gratitude. ←This really I mean really, they couldn't spring for a set of four? happened So the next time you're put on a major project, you're certainly less inclined to bust your arse. You train in the mornings before work for 6 weeks, but nothing seems to be shifting, especially your fat gut and chunky thighs, so you think, *What's the point? Fuck this, I'm staying in bed.* A new virus runs loose through the world, and you think, *All this technology, and we can't have a cure ready right now*, but then, ironically, when one turns up sooner than expected, we don't trust it because it came so quickly. Humans ... sheesh. So hard to please. You see where I'm going?

> Anything that creates major change takes time. It takes consistency. It takes realistic expectations. It takes large amounts of energy to barely move the needle, but whether you see it or not, you are creating momentum. You are moving forward.

Yeah fine, you might have only got four likes on your post, but you created the post. Yeah fine, you only got a single champagne flute, but you also proved you're worthy to lead the next major project (now you can ensure the team is rewarded appropriately for their efforts in the future). Yeah fine, you've only lost an inch of waistline in six weeks, but your heart is healthier, and you've cultivated discipline that will ultimately lead to a more value-driven life. The reason you want results *now* is because when you get immediate results, you get hits of any number of happy hormones, such as:

Okay, Veruca Salt

- **Dopamine:** Associated with rewards, pleasurable sensations, learning, memory, motor system function, and more.

- **Serotonin:** Regulates your mood, sleep, appetite, digestion, learning ability, and memory.

- **Oxytocin:** Helps promote trust, empathy, and bonding in relationships, and oxytocin levels generally increase with physical affection like kissing, cuddling, and sex.

- **Endorphins:** Levels tend to increase when you engage in rewarding activities, such as eating, working out, or having sex. ⟵ *And CEHX*

I mean, who doesn't want any one of those hormones rushing through them? The problem is, when we don't get these hits of happiness, we tend to lose sight of the bigger picture, and we're renowned for giving up 3 feet away from gold. You may not know the story, so let me enlighten you. It's a favourite of mine, and it reminds me every day to find the motivation to keep creating momentum. So much so, I created a whole group coaching service based on it. The story comes from the book *Think and Grow Rich* by Napoleon Hill. Here is the excerpt:

THREE FEET FROM GOLD
BY NAPOLEON HILL

Want to rest those weary eyes? Scan the QR code to have me read the story for you.

One of the most common causes of failure is the habit of quitting when one is overtaken by temporary defeat. Every person is guilty of this mistake at one time or another.

An uncle of R.U. Darby was caught by the "gold fever" in the gold rush days, and went west to DIG AND GROW RICH. He had never heard that more gold has been mined from the brains of men than has ever been taken from the earth. He staked a claim and went to work with pick and shovel. The going was hard, but his lust for gold was definite.

After weeks of labor, he was rewarded by the discovery of the shining ore. He needed machinery to bring the ore to the surface. Quietly, he covered up the mine, retraced his footsteps to his home in Williamsburg, Maryland, told his relatives and a few neighbors of the "strike." They got together money for the needed machinery, had it shipped. The uncle and Darby went back to work the mine.

The first car of ore was mined, and shipped to a smelter. The returns proved they had one of the richest mines in Colorado! A few more cars of that ore would clear the debts. Then would come the big killing in profits.

Down went the drills! Up went the hopes of Darby and Uncle! Then something happened! The vein of gold ore disappeared! They had come to the end of the rainbow, and the pot of gold was no longer there! They drilled on, desperately trying to pick up the vein again – all to no avail.

Finally, they decided to QUIT.

They sold the machinery to a junk man for a few hundred dollars, and took the train back home. Some "junk" men are dumb, but not this one! He called in a mining engineer to look at the mine and do a little calculating. The engineer advised that the project had failed, because the owners were not familiar with "fault lines." His calculations showed that the vein would be found just three feet from where the Darbys had stopped drilling! That is exactly where it was found!

The "Junk" man took millions of dollars in ore from the mine, because he knew enough to seek expert counsel before giving up.[28]

❡

You see, losing sight of the bigger picture because you couldn't achieve instant gratification can be detrimental to your bottom line, and your brand. So I want you to remember this story every time you think your metrics aren't moving in the direction you want them to fast enough. With the proviso that you have the right expertise in your corner, are monitoring and learning from your efforts, and are, in every sense, working towards the vision you set out, at any moment you could be just three feet from gold. Be patient and prepare to quash any Veruca Salt moments that might flare up either in yourself or your team.

METRICS SET UP TO SABOTAGE

In my advisory work, I've seen organisations apply key performance indicators (KPIs) to their teams' performance and had great success in areas such as customer satisfaction, customer retention, profits, expense lines, and so many other areas of the business. Thus, those organisations are able to share the gold with their teams, investors, and shareholders. I've also seen organisations set up metrics and measures for their teams and scratch their heads at the deplorable outcomes. Scarily, they're rarely ever willing to concede that maybe they're measuring the wrong thing at the wrong point and it all needs to be thrown in the bin and overhauled.

One such client went for blood at the end of every quarter, as no one in his teams would hit their targets. The way the founder had set up his metrics wasn't properly supporting the customer journey and was, in fact, designed in a way that set his teams up to lose. How, you ask? Well, the KPIs went something like this:

1. **Sales team** (they were an external ⟵ Not technically sales team): Sell X number of widgets *employees of the company* every week.
   a. Yes – go to stage two.

    b. No – everyone misses their KPIs.

2. **Contracts team** (they were employees of the business): Close X number of contracts sent through from the sales team.
    a. Yes – go to stage three.
    b. No – everyone except the sales team misses their KPIs.

3. **Drafting team**: Obtain sign off of X number of plans per week (the founder considered himself the only person qualified to approve plans prior to the customer being able to sign off, so they created a self-sabotaging bottleneck that led the drafting team to fail every week).
    a. Yes – go to stage four.
    b. No – everyone except the sales team and contracts team misses their KPIs.

Do you get the drift? If not, let me further explain how this implementation of metrics and measures was problematic. As mentioned, the sales team wasn't a part of the organisation. While that isn't always a problem, in this case the sales team was found to consistently oversell to customers in order to get them over the line. Once they had them, the sale was handed over to the contracts team to finalise pricing, options, and so on. In this situation, the customer would be met with a rude AF shock when the contract team explained there would be an additional cost because what they were offered wasn't part of the package and they weren't sure why they were told otherwise. Then the contract person (not the long-gone salesperson) would get abused, realising that the salesperson had overpromised and left it to them to underdeliver. At the time of advising, in over 30 percent of cases, customers would cancel their contracts and walk away as detractors of the business. ← *But the sales team still got their $$$*

Ultimately, the KPIs were promoting bad and unethical behaviours. Where there weren't necessarily bad behaviours, there were bottlenecks and poor systems and governance that saw some teams either at a stalemate with the boss or resenting their colleagues who had left them to deliver the bad news while walking away with their hefty little bonus, not caring who got burnt in the process. I'm sure you can imagine the organisational culture this created.

> It's **imperative** that, as a brand leader, your metrics and measurements **do not** encourage piss-poor behaviour to get rewards and recognition.

If they see that there's something in it for them, humans are going to human, so it's up to us as organisational leaders to create metrics that don't set us or our teams up to sabotage it all.

MIRROR, MIRROR ON THE WALL

Let's quickly touch on what are known as 'vanity metrics'. While the term predominantly refers to the measuring of marketing and advertising campaigns, they can also creep into how we feel about our CX campaigns. In short, vanity metrics are metrics that make us feel good (remember that dopamine hit conversation?) but don't ultimately translate or convert into a meaningful outcome – for example, launching a new eco-friendly product range that receives a great number of likes and comments on your socials but doesn't result in converted sales. It might feel good to know your 'audience' thinks it's excellent, but they're not following it up with a purchase. This is where vanity metrics aren't useful.

AKA the conversion into sales sucks

However, we could reframe their uselessness and use it as a trigger to learn more. For example, what's the objection to buying? Is it price? Is it a lack of social proof? Is it too close to a competitor's product that's easier to access? Something's blocking you, and this is your opportunity to learn more.

I put the word 'audience' in quotes earlier because maybe, just maybe your audience isn't *actually* your customer. This is your cue to figure that out. Also, if you're a smaller business working towards becoming a trusted and value-driven brand, consider what micro-influencers can do to help bring your brand to life. You don't need the budget for a John Cena or a Kardashian to outshine your competitors. Many brands have had excellent and sustained success working with 'real humans' who have their own trusted and value-driven brands that resonate with their audiences. So, don't be fooled by the vanity metrics – dig deeper. Work for conversion, work for meaningful and genuine relationships over transactions, work for collaborations, work for advocacy.

THE METRICS THAT MATTER

Knowing which customer experience metrics to apply can be a challenge. I work with many organisations that only really know about the net promoter score, or NPS (technically net promoter system), and think that due to its ease of use and cost effectiveness, slapping this metric on every touchpoint of the customer journey and their morning toast is all that's necessary to understand where they are on the CX Pyramid. I'm pleased to announce that there are so many other metrics available that can give you better-quality insights into a specific section of the customer experience journey than just the NPS survey question. Here's the casual hook-up to the different metric options available and why and when you might choose to use them ... in no specific order:

CSAT: Short for customer satisfaction   Measures past
score. This is a laggard metric ⟵ performance
survey question used as a transactional insight. You usually ask the question, "How satisfied are you with [PRODUCT/ COMPANY NAME]?" and provide the recipient with a scale from 0 to 5, with 0 being very dissatisfied and 5 being extremely satisfied. You use this type of survey question to identify areas of success and opportunities to improve in the CX journey and also, as the name suggests, to measure customer satisfaction. This is a great follow-up question on a support phone call or online chat, as well as after a customer has been identified as using your products or services.

CSAT Formula

How satisfied were you with your experience today?

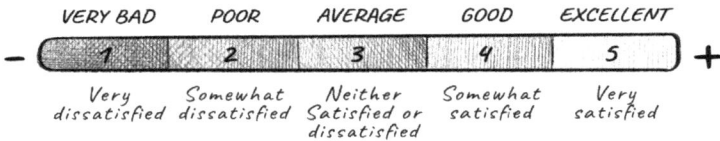

CSAT is represented as a percentage

CES: Short for customer effort score. This is a leading metric ← *Predictive measure of future performance* survey question used again as a transactional insight. The question is often worded as, "To what extent do you agree with the following statement: [COMPANY NAME] made it easy for me to handle my issue?" It's the survey question you use to help measure the ease of a transaction with your customer support or customer facing team. The scale for this survey question is 0 to 7, with 0 being strongly disagree and 7 being highly agree. The difference between this and CSAT is, in some instances, it's more imperative to understand the effort involved or how easy we made a specific part of our CX journey than overall satisfaction. This is great for support centre calls and when signing up to offers and services. ← *Or even for upgrades, downgrades, or cancellations*

CES Formula

Overall, how easy was it to get the help you wanted today?

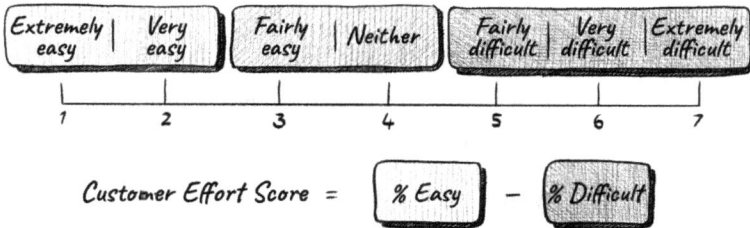

Extremely easy	Very easy	Fairly easy	Neither	Fairly difficult	Very difficult	Extremely difficult
1	2	3	4	5	6	7

Customer Effort Score = | % Easy | − | % Difficult |

CES can be represented as a percentage or a whole number.

Equation to analyse your CES.

NPS: Short for net promoter score. NPS (considered a laggard and leading metric) is often presented as the gold standard customer experience metric, but in the modern day you'll often find CX leaders debating its place on the metaphorical pedestal.

First developed in 2003 by Bain and Company, NPS is now used by millions of businesses to measure and track their customers' *perceived* loyalty. To measure this perception, the customer is asked one simple question: "How likely are you to recommend [ORGANISATION X/PRODUCT Y/SERVICE Z] to a friend or colleague?" The customer is then given a scale from 0 to 10, with 0 being not at all likely and 10 being extremely likely. Here's how to interpret the results:

- **Promoters** respond with a score of 9 or 10 and are typically loyal and enthusiastic customers. They tell others about their experiences with your organisation and are essentially doing marketing and lead generation for you.

- **Passives** respond with a score of 7 or 8. They're satisfied with your service but not happy enough to be considered promoters. They're likely not talking about you unprompted, and studies show that passives would switch quickly and without concern if a better product, service, or organisation came along. ← *Passives are the silent majority in most businesses*

- **Detractors** respond with a score of 0 to 6. They're unhappy customers who are unlikely to buy from you again and may even discourage others. They may also be out in their communities putting you down based on their experience. If detractors continue to shop with you, it's largely due to convenience and lack of competition, which causes even more resentment.

Calculating your NPS is as easy as taking the percentage of promoters and subtracting it from the percentage of detractors. However, your NPS is shown as a whole number (not a percentage). The higher the number, the better your result. Passives aren't taken into the equation. I personally consider them in the same category as detractors, as they're so neutral they may as well say, "You suck, and if a better offer comes along, I'll no sooner leave you." Recent studies approximated that for every one customer who tells you they're a detractor and leaves, there are 25 who also leave without saying a word.[29] ←

Using customer retention rate metrics is highly recommended

The other thing about NPS is there's no 'benchmark' per se. Therefore, the best way to know where you stand with customer loyalty is to compare your score to that of others in your market or industry.

NPS Formula

How likely are you to recommend buisness (X) to a friend or colleague?

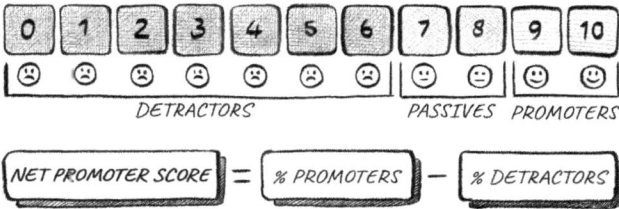

0	1	2	3	4	5	6	7	8	9	10

DETRACTORS   PASSIVES   PROMOTERS

NET PROMOTER SCORE	=	% PROMOTERS	−	% DETRACTORS

NPS is represented as a whole number.

Equation to analyse your NPS.

CCS: Short for customer centricity score. You can now measure how effective your organisation is at implementing a customer centric strategy by using the CCS scale. Your CCS comprises 15 dimensions clustered in three main groups: leadership, collaboration, and implementation. Your CCS is measured by your team and broken down into segments. While it's similar to NPS, CCS is different in the sense that it's measured by your team. It too has a 0 to 10 scale; however, instead of promoters, passives, and detractors, you have promoters, neutral, and critics. CCS certainly shouldn't be considered the be all and end all of KPIs, but it can be a great indicator of the team's perception of cut through when it comes to your organisation's mission to become truly customer-centric.

ACTIVITY: CCS SELF SURVEY

Head over to https://www.ccscore.org/en/selftest/ and bravely complete the CCS survey to receive your very own score for your business.

ROI: Short for return on investment. One of the **biggest** struggles organisations face as they scale is being able to tangibly show ROI in order to obtain the budget to improve CX opportunities. While the value of some activities is obvious, others need a bit more due diligence or homework to prove their value to the business and the customer. Technically, ROI is a lagging metric, as we use past numbers to arrive at a final figure. However, we also use this information to draw upon the potential successes or failures of CX investments. As much as we're here for our customers, it's still absolutely necessary to deliver a profitable return, for without it, we'll cease to be anything but another sad business statistic.

ROI Formula

$$ROI = \left(\frac{Amount\ Gained - Amount\ Spent}{Amount\ Spent} \right) \times 100$$

(Return on Investment)

ROI is expressed as a percentage.

Equation to understand your CX campaign's return on investment.

> " If you can't measure it, you can't improve it."
>
> — *Unknown*

As a business learning to become a trusted and value-driven brand, you must learn to love measuring. Love adapting. Love improving. Love delivering. Love being agile. This is how we *earn* the privilege of having a CEHX-y business. Sorry, you are becoming a CEHX-y brand now, aren't you? ;-)

ACTIVITY: PUT METRICS INTO MOTION

Head over to **aileenday.com.au/tjocehx-tools** to download your own 'metrics and measurements' quick reference sheet. Other metrics beyond what we've discussed will come in handy for the next few activities.

Assess which metrics and measures best align to your CX strategy and collaborate with your leadership team and team members to implement the right metrics, for the right touchpoints, for the right behavioural outcomes. ← Remember, everyone is accountable for great CEHX

TL;CBF

- Metrics matter, but use the right metric, at the right time, to tell you the right story.

- What gets measured gets done, but be sure that you align your metrics to create positive momentum, not bad or unethical behaviours.

- If you've aligned your business activities to your vision, the needle might take some time to move, but don't give up just because it doesn't move fast enough.

- You could be just 3 feet from gold, so utilise the support, resources, and experts around you to help you in your mission. Don't quit!

PART TWO

TAKE YOUR CEHX TO THE NEXT LEVEL

CHAPTER 8:
THE MODERN EX

A FRESH APPROACH TO THE EMPLOYEE EXPERIENCE

These days, there's a lot of chatter around 'employee experience' (EX) and how leaders are finding that a strategic ← *Remember, your chance to be unique* employee experience that nurtures autonomy, mastery, and purpose can deliver highly engaged and productive employees. If you haven't read Dan Pink's *Drive: The Surprising Truth About What Motivates Us*, do yourself and your organisation a favour and grab a copy and read it with the intention to learn and implement its lessons into your strategic EX. The book explains that we can do away with carrot and stick rewards and punishments and replace them with a style that's far more flexible, altruistic, and meaningful to the employee, the customer, and the business.[30]

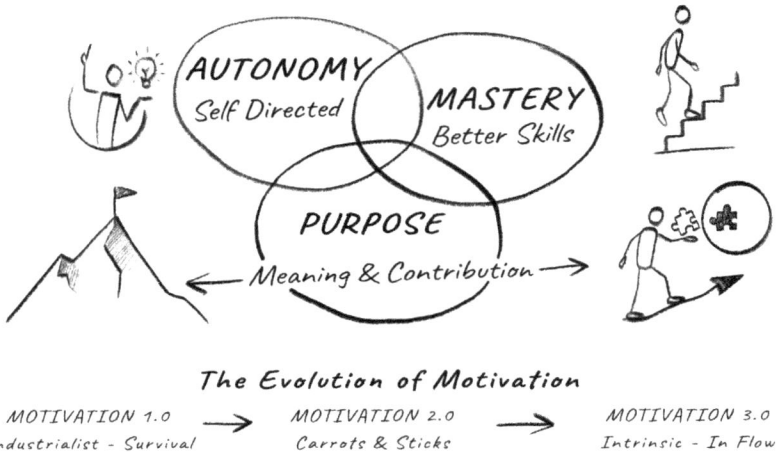

The Evolution of Motivation

MOTIVATION 1.0 → MOTIVATION 2.0 → MOTIVATION 3.0
Industrialist - Survival   Carrots & Sticks   Intrinsic - In Flow

Understanding What Drives Employees to Perform.

EMPLOYEE EXPERIENCE VS. EMPLOYEE ENGAGEMENT

The two, for lack of a better term, 'buzzwords' (employee experience and employee engagement) are often used interchangeably; however, they're not the same. Let's break it down real quick. Employee engagement is the outcome of your employee experience. Now, I hear many of you thinking, *What's my employee experience? I don't think I have one.* Well, like aresholes, everyone has one. Some of them stink, and some of them are well-maintained and regularly inspected. You're now probably thinking, *WTF did I just read?* You know what you read, and don't even tell me you didn't understand the double entendre (pronounced on-ton-dra). If you know me, you'll

know I'm intelligently crass and classy. ⟵ I'm also a lover
of oxymorons
If you didn't know me, well, now you do.

An employee experience is just like your customer experience –
strategically aligned to your brand vision and values. If your vision
is to be the world's leading innovator of microchips, you best ensure
your employee experience leans towards a culture of innovation,
open and candid communication, collaboration, and autonomy,
depending on employees' needs. You also need a big enough R and
D (research and development) budget to fail fast without consequence. You can see how an organisation that creates this style of
employee experience will succeed far more consistently than an
organisation that doesn't. Instead, that organisation is likely to use
carrots to entice and sticks to beat when things don't work out. No
one wants to be a part of that type of business anymore.

THE PEARL MODEL OF EMPLOYEE EXPERIENCE

An organisation called People Insights created a dynamic and
globally useful model to understand your employee experience
and, in turn, facilitate actionable insights to improve EX and
employee engagement. It's called PEARL, which stands for:

- **Purpose:** Understanding the organization's aims and
  feeling good about the work's purpose.

- **Enablement:** Having the resources, support, and training
  to do the job effectively.

- **A**utonomy: Having the freedom and control to make decisions about work.

- **R**eward: Feeling valued and appreciated for contributions.

- **L**eadership: Having supportive and effective leaders.[31]

I like the PEARL model because it's really good at taking something that could be made complex and helping organisations simplify their efforts. Similarly to the customer experience journey map, it helps you create clarity around the experience inputs. Using the five PEARL categories as a starting point, we as business leaders can build out the employee experience. From there, we can start to develop an understanding of the quality of employee engagement we're encouraging using behaviours such as:

- Pride

- Endeavour

- Commitment

- Advocacy

- Care.[32]

These are all tangible characteristics that can be measured and used as a baseline of expectations in any business, in any market, in any industry. If you'd like to explore PEARL further, head on over to People Insights (peopleinsight.co.uk/employee-surveys/employee-engagement).

HOW WE GOT HERE – A HISTORY LESSON

To understand the modern EX, let's do a short reflection on the historic employee experience. Peter Cheese, chief executive of the CIPD (Chartered Institute of Personnel and Development) and author of *The New World of Work*, stated in an interview that, in the past, "workers were units of labour and means of production rather than people. And if we're honest, that sort of thing was still going on for much of the last century."[33] With the industrial revolution kicking off after World War I and more women entering the workforce, the welfare of employees became more vulnerable. This saw the introduction of welfare agents, recruited to ensure the health and safety of the workforce's most vulnerable – women and children. Yes, that's right, children. History tells us that just because you have welfare agents, it doesn't guarantee the safety and welfare of anyone. During this time, the employee experience wasn't as humane as we would like to imagine.

Post World War II, some smart business owners learnt that greater employee satisfaction correlated with greater productivity and retention (usually, fewer people were causing an inconvenience and diminishing the day's outputs by dying on the job). Over the next couple of decades, wise employers and many governments around the world started working out what they could do to improve the employee experience, albeit for their own benefit, and also improve human rights in the workforce with new health and safety regulations. ← *Like regulating child labour* With so many new laws being introduced, we saw the introduction of personnel managers – people responsible for the implementation and ongoing management of all things employee-related, including ensuring adherence to new regulations. They were also tasked with working with strong trade unions, which in some industries felt more like a curse than a pleasure.

In the 70s and 80s, workers started to understand that organisations couldn't run and produce the massive profits they were reaping without the individual. We saw the introduction of what many of us now know as the 'human resources department'. Gone was the personnel department, and in most Western organisations, workers were slowly being considered human, not just *objective* units of labour. The sceptic in me says this was all bullshit and just good rebranding. But hey, as a qualified PR specialist, what would I know? The major difference with becoming a human resources (HR) department was that HR professionals now sat at the table when it came to creating organisational strategy. They were no longer just the filler-inners of paperwork; they were in charge of growing the business's talent pool, succession planning, and developing employees' skills and aptitudes to ensure a higher quality of work and a higher level of productivity.

Fast forward another 40 years (which as a Gen Y only feels like 10 years), and many organisations took their human resources department and rebranded it again. According to the Australian HR Institute, we now have people and culture departments, or people operations, or human capital management, or talent management, or if you're Airbnb, you let your imagination run wild and call it employee experience (to be honest, I'm not even mad – I love it).[34] So the question begs to be answered: Are these simply wanky PR attempts at rebranding? Or are we moving into an era where understanding what it takes to retain employees and drive them to be loyal to an organisation through their own volition is something we're actually starting to wrap our heads around? Here's my take on employee experience and where we stand as a modern workforce versus where we need to be ...

WHERE WE STAND WITH OUR EX

While writing this book, the world experienced, and probably to some point still is experiencing, 'the Great Resignation' or 'quiet quitting'. If you're in China or Japan, you may be familiar with the 'lying flat' or tang ping movement. Newer generations of workers are realising that working to burnout (which is the expectation in many countries) and leaving no time for yourself, your relationships, connection beyond your colleagues let alone fulfilling any personal dreams is brutally flawed. To show their lack of will to continue with what's essentially modern-day slavery, people protest by lying flat. In the street, in the workplace, in the parks, on the paths, individually and as a collective. The reason behind more western employment trends, such as quiet quitting ... well, to be blunt, just as employees realised in the 70s and 80s that organisations needed them to post those record-breaking profits year on year, for which workers received two parts of diddly squat, the same revolution seems to have occurred again. While some revolutionaries are from the same generation that experienced the original revolution, most are newer generations that are tired of giving their blood, sweat, and tears for two parts of fuck all. With the spicy cough era, many of us were forced to attempt work from home, often with children storming our space every other minute demanding attention; some workers only had their couch as a viable workstation, and many were expected to just get on with it – that was if they even could do their job from home. Millions were furloughed (put out of work temporarily), many sent home with no answers, no empathy, no support financially or otherwise. In many countries, workers received no support from governments, and those who did had to fall into some very obscure buckets to be considered worthy of the 'government's' money. Many were left broke, scared, and vulnerable. ⟵ Love that human experience for us

Fast forward to when the world began to return to 'normal' and organisations reconnected with their employees, and some smart business leaders knew that how they played the game moving forward could make or break their organisation and its culture, so they were kind and gentle, supporting open communication with their employees and working to learn what they needed to feel comfortable in spite of the unfortunate experiences everyone had gone through. Other less smart business leaders didn't understand the gravity of the situation, and if they did understand, they didn't care. You see, they saw themselves as the prize. They hadn't learnt that with the right employee experience, they could have been making their lives easier and their businesses run smoother. So, instead, they demanded a return to work. They demanded that there would be no more flexible time, and employees were expected back in the office, back on the floor, no exceptions, and if you tried for an exception, you'd be let go. I know this sounds dramatic, but it's literally what happened.

So here ensued a new revolution. ⟵ Plenty of good came from a shitty situation
Employees came to realise that they were built for more. Not more work, but perhaps more time for their wellbeing. More time to travel, more opportunities to connect and feel purposeful in this big wide world. So they resigned, and they did it in droves. If they didn't resign, many caught on and quit quietly, which isn't what it sounds like. Essentially, employees became desensitised to the longstanding overpromises of a corner office or a measly promotion in return for unquestioningly submitting their souls day in, day out. They quietly went about doing the bare minimum, finding reasons as to why they were unable to continue fulfilling the role of many when they were but one. And you know what? It drove the big bosses fucking crazy! All I could say to organisations that were affected was: "What a great opportunity to overhaul your employee experience. Because if it wasn't broken, you wouldn't be feeling this pain."

WHERE WE NEED TO BE WITH OUR EX

In the near future, many employers will draw the short straw, as employees who were once dealt the blows of low wages and even lower-quality working conditions are now experiencing a surging awareness of their self-worth and are taking a stand against both the poor financial experience and the poor employee experience. Where we need to go is multifaceted, and there's certainly no quick fix. As this book is a casual hook-up, I won't dive too deeply into the topic or try to solve it all here. I'll save that for my next book, *Return of the EX*, so keep your eyes peeled for that in the future.

You best believe that employees are sick of the bullshit, so their radars are cranked up to the max, and they're ready to sniff out the BS and call you out. So where do you, as an employer, place your efforts when it comes to delivering a world-class employee experience? Even if you don't yet have employees, this is still good stuff to grasp in readiness for when that day arrives.

FIX REMUNERATION

It's shocking to me that, in 2025, there are still so many people in survival mode, either working to get by on low wages or living below the poverty line. In Australia, ACOSS (Australian Council of Social Service) reported in 2022 that 13.4 percent of the population was living in relative poverty.[35] In the United States, the figure is 11.4 percent.[36] In the EU, 21.4 percent of the population is at risk of poverty.[37]

There's an age-old argument that goes, "We can't increase the minimum wage because small business owners can't afford the increased expenses, and they'll have to put their prices up, which will drive people to the big-box, low-cost operators, putting small business operators out of work." However, the reason people buy low-cost goods isn't because that's what they prefer; it's because their means don't allow them to buy anything but. So, if the minimum income was increased, people wouldn't stop shopping at small business outlets. In fact, it would have quite the opposite effect. You would now have a large segment of the population earning a liveable wage that afforded them the "luxury" of buying products and services they previously couldn't access on their pitiful income.

In 2025, Australia's minimum wage was $24.10 (about US$15.40).[38] In the U.S, it's a mess. Their federal minimum wage starts at US$7.25 (about AUD$11.30), and every state uses that as a baseline. According to the Department of Labor, minimum wages by state range anywhere from the federal minimum of US$7.25 to a whopping US$16.66.[39] However, when you look deeper, you realise that half the country has these unusual loopholes that allow, say, workers in Montana to earn a minimum of US$2.00 per hour despite the federal minimum wage. In researching this, my head was exploding. I came to the swift conclusion that it's all fucked and too many governments aren't in it for small business or any other stakeholder they claim to support. They're in it for themselves and their billionaire puppet masters. ⟵ *Okay, I'll step away from the politics*

Until we collectively start driving change by getting the humans who make our businesses what they are off the hamster wheel of survival, we'll forever keep finding ourselves at the bottom of the EX hierarchy of needs and being hurt by the latest trending employment protest – and we'll only have ourselves to blame. When just one individual or business initiates impactful change, the rest inevitably follow. (remember dancing man on the hill?)

MOTIVATE TEAMS AND INDIVIDUALS

Now, going back to the research performed by Dan Pink, author of *Drive: The Surprising Truth About What Motivates Us*, money isn't the be all and end all, but that's only when your employers have reached a point at which money flows freely enough that they can survive, feed themselves and their families, provide shelter and a level of comfort, and see past the fear of losing everything, going hungry, being cut out of the social fabric when connection and community are so, so important (even for those who don't think so). I mentioned Maslow's Hierarchy of Needs earlier. Essentially, once we get to the level of safety in the hierarchy, money is no longer the burning need when creating a loyalty-driven employee experience. As Dan explains, what motivates your employees becomes less transactional (extrinsic) and more from the heart (intrinsic).[40] What does that mean, you ask?

> Essentially, greater employee experiences are driven by employers who allow their employees to perform activities and tasks that help them build their esteem and develop their morality and sense of purpose.

Yes, money is great, but have you ever done something simply because you felt passionate about it? You expected no income, no reward except knowing that you created a positive impact with something that was important to you or someone you cared about. Well, this is the stuff real employee experiences are made of.

Heirarchy of Advocate Needs

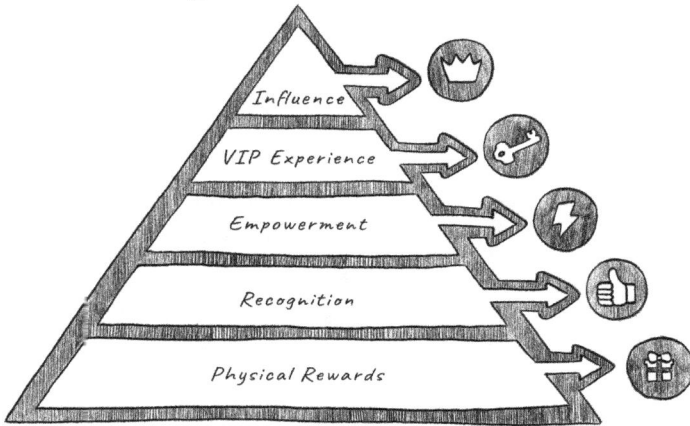

- Influence
- VIP Experience
- Empowerment
- Recognition
- Physical Rewards

Maslow's Hierarchy of Needs.[41]

Learning what drives your team collectively and as individuals doesn't have to be difficult. Simply getting to know your employees, what they do in their free time, who they care for, and who cares for them are all basic conversations you can have that will help you construct an idea around what each person values. The next step is awareness. Being aware of activities that might suit Janet, projects that might suit Tom, chairing a team meeting that might suit Vicki. It really does come down to the small things you can do to promote your employees' personal development and growth, choosing specific people for certain activities you know they enjoy. By doing this, you're communicating that you know them – you know their interests and where they excel. To you, they're more than employees. They're an integral part of your organisation. This is how you lead them to self-actualisation.

When we apply Maslow's Hierarchy of needs to the EX, we get the Hierarchy of employee needs. At the peak of the needs pyramid, employees are highly engaged. They're micro-influencers within your brand, *Imagine micro-Kardashian-level influence in your biz* and they're committed to achieving your brand vision. They feel like they make a positive impact in something bigger than themselves. This is where you build loyalty-driven, motivated, engaged, and happy employees.

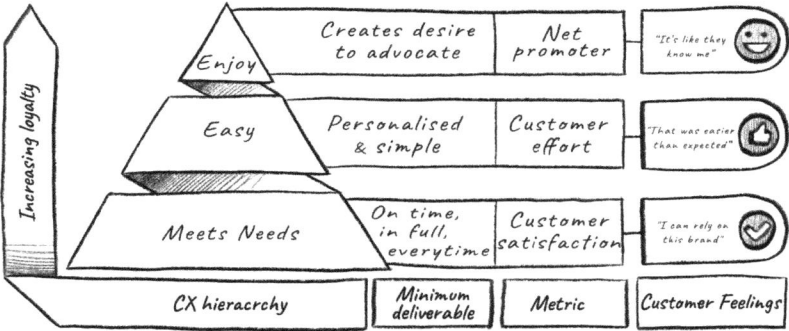

Hierarchy of Employee Needs
Leading to Positive Employee Experience.

TL;CBF

- Employee Experience (EX) is the foundation that drives employee engagement. A well-crafted EX aligned with company values fosters innovation, autonomy, and productivity, while outdated 'carrot-and-stick' approaches hinder progress.

- From the industrial revolution to now, EX has shifted from treating employees as mere labour units to recognising them as valuable assets. HR has evolved into 'people and culture', but the question remains: Is this just rebranding? Or is it genuine progress?

- Movements like the Great Resignation and quiet quitting signal a shift in employee priorities. Employees now demand fair treatment, flexibility, and purpose rather than just survival wages and burnout.

- Low wages trap employees in survival mode, preventing real engagement. Raising wages benefits businesses by increasing consumer spending and creating a more motivated workforce, contrary to fears of harming small businesses.

- Inspired by Dan Pink's research, true motivation comes from autonomy, mastery, and purpose – not just money. Once basic needs are *Motivation 3.0* met, employees can thrive in environments that offer personal growth and meaningful work. They want to feel like they're working towards something bigger than themselves.

- Companies must prioritise employee wellbeing, recognise individual strengths, and create purposeful work experiences. Those who fail to adapt will experience disengagement and higher employee turnover, while organisations who value wellbeing will build loyal, high-performing teams.

CREATE AN EMPLOYEE EXPERIENCE THAT MIRRORS YOUR CUSTOMER EXPERIENCE

Where we need to be is having organisations map out and become purposeful in the employee experience from the top down and the ground up. Why would an employee want to bust their chops creating a loyalty-driven customer experience when they're constantly faced with bureaucratic red tape, poor leadership, diminishing autonomy, and an overall sense of devalue? Short answer, they won't. Long answer, they might for a period of time, depending on where they are on the hierarchy of needs, but even then people have been known to jump ship with no life jacket if it means they can mitigate falling down another rung on the pyramid. ← *Your business shouldn't feel like The Hunger Games*

Where we need to get to is strategically executing the employee experience to drive your best to stay.

Train people well enough so they can leave, treat them well enough so they don't want to."

– *Sir Richard Branson*

That doesn't mean creating a culture of entitlement where you give and give to get nothing in return. However, it's scary how many organisations believe that if they lean towards a flexible and human-centred employee experience, all they'll get in return is low productivity and employees taking the piss. *Another great* This has been proven again and again not *reason to instil* to be the case, with productivity rates and *brand values to* employee retention increasing in many busi- *live by* nesses when the spicy cough era forced employers in many sectors to trust their teams to do their jobs remotely and autonomous- ly.[42] Also, I have to say, if you can't trust your team members, why did you hire them? What I mean is, you recruit *Legally and* the best – remember, hire slow, fire fast ←——— *ethically* – and you orchestrate the EX to mitigate the bullshit and friction employees feel every day. Now, this is no different from developing a loyalty-driven customer experience. If you under- stand that delivering a great CX improves your bottom line, you must consider that by not providing a great employee experi- ence you can cancel out any gains. Not caring for or planning out your employee experience can lead you down the path of constant employee turnover, or 'churn' as some might say. In 2025, Oxford Economics found that, in many industries, organ- isations spend an average of $58,000 recruiting and training for a single role when an employee leaves the company.[43] Lose a few good people, and tell me you couldn't have spent *Prevention is* that money more wisely simply by mitigating the *better than* bullshit from the start. ←——————— *a cure*

EVOLVE FROM PATCHWORK SOLUTIONS

The modern employee is seeking an experience where the organisation they commit to is empathetic, flexible, and provides opportunities, not just for promotion but also for personal development. The employee experience of the now and future understands that systems must be integrated and user-friendly, designed to remove friction and do as much of the boring shit as possible so employees can focus on being creative and solutions-focused. Even then, you might find that in designing your optimum employee experience, keeping some 'boring' less-pressurised work helps those in high-pressure always-on roles decompress. ← *Remember, we're designing for productivity and wellbeing*

What do I mean by integrated systems? Systems that talk to one another without the incessant need to rest, reboot, hook this thing to that thingy. Integrated systems allow your employees to just get the job done. In experience management (XM), firstly, we have the me's of the world, the CX experts. However, as your organisation scales, you'll need to expand your XM talent to mitigate the chance of simply adding to your patchwork quilt of solutions rather than creating an integrated system. For example, you'll likely need a user experience (UX) expert to ensure your online presence is designed for maximum conversion. ← *And consistency across all platforms and devices*

Ideally, you want easy-to-use, simple-to-navigate, functional, and aesthetic digital spaces. If you've ever used a website that's difficult to navigate or shits you to tears at the check-out as you cry into the void, "How hard is it to just give you my fucking money?" you've had a 'user experience', which directly impacts the customer experience. In your trusted and value-driven brand, you should ensure collaboration between UX and CX management to mitigate any problems. And when the user experience and, therefore, the customer experience is poor, who cops the tirade from overwhelmed and distressed customers? Your employees – and not even the ones who designed the website.

I can't help but think about the business *which shall remain nameless, but let's just call it CEHX-yland* ← that, when you accumulate loyalty points (their loyalty program is actually quite good), doesn't let you use your rewards at any other location. It has to be at the exact place of purchase. Being a national brand, they're not like our mates in the big green shed and prolific in every other suburb. So, to not have their loyalty program integrated in a way that allows customers to utilise their rewards in any location feels more like a punishment. They're increasing the customer effort score and minimising their employees' will to remain engaged, as they now have to grit their teeth and explain that their systems between stores "don't talk to each other."

I know, as your business scales and becomes a trusted and value-driven brand, you'll have priorities and meet roadblocks aplenty, but my wisest and sagest advice is... as you develop from the patchwork of solutions you've probably found yourself in as a micro to small business, engage your employees to gain a deep understanding of what stops them from delivering a consistent, trustworthy, and value-adding experience. There's likely never going to be just one system that does everything you need, but at least if you do your due diligence when acquiring new systems, with the needs

↖ *Think critically, investigate thoroughly, don't be impulsive*

of your employees and your customers central to your purchasing decisions, you'll likely mitigate any future catastrophes caused by patchwork solutions.

THE EMPLOYEE EXPERIENCE OF THE FUTURE

The employee experience of the future has leaders who enforce workplace and lifestyle boundaries, eradicating burnout and overwhelm. They're no longer just there to push corporate agendas and fill out paperwork. Employees feel safe speaking up about workloads and potential obstacles to success without the fear of repercussions.

The employee experience of the future understands the positive impact having a diverse workplace can have not just on the employee experience but also on the customer experience when customers see themselves represented, having a voice inside the organisation, not just on the outside.

The employee experience of the future doesn't leave new recruits with a folder of the organisation's documented policies and procedures with instructions to "read this" and "sign that" and "when you're done, go to IT to get your login details" and "if you have any questions, just come find me." Like, what the actual fuck is that? How is that displaying a sense of value to the person you just spent thousands of dollars recruiting? Putting our empathy hat on... would that make you feel welcome? You might say that's an exaggerated scenario. Sadly, I promise you, from experience, it's not – and that's just an office scenario. Scarily, far too often, we hear of workers being put on the tools, without the necessary onboarding experience. Left to fend for themselves, shamed for asking questions. Then they get hurt, or worse. These are the very real consequences of a loose or inconsiderate employee experience.

The employee experience of the future has a candid culture. Not rude, judgemental or limiting, but open, honest, and timely in its communication. Essentially, it has a culture of telling it like it is, without the ego, without the conflict, with clear friction-free communication. No fluff, no bullshit, no beating around the bush or saying one thing *We're not here* and meaning something completely different. *to fuck spiders* The Dutch, for example, are masters of candid communication and are often mistaken for arrogant when communicating with people who aren't used to self-awareness or knowing where they *honestly* stand. *Radical Candor* by Kim Scott is a great book about building a candid culture in your organisation. Kim discusses how she coupled her knack for caring personally with challenging directly and how it changed the game in every organisation she led in Silicon Valley (including everyone's favourite business case, Apple).[44]

Over the years, I've been told I'm too forthright, too quick to challenge others, but I never saw it like that. *And trust me, I've* I believe that being forthright has helped *definitely looked* everyone I've ever worked with know exactly *in the mirror* where I stand on any matter.

> My ability to challenge people no matter the gap in pay grades comes from a place of wanting to do the best job possible, and if that means I have to ask more questions or challenge someone's thinking or assumptions, then so be it.

When someone gets upset at my candour, it's their ego at play. They're pissed off they hadn't considered my points, and they feel humiliated, but that's on them. My message to them – be better prepared next time or leave your ego at the door and welcome questions and feedback. How else can we expect employees to do their very best? To be honest, I get nervous as shit when I pitch something different or new and no one asks questions. I feel like there's no way every single person made sense of it and has no questions. I also see questions and people challenging my thinking as a sign of their engagement. Welcome questions, welcome engagement, welcome diverse ways of seeing the issue or picture, welcome candid communication to resolve those issues as best you can ... together. ← *Candour is the cure for shame*

ACTIVITY: CANDID COMMUNICATION SURVEY

Head over to **aileenday.com.au/tjocehx-tools** and download your copy of the Measuring Candid Communication Culture survey. To measure your organisation's candour, complete the survey.

MOVE THE EMPLOYEE EXPERIENCE NEEDLE

When we use empathy, delivering a quality employee experience isn't as difficult as we might envisage. If you read this and think I'm full of shit, I'd guess you may be traumatised from a previous experience, and that's okay. We can try again with a different strategy. ← *Resilience in business is key*

Like with the onboarding example, we can simply put ourselves in our employees' shoes and decide if that's how we'd like to be treated. But when an EX is lacking, what do you change? Well, it's subjective. Some new recruits may like the time alone to soak it all in. Some may feel more welcome having a buddy who actively helps them get set up. Some, in my time, have boasted about turning up to their new desk to find all the tools, mod cons, logins, and systems already created, loaded, and ready to go, with a comfortable chair and a workspace that isn't a cubicle you'd expect a rat to reside in.

The point being, it's always best to ask. I'm not saying you must create hundreds of individual employee experiences, but over time you'll find patterns in what your employees prefer. With that pattern recognition, you can systemise their experiences, making your own unique tweaks along the way.

Personalisation isn't just the peak of the CX Pyramid ←

Beyond the recruitment and onboarding phase, which we'll touch on more in my next book *Return of the EX*, moving the experience needle means being invested in more than just surveys and dashboards. It means being active and no longer accepting passive results. How, you ask? You get out of your comfort zone. Get out of your industry. Learn from others. I recently had the privilege of touring the Maton Guitars factory here in Melbourne. You may not know Maton Guitars, but you certainly would have heard of the many artists who call Maton their guitar. ←

Trust, loyalty, and advocacy at its finest

Let me see ... we have Tommy Emmanuel, John Butler, Keith Urban, and let's not forget, the iconic Neil Finn, to name a few. During the tour, I learnt that Maton, a family-led business, had been operating the same way for a long time in the name of tradition and status quo. Well, while that's great, in the name of scaling your organisation and keeping up with the competition, technology, customer expectations and employee needs, some things need to change. So, what did the family decide to do? They looked outside the guitar manufacturing industry for insights into how they could actively improve their business. Where they landed was learning from some of the world's finest engineers and manufacturers at the Toyota Production System. In getting out of their comfort zone, Maton was able to learn from other industries to create an employee experience that has since become not just a gold standard in manufacturing, but a culture of innovation, pride, and advocacy. Maton Guitars now has many of the employee engagement attributes in the PEARL EX model because they dared to move the employee experience needle without compromising on quality, all the while staying true to their roots.

WHEN YOU CHANGE THE EXPERIENCE, YOU CHANGE THE GAME

According to a 2021 report from consulting firm McKinsey, a positive employee experience leads to employees being 16 times more engaged than those with a negative employee experience.[45] Taking stock of the new way of doing business not only changes the game you play but strengthens the quality of your workforce, improves your brand's productivity, and sees you become not just a destination for your customers but a destination employer as well, meaning you're more likely to attract and gain the cream of the crop when recruiting. Best of all, they'll want to stay.

Remember that Motivation 3.0 – autonomy, mastery, purpose ←

No matter your industry, no matter your market, creating a value-driven employee experience that encompasses your employees' personal values and challenges them to find their sense of purpose and belonging will propel their engagement, ultimately helping them, your customers, and, in turn, you.

← *Because you deserve a value-driven life too!*

TL;CBF

1. Employee experience = customer experience. You can't expect employees to deliver an exceptional customer experience if their own workplace experience is filled with bureaucracy, poor leadership, or lacks the components of Motivation 3.0.

2. When you have a flexible human-centred workplace, productivity and retention increase – not the opposite. Trust your people, or reconsider why you hired them in the first place. Trust, don't micromanage (I mean seriously, who has the patience to micromanage anyway?).

3. Disconnected, clunky systems frustrate employees and customers alike. Streamlined, user-friendly tech helps staff focus on creativity and service, not workaround solutions. Integrate your systems to ensure friction-free experiences for everyone.

4. Foster your workplace to be where employees feel safe to speak up, ask questions, and challenge ideas without fear. Radical candour builds trust, clarity, and engagement. Candid culture is key to a sustainable employee experience.

5. A thoughtful, well-prepared onboarding process signals respect and investment in new hires – unlike the all-too-common 'figure it out' approach.

6. To ensure they evolve rather than plateau, the best businesses look outside their industries for innovation and evolve beyond patchwork fixes.

---

7. Employee experience should be proactive, not passive, and infused with empathy and curiosity.

CHAPTER 9:
SCALING YOUR BUSINESS, WHERE SHIT GETS REAL

THE SCALING SHITSHOW

For the most part, my superpower comes into full effect when I work with organisations that are scaling. By scaling, I mean going through a growth phase where they're no longer a micro or small business and are edging their way to the next level.

You started your business in your spare room. You moved into your own office space a few years later. You got big enough to hire a team member or two. Maybe you grew enough to recruit a business manager. Time goes by, you're still a small fry in a big pond, but watch out – nek minute, you have a general manager; you have a customer support team; you have a flashy new website; you have a sales team. You're scaling, and in what feels like a whirlwind, shit is getting more real than it's ever been. Why is shit getting real, you ask? Well, in my experience, time and time again, as your business grows, you of course recruit more people to help you deliver on your promise. But inevitably, bottlenecks are created in every direction you look as you try to rein it in, treating your growing business like the little fish it used to be and watching it slip from your grip. There are not just bottlenecks, but haphazard systems and processes too. Makeshift governance, a revolving door of rules, people not playing in their lane, people not even knowing they have a lane, organisational silos, ⟵ *And not the wheat and chaff kind* poor leadership because you never really led anybody before and now you have a team that looks to you for strategy and guidance, so you just try your best to get through the day. Anyway, the list of obstacles goes on. When you're that deep in it, it can feel like an overwhelming shitshow, or my other favourite phrase – it can feel like a dumpster fire.

It's fine. I'm fine.

Everything is fine.

Dumpster Fire. We've all been there.

Now for many of us, the concept of scaling and the change that comes with it can be a hard slog. To go through it and see it to the end can be as fun as going down a metal slippery dip in the middle of an Australian Summer. It looks like a simple, possibly *IYKYK* ↗

even fun ride, but you end up getting bruised, battered, and a burnt arse on every dip, ultimately getting flung off at the end and sent flying with no safety net. If you're a millennial, your parents probably greeted your harrowing experience with no empathy and told you to just get back on the slide, ignoring the trauma, injuries, and tears. I'm not condoning generational trauma (especially as a therapist), but I will suggest we could use a little bit more tough love in the world. It makes us resilient – and remember the story about being 3 feet away from gold? Well, you could be giving up one turn on the slippery dip too early if you don't have someone in your circle pushing you back up the ladder to try the slide again. Maybe this time, you'll have learnt to put your shirt under your butt to mitigate the burn, and spread out your feet to take it a bit slower, mitigating the bumps. Maybe this time, you get to the bottom of the slide mostly unscathed. Perhaps victorious. ← *The benefit of reflection and learning some hard lessons*

The reality is, scaling and creating change need not be so traumatic. If you're an organisation that has found itself now hitting the proverbial 'ceiling', getting comfy with creating change is exactly what it takes to break through.

So how *exactly* do you break through? Well, firstly, you understand the phases of scaling and align them to the customer, employee, and human experience you want to create. I'll tell you unequivocally that if you don't wrap your head around how to scale sustainably using CEHX as your strategic pillars, you run the very real risk of becoming one of the 90 percent of organisations (global average) that shut down within their first five years of being in business.[46] So, let's get ourselves on the other side of that very heart-breaking statistic and make a case for you being among the 10 percent that not just survive but become trusted, value-driven brands. Who knows, with the right experience and great performance, your brand could even become ... a legacy.

Don't get me twisted, growing a business from a one person show to a multi-human-dependent big brand is no part-time job. I certainly won't say you can have your dream business in 70 days. ← *Damn, I hate all those promotional BS promises* Let's be real. While you can build your business through the growth phases, you don't have to die or burn out to a whisper of your former self to do it. Firstly, let's take a look at the growth phases of business, but remember – this isn't a book about scaling per se, so we'll keep it light.

CASUAL HOOK-UP TO BUSINESS GROWTH PHASES

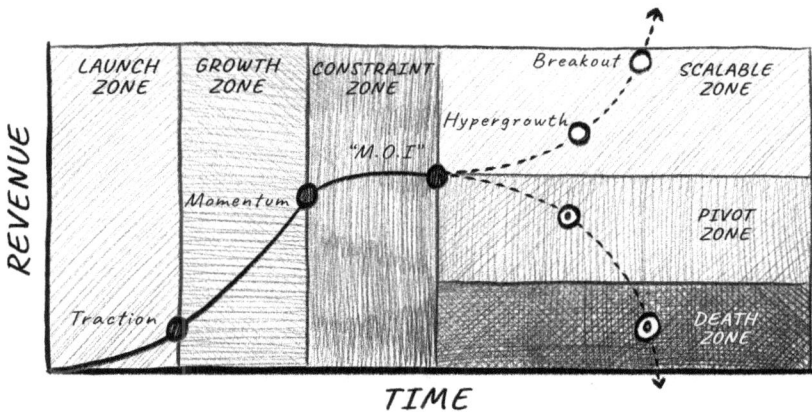

Four phases of scaling.

In a nutshell, there are four commonly agreed upon phases of growing your business. I particularly like the model produced by Scalable.co, as it also speaks to the mental arithmetic you can put yourself through going in and out of each phase.[47] Let's summarise them and align them to your CEHX maturity phases. For this, I like the Gartner CX Maturity Model, as it speaks to the potential hecticness of the launch phase.[48] To determine which phase your business is currently in, you can do an internal assessment using the following information.

GROWTH PHASE 1: LAUNCH ZONE

Signs you're in the 'launch' phase of business include:

- You're likely the only one working in your business. At best, you may have gone into business as a partnership, so you have a partner in crime or a partner in decline, as my husband and I like to refer to each other.

- You're likely trying to be everything to everyone just so someone throws you a bone. In other words, you're hustling. ← *This is where you start believing business has to be done the hard way*

- Your systems are near non-existent, and what systems you do have are likely patchworked together from your CRM (if you have one) to your point of sale to your telecommunications (you're probably still working from your mobile phone).

CX MATURITY PHASE – AD HOC

In the ad hoc phase, customer centricity and customer experience management are unlikely to be your known priorities (remember the Johari Window from chapter six?). Being fresh in business, you're less likely to be strategic, and more likely to be reactive rather than responsive. In this context, responsive means you're on the front foot, leading, not lagging. So in this 'ad hoc' phase of CX maturity, how can you ensure you start with your best foot forward?

Il migliore piede avanti ←

- Complete your customer persona (do this so you know who you're selling to and mitigate trying to be everything for everybody). ← *Energy spent the right way on the right audience*

- Complete a rough draft of your ideal customer experience journey. I say rough because, as you go through the growth phases, it will evolve.

- Create a priority matrix so, as your resources and profit line grow, you can slowly but surely implement the touchpoints that will help you take your customers from 'awareness' to 'advocacy'.

- Find touchpoints in your CX journey where you can garner meaningful feedback to learn about obstacles or objections early. Do this with the customer's needs, not your ego, at the centre. If you think it's an iD10t problem, then take a deep breath, look in the mirror, and ask yourself, "How can I take responsibility and mitigate it happening in the future?" Do you need to deliver training? Do

The IT team at Bunnings taught me that one after I thought I broke my laptop

you need to clarify your advertising? Just ask the questions and assume that because one customer said it's a problem, many others think the same – they just haven't spoken up. Most humans hate conflict and admitting they're unhappy, so if someone does offer criticism, thank them. Don't forget to implement that closed feedback loop and treat customer feedback like the ↖ *More on feedback loops in part three* gift it is.

GROWTH PHASE 2: GROWTH ZONE

I won't state a firm timeline here because while some businesses may reach the next phase within 12 months, others may sit at the launch phase for, well, years. If you're in the 'growth zone', you traditionally experience a few new things, such as:

- You're still considered a small business, but, as the label suggests, you're in a growth phase. You've hired a few new bodies, an experience you likely wouldn't recommend to your enemy in these employment markets.

- You're likely now profitable. Your income outweighs your expenses, and it feels CEHX-y.

- Business stress, although not eradicated, is now at a more func-tional level, as cash flow is more predictable and consistent.

- You're starting to learn what it means to be a leader, trust your instincts, and play risky but not reckless. However ... *Thanks to my son's parkour coach for that little nugget*

- You're probably not fully succeeding in leading new humans or forgoing recklessness completely.

CX MATURITY PHASE – ESTABLISHING

In the 'establishing' phase of CX maturity, you'll learn some hard lessons. This is especially true if you don't set yourself up with the appropriate CEHX moves. Sometimes, you'll learn the easy way, and good things will come. Other times, you'll learn the hard way, and it will seem like your blood, *So don't let* sweat, and tears were all for nothing. ← *them be for nil*

As a business advisor, I like to play a little game with my clients called the 'Reframe Game'. Imagine the Wiggles wiggling their fingers to the tune of the *Price Is Right's* 'C'mon Down' and me encouraging business owners to *Yes, we look like idiots,* "play along." So, what does the 'Reframe *but vulnerability is* Game' look like? *CEHX-y*

- At this point, you'll start hitting up more people with your goods and services. Some of them will be your people; some of them won't. To advance your CX maturity and mitigate the pain, you must learn how to reframe – that is, taking what looks negative on the surface and reflecting on what you can learn from the experience. To solidify this reflection, you may consider creating a risk register: a simple Excel document that details what the negative event or situation entailed and your investigation into the what, who, where, and why. Next, you follow up by adding details for how you'll prevent this event from occurring in the future and who's responsible for mitigation. Risk registers are common in public relations and should include any and all instances in which your business, attempting to become a trusted brand, could and does face a negative situation. The key is to reframe the negative into a lesson learnt, not a lesson burnt. ← *Remember the metal slippery dip?*

- Additionally, you could, and should, be expanding the maturity around how you gather feedback, being sure to use the right CX metrics at the right times in the customer experience journey.

- You'll also have your fresh-faced team strategically work towards developing and implementing your organisational culture, which will grow with you, with them, and with all the people you come to employ and serve. ← *You're never too small to start working on your culture*

GROWTH PHASE 3: CONSTRAINT ZONE

Phase three feels as shitty as it sounds. In a typical organisation (which you are not because you're reading and implementing this book), the constraint zone is where the fun usually goes to die. Often, this is when I get called in. I'm not going to lie – it's usually more beneficial to get me in during the growth zone so this zone doesn't mess with you so hard, but hey, sometimes we think we should suck up the pain longer than necessary. Talk about autosadism.

In the constraint zone, everything that once sparkled can now seem quite dull. Team members are becoming complacent. Innovation feels like a chore. 'Agile' is now one of the top

10 buzzwords or phrases to be banned, along with 'circling back', 'synergy', 'vibe', and 'moving the needle'. "Fuck the needle," you'll probably hear yourself say at this stage of business. "But why do I have to experience the constraint zone?" you ask. Well, in my experience, it's a great point in your business to reflect, interrogate yourself, and test yourself honestly. Questions might include:

- How successfully am I working towards my brand vision and purpose?

- How am I and my team living my brand's values?

- Are customers from the launch phase still our customers, or do we need to reassess our customer persona? *If not, then why not?*

- In what state is our tech stack? Is it still a patchwork quilt, or is it maturing with our needs?

- Is my business' culture attracting the right talent and inspiring loyalty? Am I the destination employer I want to be?

- Do my customers keep returning because they enjoy the experience, or are they here because they have no other choice?

- How do I feel? Am I feeling overwhelmed, or am I feeling underwhelmed? Am I over it, or am I still brimming with enthusiasm and vitality? *should you stay, or should you go?*

Your answers – and to be honest, if I were sitting in front of you, I'd have plenty more questions, as there's more where they came from *Like a mini therapy session* – will determine what happens next.

CX MATURITY PHASE – PERFORMING

By this stage, you're in one of two camps. The first is, you've figured out that implementing customer experience strategies is the way to go, but that doesn't stop the 'constraint' phase from kicking in. It just hurts less, and it's easier to turn the ship around when it steers off course. The second camp is, in my experience, the most common. It involves a lack of education around CX, and a culture that far too often says, "Just suck it up" and, "Business is meant to be hard." Like, what the actual fuck? No, no it's not. I mean sure, throw some curveballs and a challenge here and there, but being in business isn't meant to be your mental and physical undoing. We must stop perpetuating this culture of entrepreneurship where we only measure success by how 'busy' we are.

Many business owners and leaders aren't implicitly aware of CX, let alone how to implement it consistently in their businesses. Therefore, at the 'performing' point, we see many businesses that looked successful on the outside shut down. They go into denial, hoping that everything they did before to get to this point will be enough to get them through the rough seas. ← *My parents were in the navy, so blame them for the sea analogies* This is their ultimate undoing.

For those who realise the ship is going off course and they're about to hit rocks if they don't do something different or they may be the very few who did have an early understanding and adoption of CX management, their journey will look different. What they're doing differently, includes:

- Redefining their goods and services, possibly redesigning them to align closer to their customer's jobs to be done.

- Realigning team behaviours to the organisation's vision and values. In many cases, taking the opportunity to ethically let go of any underperformers or those who've come to the end of their journey with the business.

- Going back to the finance experts and assessing capital, assets, cash flow, and expenses, and being aware of their numbers. It literally astounds me how many businesses don't know their numbers. You *must* know your numbers. Get a good bookkeeper and accountant and have them teach you the foundations of knowing your numbers.

- Checking that all projects, including CX projects, have a clear line leading to a return on investment (ROI). ← *Don't forget the metrics and measures quick reference sheet to help you*

- Asking, "Who else can run this? Do I have the right leaders in place for my succession?" Existentially starting to question their place in the business and the mark they're leaving on everything they hold dear.

- Assessing whether the places where they show up in person and online are meaningful and still relevant to their audience. Do they really need that huge warehouse? Do the stock turns meet targets? Is that retail space still the best one now that the footpath is gone? Is their marketing still recognisable, yet drawing in new audiences?

The point being, they're asking themselves – or at least they have someone on their side asking them – questions that dig deep. Are they here for the right reasons? If they are, what has to change to get to the next phase of maturity? Once they know, are they committed to executing those changes? Or do they need to get to the point where they can exit stage left?

← *Mind you, even exiting your business takes CEHX work*

GROWTH PHASE 4: SCALE ZONE

Phase four is where the grit is. If you need more, a wonderful friend of mine named Dr Kirsten Peterson wrote a book called *When GRIT Is Not Enough*. Give it a read if you want to learn something from one of Australia's leading high-performance psychologists.

← *She helps Olympians; she can help you to*

If you've made it through the 'constraint zone', it's because you did one of two things. Option one, you decided to exit and get out of your business. Hopefully, you exited ethically, not leaving debts unpaid and a bitter taste in anyone's mouth. Sincerely, I don't judge anyone for getting out of business. Remember the field of dreams story from earlier? Sometimes the dreams just don't match reality. If your best bet is to cut your losses and leave with your dignity, then so be it. Option two is, you buckled up for the next era of your business-to-brand journey. You made some tough decisions in the previous phase. You've realigned your spending, your culture, your offerings; you're listening to your customers,

← *More intently and with renewed curiosity*

and your employees also feel heard and like they're back on the path of initiative and momentum. So, now what? Well, you look for the signs that say you're ready to scale, which include:

- Your business has a solidified set of goals and a CEHX strategy to match.

- Banks and investors see you as an investment and not a risk.

- Customers are consistently stripping your supply chain, purchasing your goods and services with minor friction points.

- You're starting to see the fruits of your advocacy, with marketing and sales showing better customer conversions and more enticing metrics. ← *Remember, advocate customers market for you*

There are plenty more signs that you're ready, but you get the gist. The ship has been turned away from the rocks, and you're now heading out to more expansive waters for a new adventure.

CX MATURITY PHASE – EMBEDDING/ OPTIMISING

Referring to the CX Pyramid from chapter four, hopefully you remember that towards the peak of that pyramid is optimisation of customer experience tactics and outcomes, which looks like:

- Efficient operations.

- Trust built within your culture and employees deeming you an employer of choice – a bloody great place to work!

- Solid relationships with supply chain partners.

- Revised and scalable customer experience journey with updated insights into your customers' needs and wants. ←——— *With purposeful dabs of personalisation*

- You and your team or teams ensuring every touchpoint mitigates as much friction and effort as possible.

- An evolved tech stack that has become mostly integrated, but with room to grow before you have to overhaul it. ←——— *It's tech – it's not built to withstand the test of time*

In the scaling stage, when optimising the customer experience becomes a priority, you now get to focus on something you might not have given much attention since the 'launch' phase, and that, my friend, is *personalisation*. Essentially, you're embedding CEHX tactics in the business and utilising the data to do more than make your dashboard look good, taking that data and converting it to actionable change. You're now mature enough in your customer experience to invest in making your goods and services, dare I say, consistently enjoyable to your customers, to your employees, to the humans who advocate for your trusted and value-driven brand.

SCALE WITH GRACE AND AN EARLY UNDERSTANDING

I know, I said we'd keep it light, and that was more like heavy cream, but at least now you can better comprehend the phases of business growth and how they align to the phases of CX maturity. When organisations have this knowledge early in their growth phases, there's no need for them to hold off on applying their

CX strategies. Every tactic they implement *Making business* early helps them get through the next phase *feel like the 'joy* a little less burnt for the experience. ←— *of CEHX'*

If you're an organisation that has gone through several of the growth phases and you're thinking, *Well, I haven't done any of this, and I'm making money hand over fist*, I say, well, all power to you. I would then ask: How often are you putting out fires? How often do you need to have 'serious conversations'? How well are you balancing work with life? These are the areas where a CX strategy can make a difference. It's not a miracle, silver bullet, or unicorn, but it will certainly help mitigate some of those grey hairs coming through and the bubbling resentment you may feel about being a leader or an owner in business.

TL;CBF

- Growing a business can be tough, and it takes comm tment. However, it doesn't need to be your undoing.

- Learning and implementing customer experience strategies early that are aligned to your growth phase can circumvent feeling unnecessary pain in the future growth phases, where things can take a turn and get rocky.

- In the journey of growing your business, you'll find yourself, your team, and your goods and services evolving and innovating, and if you develop your business to consider the customer in every decision, you'll find yourself more successfully achieving expansion.

- If everything is going to shit in handbasket, ⟵ Aussie invest in calling in some experts who have a good saying reputation for making impactful and ethical change. Otherwise, cut your losses and exit your business.

ACTIVITY: CX MATURITY SURVEY

Visit **aileenday.com.au/tjocehx-tools** and download your CX Maturity Survey to create clarity around your understanding and current implementation of customer experience strategies within your business.

CHAPTER 10: LEADERSHIP, NOT JUST A BUZZWORD

THE PROBLEM WITH TRADITIONAL 'MANAGERS'

In all my years working and even well before, I've been acutely aware of the concept of leadership. My dad worked full-time in the Australian Defence Force; therefore, I was exposed to ideas such as the chain of command and hierarchies well before I imagine the average person was.

The concept of leadership has been well-covered and scrutinised over the years, with its civil war against the concept of management and the debate over which mode of influence works best. Newsflash – they're both equally necessary when you lead or run a business, and they're even more imperative to those working to develop their own trusted and value-driven brand.

When I started working (at 13 years old for cash under the counter), leadership *wasn't* a thing. I'm talking about the early 1990s. It was all about management. In many organisations, leadership was deemed 'soft skills' – skills that demonstrate human traits like empathy, active listening, self-awareness, reflection, and so on. All very rare birds back in those days.

By 1998, after graduating high school and successfully completing 2 years of a business management and commerce course, my drive was to be a manager. According to my schoolbooks, managers get shit done. They make change happen. They corral the troops and earn respect and authority. If you didn't know, I'm the oldest of six children. That's how I grew up – in charge. So it made sense to start doing it for money.

By 1999, I got my wish. I was the trainee manager for a major supermarket chain that shall remain nameless for reasons, as you'll see. What I quickly learnt was that being a manager *sucked*. I quickly determined that I wasn't a very good manager, getting called into my store manager's office for the umpteenth time to discuss how I was managing my team. "You're not there to teach them, Aileen. You're there to give them a fucking list and get back to your job." ← *I actually did want to be a teacher growing up*

Now the predicament with that was, I was managing several other teens. None over 16 (yes, I know, but I was only 18). However, when I did as directed – when I did the 'manager's job' – tasks wouldn't get done as expected, in the right way or in time. Therefore, I would have to run around after the team had left or arrive the next day hours earlier than rostered to fix errors. *So, I thought, what if I pre-empt the errors? What if I provide feedback and help the team understand what's expected by walking them through each section of the department and explaining their tasks until they feel confident and are deemed proficient?* Even if that meant putting in some extra effort at the beginning, surely the outcome would be a smoother finish ...

Well, that's not what management was ← *Well, would you believe it, it worked* about. According to Michael, the store manager, "If they can't stack shelves, they should be fired." He would shriek at me, "They're here to do a task – how hard is it?" Well, Michael, it seems for a kid who's never worked before, it's actually *not* that hard *after* they've been properly trained. But Michael and many other 'managers' over my career fell into the same "how fucking hard is it to do your job?" trap, believing that people should just inherently know what to do. I would argue that, with the exception of breathing, there's nothing a human does inherently without first being taught (directly or indirectly).   ← *Don't @ me if I'm wrong*

I lasted 11 months and 12 days with this employer, as I realised that what I was being punished for wasn't my inability to manage – it was my *ability* to lead. My employer didn't value subordinates trusting the people they reported to. Subordinates weren't humans; they were moving objects. They were there for a task. To fulfil a duty. That was it. If you couldn't do that, you were worthless to them.

By 2000, I moved on to another of Australia's largest retailers, this time in home improvement. I would spend the next 14 years with this employer. Although I took a step back when I made the move, after dealing with the bullshit and fuckwittery of my previous employer, for my mental health, it was 200 steps forward in the long run. Despite not starting in a 'management' position, I still felt a resounding urge to take the reins and lead the way. Regularly, over the   *Oldest-child syndrome* years, my team and co-workers have called me Mum, sometimes endearingly, sometimes facetiously. With my new employer, I realised very quickly that although there were 'managers' in the

building, everyone was expected to behave like a leader. This concept boggled my tiny mind as I watched frontline team members make decisions without permission. A term I came to know as empowerment later turned into another buzzword by other organisations. I watched team members manage their own task loads around their other responsibilities without being directed, ← *Fancy that ... autonomy on show*
I later learnt this was what autonomy looked like.
I saw managers collaborating with their teams without disciplinary action being taken against them. Before that, the only time I'd seen a manager working as a team with their employees was ... oh, that's right, it was me. I saw managers teaching their teams new techniques to help make their tasks easier and less cumbersome, while having the team lead discussions and put forward ideas. ← *With leaders eagerly leaning into learning*
Who knew I'd be watching those 'soft skills' in action day in, day out?

I saw feedback being provided in both directions without egos getting butthurt (well, most of the time). I saw store managers walking around, talking to team members and helping them with their tasks as they chatted. When I enquired why they would do such a thing, it was explained to me that working together, despite your authority level, was a great opportunity for the store manager to get to know their teams and build trusting relationships.

I saw people talking about the values and the vision they had for themselves and the organisation. People were proud of their work. They felt like they were actively applying themselves to something bigger than themselves, and they valued being in an environment that ensured they weren't in survival mode every day.

In comparison to my previous employment experience, it was a damn utopia, and all because of *leadership*. Not the tyrannical example of management I had experienced and been forcibly encouraged to deliver. When I made my first mistake after being hired, I knew I'd found the place I wanted to be. I got called to the store manager's office and was asked to explain which error I thought I'd made. Following my confused explanation, my manager sincerely apologised for not giving me all the information I needed to complete the task properly. That humility, sincerity, and personal accountability were – and still are – traits I valued highly. It was the dawn of a new era.

TL;CBF

- I was blessed to learn and experience early on in my career the difference between poor management behaviours and purpose-led, employee-centric leadership.

- There's nothing soft about soft skills. Both soft skills (interpersonal qualities and traits) and hard skills (technical skills that require a form of formal education) require commitment, agility, integrity, and high levels of accountability. It's the delivery that makes all the difference.

LEARNING FROM OUR HISTORY – THE EVOLUTION OF MANAGEMENT AND LEADERSHIP

In my early career, in the wider world of business, the leadership style of people management was still largely unheard of, let alone experienced. Businesses were still largely stuck in aggressive micromanagement mode. Living and dying by the business's needs. Seeing employees as tools for the organisation's bottom line and completely replaceable.

We've all likely heard someone say or curse, "There are plenty more people who want this job. I can replace you in a second." How they saw customers was, in many cases, even worse. Ever since the end of World War II, the global goal was to accumulate and consume, and it was every organisation's aim to capitalise on this new economic behaviour. Their methods came with minimal to no concern for factors such as the environment, the community, their employees (management or otherwise), and certainly minimal to no care for the then exploitable consumer. However, over time, like we saw with the evolution of human resources in chapter nine, management and leadership also took its own evolutionary journey.

At least I have

The 21st Century has brought all manner of change to the way we view and do leadership, and management, for that matter. We're now in a more globalised and digitally connected world than ever, with communication methods far outreaching the capacity of those of our elders. Nowadays, we don't need millions of dollars to

Physically and emotionally disconnected

start up a business. We simply need a laptop and a marketable idea. The 21st century has seen women stop being bystanders in the boardroom and start being the leaders of it. We've seen employees, especially since the spicy cough era, take a stand for what they value, and it seems it's not sitting in 3 hours of gridlock traffic each day to get to the office, just to be made to feel replaceable. We see technology surpass itself every other day, sometimes aiding us to lead better. Sometimes inhibiting our ability to lead at all. We've seen jobs come into reality that never existed even a few years ago, such as social media influencers, blockchain analysts, contact tracers, eSports coaches, and so many more.[49]

Despite all of the world's growth and so-called efficiencies, there's still one thing organisations don't do consistently: train their leaders to be leaders and, in some cases, teach them when to be managers.

> The reality is, management and leadership have different meanings and yet are often used interchangeably.

Let's take a squiz at some of the core differences between leadership and management traits.

Organisational Activities and How Leaders vs. Managers Deliver

Workplace Activity	Leadership Approach	Management Approach
Setting Direction	Establishes vision and purpose, inspires with compelling future, focuses on 'why'	Develops specific goals, plans, and targets; focuses on 'what' and 'how'
Decision-Making	Encourages input and participation, considers broader impact, makes value-driven decisions	Analyses data and metrics, follows established processes, makes efficiency-driven decisions
Problem-Solving	Challenges assumptions, seeks innovative solutions, views problems as opportunities	Implements systematic approaches, applies proven methods, focuses on resolutions
Team Development	Coaches for growth, builds on strengths, develops future capabilities	Trains for performance, addresses weaknesses, focuses on current skills
Communication	Tells stories, connects emotionally, communicates values and meaning	Shares information, provides clear instructions, communicates expectations and timelines

Workplace Activity	Leadership Approach	Management Approach
Change Implementation	Creates urgency for change, addresses emotional responses, inspires adaptation	Plans steps for change, manages resistance, ensures compliance
Conflict Resolution	Explores underlying issues, focuses on relationship building, seeks win-win outcomes	Applies policies, focuses on immediate resolution, maintains productivity *Remember this when we discuss an outward mindset*
Performance Feedback	Has development conversations, discusses growth trajectory, connects work to purpose	Conducts reviews, measures against standards, addresses gaps
Risk Management	Takes calculated risks, embraces uncertainty, creates psychological safety	Mitigates risks, establishes controls, ensures compliance
Innovation	Creates space for experimentation, encourages creative thinking, tolerates failure	Implements improvement processes, measures outcomes, ensures quality
Meetings	Facilitates dialogue, explores possibilities, builds consensus	Sets agendas, tracks action items, maintains focus
Resource Allocation	Invests in potential, aligns resources with vision, thinks long term	Optimises efficiency, manages budgets, ensures immediate needs are met

In truth, the evolution of leadership has become even wider in scope. When

There are even more leadership styles

I speak to colleagues who live and breathe leadership, they use phrases such as, "Leadership is the creation of inspiration for a person or a group of people." They exclaim that leadership is about supporting and guiding others' interests, not one's self-interest. They're often heard discussing how those in true leadership positions are humble, active listeners, and there to create a culture of engagement, momentum, and loyalty.

In the discipline of customer experience, leadership is a key maker or breaker of your organisation's ability to feel the joy of CEHX. Your people's ability to self-lead, be led, and be managed all combine to align your organisation's values, strategy, sales goals, customer – and for that matter, employee – engagement. It has the ability to mitigate an 'us vs. them' attitude and keep everyone aligned to stay customer-obsessed, not self-obsessed. Remember your vision, the one you pointed your brand towards? Achieving it takes leadership.

In my experience, it's never enough to just say, "Oh, do this and you're a leader." Becoming a leader with a keen awareness of self and others takes time. It takes practice, and it certainly takes the privilege of knowing a great leader whom you can model your own behaviours on. I'm a huge advocate for taking on a mentor. In my career, I had somewhat of a mixed bag. I certainly was privileged to learn from some wonderful, caring, and servient leaders. Now, don't take the term 'servient' to mean submissive or to imply my mentors were walkovers. What I mean is, they had no ego that stopped them from understanding that they were there to serve a group of people and that those people were business-critical to the success of the company.

In hindsight, I also had the privilege of learning from many less than ideal examples of leadership. I remember coming home to my family on occasion and remarking, "Today I learnt how not to behave/react/respond," and that lesson, my friend, can sometimes be more important than anything you can learn from a great leader. You get to see the flip side of great leadership and great management – *poor* leadership and *poor* management. The ugliness of making another person's human experience seem less important than your own. In these instances, you often find that the 'leader' was elevated because they were the high performer in their area of work. The pragmatic next step was, of course, to have them lead a team to influence them to be as high-performing as they were in their role. The real, and I mean *real*, predicament here is that not everyone is cut out to lead, to manage, to be a major influencer of others. Sometimes, we need to look hard at the roles we're expecting these high performers to take on and ask ourselves, as the business owner, CEO, general manager, CXO, whoever we are, if that high performer is set up for success in that leadership role or set up for failure and, in failing, likely to take others down with them.

People leave managers, not jobs

> Not all managers are wankers, and not all leaders are influencing gurus.

LEADERSHIP – THE GATEWAY TO A VALUE-DRIVEN LIFE

Finding the balance between managing and leading can be tricky. Worldwide recruiting website Indeed recommends taking on more of a management mode in moments of crisis or emergency, when training new team members, in times when delegation is necessary, and where a situation requires a specific result, such as annual report preparation and the like.[50] On a micro level, I tend to agree. In general, however, using a mix of management and leadership gets the best results. As I mentioned earlier, in a previous role, I experienced team members successfully completing tasks how and when they saw fit without the micromanagement or instruction of their leader. Why was this approach so successful? Well, when first training new team members, their leader leant towards the manager role, helping them understand deadlines and become proficient at their tasks, while giving them the space to make mistakes and learn from them without fear of repercussion. ⟵ *That part is leadership* Once confidence and proficiency were demonstrated consistently, the team member was given the space to manage their own workload – empowered to choose how they delivered outcomes based on the organisation's vision, values, and their own competencies.

From this point, leadership can be the main mode of execution. When you lean more towards leadership, your team looks for opportunities to collaborate with you. They're open to learning and listening, as these are the same traits you've demonstrated to them. When tough decisions must be made or delegation is required, you find that your team either already recognises a viable solution or opts to take on the additional workload if required.

At this point, you know leadership isn't just a buzzword – it's a way of life. I say 'life' because good leaders don't stop being leaders once they walk out the door at the end of the day. They take the skills of values-based and strategic thinking, consideration, candidness, and a commitment to improvement to self and others out into the world with them. They take what they've learnt about creating a value-driven brand through leadership and use it to develop their own value-driven lives. They learn to listen to their kids. They value the thoughts and opinions of others, whether they agree or not. ← *we could seriously use more of that right now* They become open to learning more about themselves and the impact they make in the world. They look for a bigger purpose than themselves. They begin to show the rest of us what a positive human experience looks like, inspiring others to emulate them and become better themselves. Just look at the Mel Robbins, the Brené Browns, and the Tony Robbins of the world – they've become inspirations for those aspiring to take their own life challenges and turn them into valuable life experiences. They're actively creating their own value-driven lives.

One of my favourite conversations about leadership occurred in 2021 with an old colleague, Danny Ginsberg, who at the time was an advocate for the Arbinger Institute. We chatted on my podcast, *The Value Driven Brand*, about the concepts of inward and outward mindset. To me, these mindsets were a key part of a strong leadership foundation. He explained how anyone with an inward mindset is essentially only serving their own needs. However, an outward mindset is one where the person recognises that despite needing to have a difficult conversation or make a decision they disagree with to appease the majority, it's the right course to take. Essentially, it's outwardly thinking of others before acting in a way that only serves yourself. If you get a chance to listen to the conversation, you'll see how applying these concepts not just breeds new life into leaders' behaviours but also their teams, as they're encouraged to adopt the same mindset, helping them self-lead and supporting a more honest and open culture. ←

There's that candid culture for the win

Listen to my Value Driven Brand podcast with Danny Ginsberg here (or anywhere podcasts are available):

One of my favourite leadership quotes is ...

> A leader is best when people barely know he exists, when his work is done, his aim fulfilled, they will say: we did it ourselves."
>
> *– Lao Tzu, Chinese philosopher*

EMPLOYEE PERFORMANCE APPRAISALS AND SUCCESSION PLANNING

Succession planning and employee appraisals are two business activities many groan at. They mean more effort, more attention to detail when you're already feeling choked under the weight of your workload or, in some cases, you feel potentially threatened. Don't make me tell you the story about the 'manager' who read my answer to the question in my performance appraisal ... *Where do you see yourself in 3 years?* From that experience, I learnt the hard way not to assume that when you say, *Doing your job*, they'll take it as the compliment you believe it to be.

The point? Not everyone wants to move to the 'next step'; not everyone is built for leading teams, and you, as the person running the show, must take stock of your people's personalities and strengths to determine which opportunities you're willing to give them to ensure their ongoing engagement and success. Aside from remuneration, this is the main area where employee performance appraisals help. You need to understand your employees' performance against your now human-centred and behaviour-based metrics because the insights in these appraisals directly support the successful outcomes of succession plans.

As for succession plans, more specifically, they help you mitigate future shit fights (to the degree you put in the real work). This issue never felt more real than when I was training to become an accredited family business advisor through Adelaide University and, in turn, join the Australian/New Zealand Family Business Association. Every other week, I heard stories of business advisors working with family businesses where the patriarch was on death's door, refusing to consider a successor to their now third-generation business. Talk about holding out.

In any business – family-run or otherwise – investing the right amount of energy, resources, and time in deter- *Letting go can be scary if your identity is grounded in your business* mining a successor can be the difference between unrest and collapse. ~~While many~~ larger businesses may be lucky enough to have a board of directors or a family council to assist with the replacement, the process can be forced, rushed, and the successor might be ill-prepared. There may be no one in the organisation qualified, creating the need to navigate external recruitment. What a potential shitshow!

I get that your business is the equivalent of your 'baby', especially when you founded the business, built the relationships, built the wealth, and it's your entire identity, but at the beginning of your recruitment and team-building journey, you should get into the habit of performing at least biannual employee performance appraisals, maintaining an outward mindset and ensuring that no feedback comes as a surprise. If you feel extra brave, have your team deliver a candid perfor- *Twice per year* mance appraisal of you. Then start formulating a succession plan, even if only to ensure you have the right people at the helm should you want to take a well-deserved break! With the right people in the right roles, the ship should sail smoothly in your absence.

ACTIVITY: SUCCESSION PLAN

Head over to **aileenday.com.au/tjocehx-tools** and download your succession plan and employee appraisal templates. Review the templates and schedule time to deep dive into their impact and discuss their implementation in your business with your senior leadership team.

TL;CBF

* There has been a historical shift from rigid, control-heavy management styles to more human-centred, values-based leadership, emphasising the difference between managing tasks and inspiring people.

* True leadership drives employee and customer engagement by aligning vision, values, and behaviour, with leaders expected to lead by example in and outside of work.

* Many organisations still fail to train managers in leadership, often promoting high performers without assessing their readiness or suitability for people leadership roles.

* Succession planning and performance appraisals are essential but often overlooked tools to maintain business continuity and employee development, requiring ongoing, honest feedback and an outward mindset that prioritises the team and business sustainability.

CHAPTER 11:
CULTURE, VALUES,
AND CREATING A
TRUSTED BRAND

CULTURE – THE KEY TO EVERYTHING

When I started writing this book, I was also creating some courses named 'CX in Concept (CXiC)' and 'CX in Action (CXiA)'. My learning and development designer Kris Kimberley and I had a field day discussing the realities of creating a truly customer-centric organisation. What kept coming up was how next to none of the disciplines of customer experience design, human-centred or systems design, or the pillars of CEHX can ever be sustained without the same energy being placed into creating a human-centric culture – using the values those humans live and breathe and, in time, developing a trusted brand. It truly felt like an infinity loop where *this* can't work unless we have *that*.

That's the ultimate goal, right? To create your very own trusted and value-driven brand. To transform from a business into a brand. To feel the intrinsic joy of CEHX. This is your pathway to becoming a legacy brand. The Nikes, the Apples, the Zappos, the Bunnings, the Kmarts, the Tiffany & Cos, the Pandoras, the Dom Perignons. You get where I'm going. These brands service multiple audiences. Some are considered a luxury, some not, proving you don't need to be a world-famous designer to become a legacy. You just have to be for the people, whoever your people are. When you're for the people, the people show you their appreciation by buying from you; therefore, being for the people is your profit strategy.

A common consensus among CX professionals is that without the right culture, leadership, and values, no customer experience initiative can flourish. Instead, it's forever destined to be abandoned too soon. Not implemented in a way that manages the need for adjustment or revision. Not supported by the entire organisation. Politicised. Lucky to be measured appropriately or given the attention it requires to develop and prove its worth. This is because your organisation's culture shows up in ↑ every aspect of customer experience design, the *Then CX is blamed for shit results* foremost important aspect of its success. How you influence your team to get on board, how you develop their trust to speak up and be candid about product and service intricacies, and so much more can make or break your whole CX strategy. In fact, *any* strategy.

NOURISHING VS. TOXIC WORKPLACE CULTURES

Let's take a quick gander at culture in organisations. What it means, what it looks like, what it feels like. If we look to our mate Merriam-Webster, ← *AKA the dictionary for my gen Z friends or younger* it defines culture as "the set of shared attitudes, values, goals, and practices that characterises an institution or organisation."[51]

Organisational awards website Comparably mentions numerous organisations on its 'best company culture 2024' list – voted on by employees of each organisation – including Adobe (tech/business services), Volvo (car manufacturer), and blow me down, even Tinder (online dating app) is on the list.[52] These organisations are measured on aspects *They clearly understand* such as diversity, leadership, employee net *great CEHX* promoter scores, CEO scores, employee reviews, employee benefits, and several other metrics. Reviewing these metrics gives us the implicit understanding from the outside looking in of what it feels like to be a part of these cultures.

Now, you might be sitting there thinking, *Well, what the team thinks can be highly subjective*. That's my point entirely. You're absolutely correct in your critique. However, their subjectiveness is what helps tell the story of an organisation's culture. How different peoaple experience the same or similar environment based on their own personal experiences. Based on their own personal goals and ambitions. Based on their own personal biases and expectations. This is culture. This is the human experience. No two of us are the same. I mean, have you met my twin sister, Nerida (or womb mate, as we refer to each other)? We are chalk and cheese. So why would we ever expect a group of strangers who come together to work towards a common vision to be anything less than variable and subjective in what they bring to the table?

There are, however, people who expect complete uniformity and to command a workplace environment like an authoritarian overlord. Here in Australia, there are several organisations that have been quite publicly reported to not just know they exert a toxic culture but to also not care enough to invest in changing it. For reasons that can only be put down to profits and no time to give a shit about the humans in the workplace, workers in one particular industry are reported to experience high levels of workplace bullying and trauma and have a much higher suicide risk than workers in any other field, yet the toxic culture prevails.[53]

> The problem with toxic cultures is they reverberate outwards. They increase chances of employees turning to addictive substances. They increase cases of domestic violence. They can lead to internal and external workplace ostracism, pushing employees closer to the edge of destruction. *It's an organisational cancer*

It may sound dramatic, but just take a squiz at the Fair Work Australia website or the equivalent in your *If it hasn't been dismantled* country and see for yourself the number of claims of bullying, harassment, and unfair dismissal in any given state on any given day. Toxic cultures come in all shapes and sizes. Some are global entities; others are Mum and Dad businesses. It's up to you as the leader in whichever role you play to create a culture you can be proud of. *Why is it up to me?* you ask. Well, plainly, the fish rots from the head first. The leaders are there to lead, not leave it to everyone else. *That's management*

So what does it even take to create a high-performing culture?

USING SCIENCE TO CREATE A HIGH-PERFORMING CULTURE

As mentioned previously, one of my favourite books about the employee experience and what drives employee motivation and, in turn, employee loyalty is Dan Pink's *Drive: The Surprising Truth About What Motivates Us*. Dan explains that, for hundreds of years, we've been trying to drive our employees the wrong way. He says empirical scientific evidence shows that when we create a culture framed by what we all know as carrots and sticks,

I know, this guy again

Which could explain the lack of positive results for some of us

Evidence gathered through direct observation and replicable experimentation

we're never as successful in our endeavours when compared to organisations that drive a culture of values. "What does that mean?" you ask. Well, as Dan explains, the science of humans isn't always as straightforward as it is for, say, a pet dog, but many businesses still treat people like pets. "Do this job well, and you'll get a treat" (dangling the carrot). "Don't do this job well, and you'll get punished" (threatened with the stick, metaphorically speaking). Dangled treats and threatened punishments aren't what humans want. Instead, we require what's known as Motivation 3.0:

We hope

This is known as Motivation 2.0

1. **Autonomy** – the desire to direct our own lives.

2. **Mastery** – the urge to make progress and get better at something that matters.

3. **Purpose** – the yearning to do what we do in the service of something larger than us.[54]

Many organisations have tested the science and created organisational cultures that, above all else, provide value to their employees, rather than the outdated one-way street approach where only the organisation benefits. *Fewer my way or the highway traits* Over the years, we've seen evidence of this ineffective approach, with the likes of Elon Musk directing his teams to return to the office full time or 'pretend' to work elsewhere. Literally, he said "pretend to work."[55] This is despite every study delivered since the post spicy cough era detailing that teams have become more productive due to flexible work arrangements. *In many cases, employees were found to increase output*

We've touched on the Great Resignation, right? Another post pandemic pandemic where industries found themselves in the shit because they'd spent so many years under-valuing their employees that, after such a major lifestyle shift, millions of people around the world woke up, looked out the window, and thought, *Fuck it, I'm done.* Questioning why they give and give and get nothing but sticks or shitty flaccid carrots in return. Questioning if their boss will be delivering the eulogy at their funeral when they die of burnout. Well, of course they bloody won't be. So why should an employee continue being subjected to all that bullshit?

Finally, employees have found their voice. They know their value, ← *Albeit the odd employee might be somewhat deluded* and they're leaving shithouse cultures in droves. They're now being headhunted, and some organisations are willing to do whatever it takes to get them and keep them. Most employees want flexibility, wellbeing, and purpose on top of competitive pay, ← *They're sticking it to being in survival mode* good working conditions, and skills development.[56] It's as simple as that.

At this stage, my intuition tells me, as a business owner, you too feel unduly pressed by the 'revelations' of employees, realising you want to lure the best, show them they're valued, and retain them, but you have additional red tape fucking up your plans. You have compliance burdens, payroll taxes, exorbitant rental costs, overheads, insurances, and so much more. However, I'll tell you this: the internet is littered with examples of organisations that have popped off in hard times, and it's that high level of innovation, leadership, and resilience that separates the wheat from the chaff. An appropriately motivated workforce can make the burdens of business feel less oppressive and more successive.

A CULTURE OF RISKINESS, NOT RECKLESSNESS

In creating a loyalty-driven workplace culture, there's the unavoidable need to also work out how you can sustainably deliver what each of your employees values. As we've seen, it could be anything from flexible work arrangements to applying resources to an important social cause (locally or otherwise).

> Your employees want to feel that they have a purpose and are connected to something bigger than themselves.

While they may value the opportunity to increase their take-home income, as proven, as long as their income covers the cost of living and provides forward financial momentum, in most cases, money is no longer a primary motivator.

This is where you, as the employer, wanting to attract the best of the best, have the opportunity to be different. For example, should you adopt the Atlassian style of *There's that being* difference, where they provide one day *strategic again* per quarter for their employees to work on solving a problem of their choice? In this example, they can either work solo or in teams. The only rule – the solution has to be delivered in 24 hours; thus, they call it a ShipIt Day, formerly named a FedEx Day.[57]

Dom Price, Atlassian's head of R and D and work futurist, explained that scaling the organisation's internal culture using ShipIt Days was one of the greatest benefits of the value-driven innovation.[58] With their mission to be famous for being awesome, Atlassian needed to mitigate one of the biggest killers of businesses who scale – losing the will to take calculated risks. Creating the ShipIt Day ritual to scale culture, innovation, and values has seen what started as 14 Atlassian ShipIt Day participants grow to over 1,500 (as of 2017). In Atlassian's culture, their employees are at the centre of the solution, and their customer, employee, and human experience as well as brand trust and advocacy are the winners.

While you're developing your best in-show culture, you'll need to get comfortable with taking risks. Your reaction to that statement will depend on which business growth phase you're in. Commonly, when we're in the early years of business, taking risks feels necessary and possibly exhilarating. However, as businesses grow, risk-taking starts to seem all too reckless; therefore, taking risks becomes a thing of the past. We install strict governance or red tape to ensure the status quo isn't damaged, but when taking a strict risk-averse approach, many businesses start to see shit going sideways.

The Governance Institute of Australia works on the basis of behavioural science and states that when creating a risk-tolerant culture, it's important to start in the right place.[59] That means assessing *how* you get your employees to do the right thing, rather than just helping them know *what* to do after the fact. To create a culture of risky, not reckless, you need to conceive a program that helps employees feel safe around risk. For example, *My son's parkour coach's mantra* there's no point letting them loose to take on an Atlassian-style ShipIt Day if they then get grilled for not meeting a deadline, or taking a call, or whatever the fallout might be. Helping the team understand 'how' to do risk appropriately may involve a set of guidelines around workload, and communication of intentions and any perceived risk rather than, after a risk event, those involved simply hoping they won't be scrutinised.

AUTHENTIC, ENGAGED, AND SAFE

Another great opportunity to practise candid communication

Building a culture central to the human experiences your employees value is fundamental in not just the growth phases but every day thereafter. While writing this book, I had the pleasure of learning about culture quality from many experts. In light of these conversations, current research, and lived experience, I created a list of five tactical, practical, and proven activities you can deliver in your own organisation. No carrots or sticks required. An investment, sure, but when your ROI is employee loyalty and improved engagement, which flows on to your customer experience, the investment is worth it. Some of these ideas may feel left of centre, but remember, the key is to first determine what the humans in your organisation value and create your culture from there. The aim is to be authentic, engaged, and to make your employees feel safe. ← *Feeling safe breeds innovation – it's CEHX-y*

CULTURE-BUILDING TIPS

1. **Create your own ShipIt Day.** There are many, many organisations who, after seeing Atlassian's success, have now taken it upon themselves to create their own versions of ShipIt Day. Many report that this simple investment of 24 hours has changed the culture game for them.

2. **Eat with your team.** That's right. According to Sharon Natoli, author of *Eating Together* and expert in creating human connections within the workplace, "Eating together is a humble, yet surprisingly powerful ritual that easily fits within the rhythms of an organisation. It is a simple, yet highly effective means of building workplace cultures characterised by connected and cohesive teams that in turn will drive future organisational performance." She discusses how other well-known and trusted brands, such as Canva and cereal maker Carman's Kitchen, have taken on the ritual of eating together to reap the rewards of an engaged and accountable culture.[60]

Ask me about the success of my monthly lunch event DBSS

3. **Create a set of values and vision for your organisation.** Coming from Bunnings where this was a given, I was stunned to see it isn't the case in most organisations. The beauty of having your brand's vision and values is that your team collaborates to determine what working in the organisation means to them. Together, they decide what their vision of success looks like, feels like, and who it serves. Once your vision is clear, you have a tool with which to support your team, support your growth, and provide that elusive 'purpose' Dan Pink flags as a necessary element of organisational motivation. Even if you don't yet have a team, do this for yourself, and make it the drawcard for your future brand advocates.

4. **Give your team the opportunity to venture out of their day to day.** Help them take on the role of someone in a completely different setting within the organisation. One of the best ways to mitigate organisational silos, mitigate the 'us and them' mentality, *where the left* ↑ and mitigate the "that's not my job" *hand is clueless to* or "I dunno" moments is to facilitate *the right hand* regular job swap opportunities. While this activity can seem a little out of left field, for your team and your customers, it can create precious outcomes where everyone has a little more empathy for those in different roles from them. In time, your customers start to experience a more congruent team. In addition, your innovation goes wild as team members return to their everyday roles a little wiser, or sometimes a little more driven to create improvements in areas of the business other than their own. For a minimal disruption and drop in productivity (as people take on roles they're not exactly qualified for), you'll see the return on investment in every other area of your business, which makes it a worthy endeavour.

5. In a world of instability, find ways to be stable. Now, I realise this might come as a surprise, but one of the best methods for building a trusted and loyalty-driven culture is to ... **be consistent.** ← *Who knew?* This also applies to your customer experience. Nearly gone are the days where 'experts' are out there screaming about how to make people love you by *wowing* them

with every interaction. Truth be told, it's fucking exhausting to deliver and even worse to be on the receiving end of.

Your employees, like your customers, are all their own type of human. Trying to guess what will deliver the *wow* today and then again tomorrow is almost impossible. If you come across someone instructing you how to make 'raving fans' of anyone, let alone everyone, walk the hell away. You don't need that type of bullshit hyperbole in your life. However, in reality, what all humans do love is a bit of consistency. Knowing what to expect. Feeling a sense of belonging. When you're delivering a culture based on your brand's values, this is made even easier, as you and your team, and your customers for that matter, can expect integrity, teamwork, and perhaps a bit of fun every now and then. Maybe they can expect timely, open, and candid communication. Maybe they can expect consistency in the way recognition – and discipline for that matter – are provided. One of our basic human needs is stability ← Fuck knows we could use more and certainty, and everything else we of that too believe motivates us as humans comes secondary.

ACTIVITY: BECOME A DESTINATION EMPLOYER

Write a list of the things that would make you want to be an employee in your business. Based on what you've learnt about the employee experience, what opportunities do you have to deliver a culture that will make you a destination employer?

TL;CBF

- Culture is the foundation of customer experience success. Without a values-driven, human-centric organisational culture led by authentic leadership, your customer experience (CX) initiatives are likely to fail, no matter how well-designed.

- Dan Pink's research highlights that employee motivation is driven by autonomy, mastery, and purpose, and moving away from 'carrot-and-stick' approaches of human motivation and towards deeper fulfilling human drivers leads to higher engagement and loyalty. Otherwise known as Motivation 3.0.

- Authentic culture requires consistency and inclusion. Practical strategies like ShipIt Days, team meals, cross-functional job swaps, and co-creating values help build trust, safe connection, and a shared sense of purpose among employees. Organisations with poor cultures not only harm employees but also damage brand trust and customer experience – proving that internal culture and external reputation are inseparable.

PART THREE:

TAILORING CEHX FOR HUMANS

CHAPTER 12: THE MISSING PUZZLE PIECE

TO BE OR NOT TO BE? THAT IS THE QUESTION

To be or not to be? A question poured over so deeply in Shakespeare's *Hamlet*, where Hamlet considers the mortal question of life and death and goes on to ask about his own morality and the human experience.

What does 'human experience' even mean? Well, it's subjective. As human beings, we live our lives in moments. We experience moments; we memorise moments; we live for moments; we share moments. These are the moments that matter. All the rest are either filed, forgotten, or not even registered. How we remember our experiences, or these 'moments', is determined by the emotions associated with the most intense part of an experience (the peak) and the end of an experience (the end).[61]

Or in quarter miles if you've Dom Toretto

Our human lives have several characteristics unique to our species. These include, but are not limited to:

1. Complex language.

2. The existence of a soul or spirituality.

3. A capacity for rational thinking. ←— If only we had more

4. Ideas and memory.

5. Simple and complex emotions.

With the modern world spinning around us the way it does, it's estimated that the average adult comes into contact with 34 gigabytes of data every day![62] Want to compare that to something more relatable than a computer? Well, you could say it's about the equivalent of scrolling through 11.3 million social media posts. Or it would be like standing under a fire hydrant while trying to drink from it; meanwhile, your conscious mind only captures about a cupful. So how do we cope? We rely on the brain's prefrontal cortex to act as our executive filter, keeping the noise manageable. Without it, we'd be in a state of sensory overwhelm, basically potatoes with wi-fi.

Now, here's the kicker: the old way of explaining the brain – triune models, or tidy 'survival-emotional-executive' compartments – sounds neat for teaching, but modern neuroscience has moved on. The brain isn't three stacked layers. It's a living, breathing network of 86 billion neurons that's *plastic*, meaning it rewires constantly in response to experience, learning and environment.[63]

This matters for business because it changes how we think about customer experience. You're not designing for three fixed brain states. You're designing for an *adaptive brain* that:

- Predicts what will happen next

- Associates meaning with emotions and memory

- Reshapes itself through repeated experience (AKA neuroplasticity)

- Can have rational processes overridden by perceived threat or stress

That last point is gold for brands: when people feel unsafe, stressed, or undervalued, their rational brain is hijacked. They won't hear your 'value prop'; they'll just bolt. But when you design experiences that foster safety, meaning, and connection, you literally help customers' brains stay open to engagement and trust.

In business terms:

- **Predictive brains want anticipation.** Design experiences that feel one step ahead of the customer.

- **Plastic brains want reinforcement.** Repetition of positive touchpoints rewires perception in your favour.

- **Emotional brains want safety.** Stability, trust, empathy. These are your currency.

The practical takeaway? Neuroplasticity gives us a road map. Every customer interaction reshapes how they see you. Every touchpoint either strengthens or weakens the neural pathways of trust, loyalty, and advocacy. That's why being human-centred isn't just fluffy 'nice to have'; it's the only way to build a value-driven brand that survives the test of time.

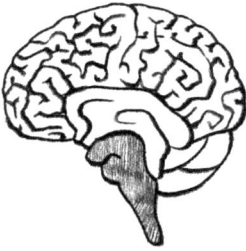

Survival State
BRAIN STEM

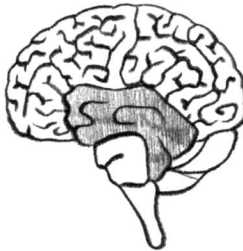

Emotional State
LIMBIC SYSTEM

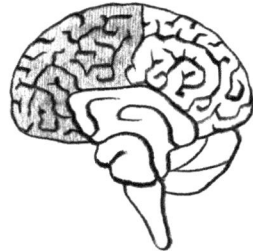

Executive State
PREFRONTAL LOBES

THE IMPACT OF CEHX ON THE HUMAN EXPERIENCE

In chapter six, where we designed your customer experience journey, we touched on the concept of designing for the human experience. Many business leaders rarely consider the human experience, meaning they rarely sit back and think about what's going on in their human customers' lives. Thus, designing and delivering a brand that's motivated by the human experience is the missing puzzle piece to feeling the joy of CEHX in your brand.

Which is how we got here

When does a business ever take time to ask which human experiences have moulded their customers' perceptions, inhibitions, and ambitions? What are their jobs to be done? What pressures are they experiencing? What intrinsic and extrinsic values have shaped and now motivate them? What could help them feel safe and open to what you want to share with them? So many questions and so little consideration, *And yes, it is* let alone answers. ⟵ *that deep*

If we're designing a business to become a trusted and value-driven brand, we must be unique. ⟵ *Remember, that's* We must be different from our competi- *what strategy is* tors. We must be different in our market, in our industry, and to do that, we must consider and design with the human experience central to our brand. Even the best AI brands know they need to be human-centric because, at the end of the day, humans are the customers. ⟵ *For now*

So taking what we know, and remembering that this is the casual hook-up, not the be all and end all of designing for the human experience, let's examine the principles of human-centred design and the CX journey. Instead of designing touchpoints for 'survival brain', 'emotional brain', or 'executive brain', let's talk about creating *adaptive experiences* that learn, adjust, and build game-changing trust over time. Building customer experience journeys that mirror how our brains work – interconnected, predictive, and collective – gives you not only originality, but also strategic profit, longevity, and loyalty.

Here's how to apply modern, human-centred design with updated neuroscience frameworks:

1. **Adaptive, predictive design (not reactive compartments):**

The brain doesn't wait for a stimulus; it predicts and adapts. Designing touchpoints that anticipate needs, context, and states creates smoother, deeper interactions.

2. **Neuroplasticity as a design principle:**

Brains physically rewire through repeated, meaningful experience. You can respect this by designing experiences that progressively build trust, reinforce value, and encourage deeper engagement.

3. **Systems, not silos:**

Emotion, cognition, and survival aren't isolated; they're interconnected systems. Your CX journey must reflect that integration – not three separate states, but one adaptive process.

4. **Co-creation and iteration, neuro-style:**

Let your customers literally help shape the brand's neural pathways. Co-design, pilot, refine. The brain thrives on feedback-loop learning.

5. **Contextual and environmental sensitivity:**

The brain's brain – its processing – changes based on context. Observe real usage and create flexible experiences that adapt to surroundings, moods, and modes of processing.

6. **Inclusive, accessible experiences:**

We all process differently: visually, auditorily, kinaesthetically. Designs must adapt to varied neuro types, just like a plastic brain adapts to injury or change.

7. **Culture of continuous adaptation (corporate neuroplasticity):**

Organisations, like brains, must build adaptability into their bones. Design learning environments, immersive training, and habits that prime teams for change and innovation.

By ditching the triune brain (separate, static layers) in favour of an adaptive, neuroplastic-inspired model, you're not just selling a product or service. You're building a brand that *learns with the customer*, evolves with them, and becomes trust-rich in the process. That's the real joy of CEHX.

FROM BUSINESS TO BRAND – A HUMAN-CENTRED APPROACH

When transforming your business into a brand, consider applying what you've learnt so far and turning it into a simplified human-centred implementation framework. While the size of your business will determine which stakeholders are relevant to each part of the framework, designing for the human experience is size agnostic. ←

I've told you, when it comes to having great CEHX, size doesn't matter

THE HUMAN-CENTRED IMPLEMENTATION FRAMEWORK

Research Phase: Understanding Your Customers

- Watch real customers interact with your business: Observe where they hesitate, what makes them smile, and when they seem confused.

- Ask about feelings, not just facts: Have timely conversations about how customers feel at key moments, such as first visit, check-out, and after purchase.

- Spot the sticking points: Identify where customers get overwhelmed, confused, or frustrated.

Design Phase: Creating Experiences That Connect

- Bring your team together: Discuss what you've learnt about customer reactions and brainstorm improvements.

- Address core human needs: For each touchpoint, consider:

  - How to create a sense of safety and ease (keeps the brain open instead of defensive).

  - How to make it emotionally satisfying (reinforces positive associations and rewires loyalty).

  - How to make it clear and logical (supports better decision-making and reduces cognitive load).

- Review your ideas: Ask, "How would this make customers feel?" and, "How would it make them remember us?" before implementing changes.

Testing Phase: Making Sure It Works

- Watch for comfort signals: Notice body language, facial expressions, and stress indicators when customers use your new approach.

- Check the emotional temperature: Simply ask, "How did that make you feel?" after interactions.

- Follow the thought process: Ask customers to talk through what they're thinking as they navigate your business. Their comments are gold nuggets.

Implementation Phase: Making It Stick

- Train your team to recognise signals: Help the team identify when customers feel unsafe or rushed, when they're emotionally engaged or frustrated, and when they're calmly evaluating.

- Track what matters. Create simple measures for each human need:

  - Safety metrics: Abandonment rates, help requests, frustration points.

  - Emotional metrics: Satisfaction scores, positive comments, excitement levels.

  - Cognitive metrics: Understanding of offerings, ease of decision-making, jobs to be done.

- Keep improving: Regularly review customer feedback and metrics to make continuous improvements.

Now, we haven't gone into too many specifics around what CEHX would look like ⟵ *We'll cover the feedback loop in chapter 15* for different business types. Predominantly because, well ... one, it looks different in different businesses but also ... two, because CEHX is applicable to every business. Let's take a moment to look at some practical applications for a few core business types.

Practical Applications Across Business Types

Retail Stores

- Safety: Clear signage, visible staff, easy-to-navigate layout.

- Emotion: Warm greetings, engaging sensory experiences, celebration of purchases.

- Cognition: Logical product groupings, clear comparisons, helpful information.

Service Businesses

- Safety: Transparent pricing, clear timelines, no hidden fees.

- Emotion: Warm welcome, recognition of concerns, celebration of results.

- Cognition: Simple explanations, process overviews, expected outcomes.

Online Businesses

- Safety: Fast load times, secure check-out, easy return policies.

- Emotion: Appealing visuals, positive language, customer stories.

- Cognition: Clear navigation, helpful filters, straightforward information, transparent expectations.

Simple Starting Points for Any Business

Where tactile selling isn't possible, social proof is a must

- Map your customer moments: List every interaction, from first awareness to loyalty and advocacy. ←———— *DIFOT is still one of my favourite transparency metrics: delivered in full, on time*

- Rate each moment: How well does it address safety needs, emotional needs, and cognitive needs?

- Fix the weakest points first: Start with moments that trigger ← *Chapter six if you haven't already created your customer journey map* negative reactions.

- Ask and observe: The simplest ← *It's that deep* research is just watching and asking, "How was that for you?"

- Make one brain-friendly improvement each month: Small, consistent changes add up.

These are the moments that matter.

TL;CBF

- The human experience is subjective; no two people process the same moment the same way.

- By understanding how the brain constantly rewires itself around three core needs, you can design customer experiences that stand out.

- The three needs are:
  - Safety (keep the brain open instead of defensive)
  - Emotion (create positive associations that stick)
  - Cognition (make things clear, logical, and easy-to-decide)

- Applying these principles to human-centred design gives you an edge over your competitors.

- Mapping experiences against these needs reveals opportunities to become a more profitable, trusted, and value-driven brand.

ACTIVITY: DESIGN FOR BRAIN-FRIENDLY EXPERIENCES

Step 1:

Add a new line to your customer journey map. Label it Customer Brain Needs.

Step 2:

At each stage of the journey, tick off how well you address the three needs.

Stage of journey	Safety (felt secure, not stressed)	Emotion (felt positive, valued)	Cognition (clear, easy-to-decide)	Notes/ideas for improvement
Awareness	☐ Yes ☐ No	☐ Yes ☐ No	☐ Yes ☐ No	
Consideration	☐ Yes ☐ No	☐ Yes ☐ No	☐ Yes ☐ No	
Acquisition/ purchase	☐ Yes ☐ No	☐ Yes ☐ No	☐ Yes ☐ No	
Retention	☐ Yes ☐ No	☐ Yes ☐ No	☐ Yes ☐ No	
Advocacy	☐ Yes ☐ No	☐ Yes ☐ No	☐ Yes ☐ No	

Step 3: Reflect.

* Which stages are brain-friendly, and which trigger friction?

* Which 'no' boxes can you turn into 'yes' with small tweaks?

* Where could you add a moment of safety, joy, or clarity that rewires customer loyalty?

Step 4: Story it out.

Write a quick story (even as a fairytale) of a time a business made you feel safe, emotionally connected, and clear-minded. What did they do? How can you replicate it?

STRATEGIES TO SUPPORT THE HUMAN EXPERIENCE

In the broader and pragmatic realms of CX management and design, there are multiple ways you, as an organisation, can support your customers and employees to feel like they belong, as opposed to just having to 'fit in'. In my experience, effective strategies include:

A hugely important human need ←

1. Having an inclusive and diverse group of humans working together, utilising their individual skills, experiences, cultures, educations, and whatever makes them unique. This collaboration of differences correlates to improved profit, performance, innovation, creativity, talent management, engagement, and wellbeing.

2. Developing your organisational skill sets doesn't just include the field of human-centred design but also what's known as systems design. Both design methodologies make you, the organisation, consider:

    ← Get David Jenyns' book SYSTEMology

- A holistic perspective: Both methodol-ogies reject reductionist approaches and understand that the whole experi-ence or system is greater than the sum of its parts.

  oversimplifying ← complex systems

- Understanding interconnections: Both recognise that connections and relationships are often more important than the individual components themselves. ←

  Relationship over transactional

- Embracing complexity: Both value continuous learning and adaptation over one-time solutions.

- Root cause focus: Both dig deeper to find fundamental causes rather than quick fixes. ←

  Candid communication is great here

- Context sensitivity: Both acknowledge that context dramatically influences outcomes.

- Collaborative methodology: Both value multiple viewpoints to create more complete understanding. ←

  Fuck off the silos

- Being empathy-driven: The most important human value in achieving the joy of CEHX. Both methodol-ogies acknowledge that understanding and addressing human factors are essential to success.

- Installation of strong systems: Allow trust-building, innovation, Motivation 3.0, and as a brand leader, the ability to achieve not just a value-driven brand but a value-driven life.

- The value of systems thinking and human-centred design: Both can support your shift from a workforce dependent on you to a brand of independent, autonomous, and innovative humans, creating and sustaining a culture that elevates the human experience. This means delivering strategies and activities that develop your ongoing user centredness in the HX areas of physical, cognitive, ↑ social, cultural, and emotional. As discussed *Customer or* in chapter 11, when it comes to creating a *employee* trusted and value-driven brand, culture is everything.

3. Building a connected and engaged brand community is a marker of a successful human-centred organisation. Understanding how to bring your audience together in a genuine and value-driven way where they feel a part of the brand can set you apart. The brands that get this right communicate using their audience's preferred *We'll discuss* method via channels that allow two-way ← *this more in* communication. They're brands that invite *chapter 15* their audience to test and give feedback on upcoming products and services. Brands that encourage experiences worth sharing and celebrating.

The use of human-centred and systems design is how we create unique customer, employee, and human experiences, showcasing our understanding that our customers and employees are at the heart of everything we do.

The one similarity we all share, which needs definitive attention, is our humanity. We're all human beings. Even if your organisation is geared towards animals or inanimate objects, the team creating for the end user is human, and the people experiencing the sales journey are also human. Designing the human experience is your opportunity to be strategically unique, just like the humans you serve.

No one expects your organisation to have everything working cohesively from the get-go, but, in business, the strategies we've discussed will eventually be necessary to outpace the competition. So, if you're reading this as a solopreneur, thinking, *Meh, I'm not big enough to worry about this*, I call bullshit. This is exactly where you need to start working on these strategies – when it's just you, yourself, your flexibility, your agility, and your ambition. ←— *And your natural affinity to be risky, not reckless* If you're already growing, you need to get the engines revving and apply these strategies, tactics, and brand-building behaviours to your business now. At your next turn, your customers and your employees will likely expect it. That's right – the time to develop these areas of your organisation is *now*. Because if not now, then when?

CHAPTER 13:
DELIVERING HX
IN AN AI WORLD

AI ... IT AIN'T ALL IT'S CRACKED UP TO BE

I could start off by announcing the latest figures relating to artificial intelligence (AI) utilisation within organisations. However, by the time I research the numbers and this book goes to print, that data will be outdated.

So, here's what I *will* tell you: AI is popular, but its implementation hasn't been as successful as many businesses believe it should have been. In addition, the customers of those businesses feel less connected to the outcomes AI delivers than they do to human-delivered outcomes.

At least for now

The crux of this – which I find every single time I have a conversation with an organisation about optimising how they do what they do – is they're looking for a silver bullet. A magic answer to all their problems. The reality is, a silver bullet to anything is always bullshit and often causes more headaches when you realise it shot you right in the foot. Think about it. There's no silver bullet

Look up the Klarna bot debacle

answer to optimising your health. No silver bullet for improving your personal relationships. Certainly, no silver bullet to fix years of childhood trauma. The reality is that business, like life, can be challenging.

> Getting to a place of optimisation and, for that matter, optimism takes time, energy, commitment, resources, and patience.

It takes the will to sustain, ask questions, ←——— We need to stay curious

and face up to egos and not only your experiences but also others'. It also takes massive vulnerability – something we, as business leaders, are known to struggle with expressing.

There's no singular activity you can buy, complete, or implement that will improve the CEHX in your business. So fuck that idea right off. As our businesses grow, it's important to also grow in our desire to deliver a human experience (HX) that not only helps our customers but also helps our teams, and if we're genuine in our attempts, it will also help us.

We didn't go into business ownership to lose our lives to bullshit processes and putting out unnecessary fires. We did it to enrich our lives. To create flexibility. To give us the opportunity to do what we love, when we love to do it, with the humans we love to do it with. Therefore, it should be natural to do whatever improves your business and, in turn, your life. Remember, a value-driven brand creates a value-driven life.

So, how do we create a value-driven brand in a world that

blasts AI in our faces, offering quick fixes and no-pain, all-gain solutions every day? Well, to deliver a human experience in an AI world, you need to understand what makes us humans tick.

THE TRUTH BEHIND OUR HUMAN LIES

So, what do we know of the human condition? Well, we know plenty, yet in business we utilise little. I'm always reminded of the catchphrase coined by Dr Gregory House (actor Hugh Laurie) in the naughties television drama, *House*. "People lie," Dr House says, episode after episode, to explain his miraculous outcomes. In the show, in every known scenario, including those involving life or death, people lie. Now, as a teen growing up watching this, hearing this regularly, and being of an age where I, of course, told little lies often to get away with doing whatever teenagers do, the phrase not just stuck with me, but it resonated as true. Fast-forward some years, and I've come to learn in my therapy practice that what we, as humans, are more likely doing is one of three things: we're distorting the truth; we're deleting the truth, or we're generalising the truth. "Say what?" you ask. Let me give you a short lesson in 'natural language processing', or 'NLP'.

Humans, as subjective as we are, perceive the world as only we can. When someone distorts, deletes, or generalises, their brain has likely processed information differently from yours, even if you shared the same experience. In more detail …

- **Deletion:** With so much information being processed every waking moment, the brain must 'delete' information it doesn't deem important. However, the brain can also use this filtering method to selectively pay attention to certain aspects of our experiences while, at the same time, ignore others.

- **Distortion:** This occurs when our conscious brain misrepresents or distorts the reality of our experiences. Our beliefs are based on interpretations of our experiences, not necessarily objective truth. Humans are almost incapable of having an objective view of reality, as our memories and past experiences determine our current perceptions.

- **Generalisation:** When we selectively take one component of an experience and apply it to other experiences, our brains are generalising. We form biased beliefs based on previous lived experiences. It's why we're able to notice patterns, draw assumptions, and create stereotypes.[64]

Essentially, distorting, deleting, and generalising are linked to our perception of reality, which makes so much sense when you consider how humans behave regarding telling the truth. For the most part, however, humans lie for self-preservation. They anticipate a reaction rather than a considered response from their audience, and they fear being viewed unfavourably (fairly or not), so they determine that a lie will be better received and help keep their social standing safe. In my career, knowing this was a valuable skill ... but not for the reasons you might imagine.

To get people to be honest with you, you must first train yourself to be ready for the truth. The whole truth, not just the part that doesn't hurt your feelings. Remembering that people are likely lying either to serve you and your ego or to protect themselves, consciously or not.

So, what reaction are they anticipating that motivates them to tell mistruths? Have they seen you lose your shit at someone who lied to you in the past? Do they believe *There's that* you're not equipped with the emotional ← *empathy again* intelligence to cope with the truth? Do they feel restricted in their capacity to have candid and honest conversations about problems you've potentially caused? The other thing we rarely consider (because we always think it's about us) is, did they grow up lacking experience in managing confrontation? Or are they a people pleaser? Have they experienced manipula- *The survival* tion or abuse and learnt that lying is the way to get *brain at* what they want or to see out another day? ← *work 24/7* The questions are endless, yet we rarely take the time to consider them. In fairness, we often don't know what to consider in the first place.

See, it's not only about knowing *when* people are lying; it's also about knowing *why* they're lying. From there, you can create a culture where people feel comfortable expressing the truth – that is, telling it like it is.

PRACTICE MAKES POSSIBLE

Understand that without *earning* people's trust, you may be the recipient of more bullshit than truth. So, *So you can ask* how can you learn to sniff out mistruths ← *better questions* or, even better, mitigate lying in the first place?

Earlier in this book, we discussed the act of developing an

outward mindset – a purposeful mindset that teaches you how to express uncomfortable truths that genuinely become meaningful once said. Well, as you develop these skills for yourself, it's an ideal opportunity to train those around you in the same skills. There's no point just you being on the ball.

> Always lead by example, but also teach when possible, as teaching others is the best way to learn and reinforce any new skill.

Remember, mitigation is key, and to have the best chance at success, everyone must be as skilled as you.

While it may be clear how understanding humans can set you apart when it comes to leading your team and cultivating a favourable culture, you may be wondering how it can help with the customer experience, specifically how it relates to the choice to utilise AI – or not. Well, as you delve deeper into your need for new systems, you'll hopefully get out on the street and start asking your customers what they want, what they need, and what they expect from you to stay advocates well into the future. This is where you'll quickly learn, intentionally or not, *people lie*. In my over two decades of experience, I've witnessed, more often than I can recall, customers lying. The most common reasons – they don't know the answer; they don't want to hurt your feelings; they need to protect themselves, or they're genuinely convinced their lie is the truth. Over the years, this has led me to practise specific behaviours that, more often than not, get me to the root of the issue, all while maintaining trust in myself:

1. **Ask questions differently.** Using open-ended questions (questions that can't be answered with just a yes or no) makes a huge difference in the quality of responses. Stay focused on what people are saying and actively listen. Don't just listen to respond – you'll miss the detail and make mistakes. Stay patient, calm, and ← Ego-led rookie considered with the next question. ← mistakes Remember, you could be three feet from gold!

2. **Observation over conversations where possible is a brilliant way to ascertain anything.** I mean, I love people watching, but in your business, it could just simply mean sitting quietly and watching how people move around your store. It could be watching how many times your team has to get up to the filing cabinet, or observing how your customers interact with your product or service. A bit like mystery shopping, but you're just there absorbing and observing. No false memories or perceptions, no, "Oh yeah, I buy your product and use it all the time," which could equate to, "Yeah, I waited for it to go on sale, then I used it once." What people say and what they do rarely align exactly. I'm not trying to imply that humans are just out there talking shit, but at the same time, much of what they say is based on individual distortions, deletions, and generalisations.

3. **Qualify responses further.** This means digging deeper. Don't just accept someone's first answer, let it lead you to a new question that gets you closer to the root of the concern. Separate the wheat from the chaff. Questions might include, "So what happened then?" or, "Can you tell me more about that?" or, "What made you decide to choose this over that?" You can ask useful questions without making the customer or employee, whoever you're in conversation with, feel like they're being interrogated or having their integrity attacked, helping to keep the interaction calm, two-way, and respectful.

4. **Don't take it personally.** It's easy to get defensive over your business when you hear feedback you disagree with; however, as the leader, it's in your best interest to not take it personally. Remember, feedback may be more perception than fact, but this is part of the human experience. Humans are renowned for having subjective perceptions. You can't really argue with someone else's perception because that's exactly what it is – *their* perception. They have theirs; you have yours, and then there are the facts. Whenever you feel yourself getting defensive or taking feedback personally, aim to address the facts with an underlying foundation of empathy and integrity (or use the feedback to your benefit).

5. **Change who asks the questions.** In my experience, using third-party agents – as opposed to employees – gets the most honest and up-front feedback because the agent doesn't work in your organisation. Therefore, the customer isn't concerned with hurting that person's feelings. They're ready to deliver their honest thoughts and feelings on the customer experience based on their *You need* perception. You tend to get the savage truth *all three to* – the good, the bad, and the ugly. ← *deliver the joy of CEHX*

6. **Look for patterns.** Actionable feedback tends to show a pattern. It's so important to ensure that as you collect customer or team feedback, you're analysing it to understand the patterns. People are more willing to spend

↖ *Please don't just collect feedback then do nothing with it*

time helping you improve if you can genuinely show that you're working towards learning more and taking positive action.

Practising these steps to mitigate feelings of nervousness and distrust and promote a culture of candour has saved my employers and clients millions of dollars *Because we've* and untold amounts of time and energy. ← *tackling what* *matters by* Having insight into how your customers *eliciting the* and employees perceive their world can greatly *candid truth* support your due diligence when innovating your business. Without these insights, you could burn yourself out and likely break the bank trying to please everybody. The more truth you can garner, the better you'll understand the path forward – and practice makes possible.

IT JUST ISN'T HX WITHOUT EQ

Let's talk EQ. When I was growing up, there was so much weight put on being smart. Having a high IQ. Some places, like the US, taught their kids that if they didn't get a university or college degree, they would be rendered useless, unfit to compose the fabric of society. Imagine that. In the '80s and '90s, there was never any real talk about anything other than IQ, and if there was, it was usually some adult attempting to justify their lack of intelligence by stating they were street smart rather than book smart. To be honest, growing up, street smart always sounded more impressive to me. Back then, the closest we got to learning about EQ was the good old adage, "Treat others the way you want to be treated." How many times in the playground would you hear, "I wouldn't do that *Dobbers wear* to you, so don't do that to meeee, or I'll dob"? ← *nappies haha* Most of us have since grown up and moved on from those times. However, reading this, you may now understand the 'IQ generation', which may include your parents, a little better. We've now transitioned from focusing on IQ to understanding the importance of EQ when it comes to delivering a quality human experience.

EQ is short for 'emotional quotient' – or you may have heard the term 'emotional intelligence' – just as IQ is short for 'intelligence quotient'. IQ is determined by completing a standardised intelligence test that measures areas such as working memory, verbal comprehension, processing speed, and perceptual reasoning. The problem with IQs is they change with age. What you would score now is likely different from what you would have scored 20 years ago. *Better or worse,* The same may be true for EQ, as our life *depends on the* experiences, natural curiosities, and personal *individual* traits can evolve our emotional quotient.

Developing a strong EQ means developing the skills that allow you to connect with emotions on a deeper and more intuitive level. Now, I'd put money on some of you *Those* thinking EQ sounds great and others *so-called* thinking, *No thanks, I don't need to get* *'soft skills'* *in touch with other people's emotions.* However, EQ is first and foremost about being in touch with your own emotions.

For example, I know that when my 2-year-old son, who thinks sleep is for the weak, won't go to bed at night, *Still scary for some* if I can't keep *my* emotions in check, it will trigger his emotions. It's like understanding that when sales are down and you want to go on a blame rampage, *Insert shitstorm where we both act like toddlers* your emotions – or your EQ – have regressed to those of a child. As your self-awareness and emotional regulation falter, your own emotional intelligence is drastically reduced. Ideally, we don't want to be throwing toddler tantrums in our businesses ... or anywhere, for that matter.

Let's now dig a little deeper into EQ, which includes five components:

- **Self-awareness:** Your ability to understand your emotions and behaviours and how they impact you and those around you.

- **Self-regulation:** Your ability to control your impulses and mood, along with your ability to stop and think before acting upon any negative experiences and regulate back to centre (homeostasis) after a negative event.

- **Motivation:** Your ability to be intrinsically motivated to achieve your goals and dreams outside *Say no to* of external rewards. *cosmetic metrics*

- **Empathy:** Your ability to recognise yourself in others (put yourself in their shoes) and consider what they're experiencing from their point of view.

- **Social skills:** Your ability to develop rapport, build meaningful relationships, navigate social interactions, and the one so many of us need help with … communicate effectively with others.

In business and in life, developing an understanding of these five components can grant you serious guru status. Think the Tony Robbins, Peter Druckers, and Dalai Lamas of the world. Now dial it down just a notch, and with consistent practice, you can be just as 'in touch', enriching your life and the lives of others. Again, we're working on developing a value-driven brand where amplifying the human experience is our unique differentiator. When, in business, you connect to your own motivations, tune in to your emotions, and practise empathy, these practices spread to your personal life, amplifying that value-driven life. Remember, just like sex, business is meant to be pleasurable, and if it isn't, well, it's up to you to change that. ←——————— *This is why great business feels like great CEHX*

When you're in business, you want to attract high EQ employees and, ideally, high EQ customers – but let's start with employees. I mean yes, IQ can also be very helpful, but in this day and age where the human experience is near forgotten, businesses like yours who commit to bringing it back and making it your unique value proposition must have a community of emotionally intelligent people around them. ← *We're creating a high EQ herd* Let's examine why.

Dimension	High EQ Employee	High IQ Employee	Impact of EQ on CEHX
Communication	Listens actively, reads emotional cues, and responds with empathy.	Communicates facts clearly, but may overlook emotional context.	Customers and coworkers feel heard and understood, leading to trust and loyalty.
Conflict Resolution	Manages emotions, diffuses tension, seeks win-win solutions. ↗ *But also has an outward mindset, helping mitigate conflict.*	May focus on logic over feelings, potentially escalating interpersonal issues.	More harmonious team dynamics and better customer recovery in tense situations.
Collaboration *Where everyone feels safe to be themselves* ↗	Builds rapport easily, values team input, encourages psychological safety.	May prefer independent work, can appear dismissive of others' ideas.	Teams function more smoothly, fostering innovation and employee retention.
Customer Experience	Anticipates emotional needs, personalises interactions.	Offers technically correct solutions, but may miss relationship-building opportunities.	Customers feel cared for, increasing satisfaction and brand loyalty.

Dimension	High EQ Employee	High IQ Employee	Impact of EQ on CEHX
Adaptability and Resilience	Stays calm under pressure, adjusts tone/approach based on people's needs.	Sticks to facts and established processes, may struggle with ambiguity or emotionally charged changes.	Better able to navigate crises or change with empathy and support.
Leadership Potential	Inspires and motivates through empathy and authentic connection.	Leads through logic and vision, but may struggle to emotionally engage teams.	Employees feel valued and motivated, improving morale and performance.
Employee Experience	Fosters inclusive, emotionally safe work environments.	May unintentionally create competitive or isolating atmospheres.	Higher job satisfaction, lower turnover, and stronger culture.
Brand Differentiation *Even in a digital space* ↗	Makes the business feel human, personal, and values-driven.	Emphasises expertise and intelligence, but can feel detached or impersonal.	Helps the brand stand out in a market saturated with impersonal, transactional service.

Ultimately, we must understand that humans, customers, employees, whoever remember how we made them feel. They'll pay good money (even in hard times) for an experience that resonates with them. When your customers and, for that matter, your team feel emotionally connected to your brand, you're on the front foot of generating advocacy through emotional resonance.

That's not to say we no longer need IQ. I mean, of course we need the brains to go with the heart, but helping your high IQ people understand and practise emotional intelligence and awareness helps support them in developing what could start as an intelligent solution but turn into an *Also remember to let them be their authentic self* impactful human experience. ←

SUGAR AND SPICE AND EVERYTHING NICE

A little while ago, I had the privilege of teaching a number of business leaders the art of assertiveness. When it comes to emotional intelligence, assertiveness is a game changer. For years, I was told I was too aggressive. But what was the alternative? Others around me were either too 'nice', thinking it would serve their agenda, willing to throw you under a bus in a heartbeat, *Nice = red flag* or too passive (even submissive in some cases), constantly getting walked all over. When people said I was too aggressive, I didn't exactly like that feedback, which meant I had a choice to make. I could either change the perception of my so-called 'aggression', or I could get butthurt and keep getting nowhere. I don't want to see you, as a business leader, fall into the trap of defensiveness in every situation, *Different to* or worse, being railroaded in your own business. ←*collaboration* So as we develop our emotional intelligence practice suite, producing a human experience worthy of our customers' and employees' loyalty, let's examine how EQ plays out in real life and in real business.

For me personally, it started with developing a greater self-awareness and learning when to stop talking. ← *Still practising this* It meant analysing and replaying events and conversations and being really fucking honest with myself. Eventually, I could do it in the moment. I would detach ever so slightly, watching myself from the other side of the room. Checking my mannerisms, checking my facial expressions. I would check where my eyes and brows were. I ⤺ *They're a dead giveaway to my thoughts* would then get back into myself, back into listening, and make any adjustments that 'outside me' deemed necessary. Over time, I developed the ability to do this without dissociation. When first practising a change like this, there's an exhaustive checklist running through your head. However, through practice, you can gain self-awareness, and the practice becomes second nature. You're 'in the moment', aware of yourself, aware of those around you, working to anticipate their emotions and needs, and people notice the change.

Once my self-awareness practice started showing dividends, I moved on to practising empathy. Sometimes I find that I'm a walking conundrum when it comes to empathy. One minute I'm a sobbing mess, imagining what life must be like for a parent who lost their child; the next minute I'm agitated at my teenage son because he still can't get up when his alarm goes off and complains about a bad night's sleep due to growing pains. Now ... I never had growing pains. I don't know what they feel like. I haven't grown since I was 14 years old, and I never had any major growth spurts to personally understand his pain or frustration. However, it's a reminder that, despite never experiencing my son's pain, I could certainly still take a deep breath, put myself in his tired and weary size 13s, and show him empathy. Showing him ... *I'm willing to try to understand you because I value you and your human experience. I want you to feel like you belong, and I want to learn about you so I can enrich your life and help you add value to others because* you *feel valued.* It's the opposite of a vicious circle. It's a victorious cycle.

Over time, other leaders made comments about how they had noticed something different in me. How they could 'feel' a shift in the way I showed up. Only I truly knew that it was because I was practising my EQ skills. I didn't want to be 'nice'. Fuck nice. In my experience, people who are 'nice' always have ulterior motives, and nice shouldn't be mistaken for kind. They're two different things. I choose to be kind, and to paraphrase our messiah Brené Brown, to be *clear* is to be kind, and in my books, to be clear is to be assertive, which means you and your team must practise:

- Expressing yourself confidently and clearly without being passive or aggressive.

- Showing empathy and respect for others. Put the shitty assumptions, disparaging judgements, and personal projections in the bin where they belong.

- Acknowledging other people's feelings and being prepared to adjust your own behaviour to make a more positive impact. ⟵ *This isn't walking on eggshells but being aware of the impact of your behaviours*

- Being prepared to uphold your personal boundaries – something too many humans are generally shit at, leaving all sorts of messy situations to unravel.

- Boosting or maintaining self-esteem, knowing you're doing everything in your control to create a value-adding human experience. ⟵ *We can't control others – therapy 101*

Having a brand that embeds emotional intelligence into the way it does business is the definition of *smart*. It's how, in a world obsessed with tech and AI, you can still build candid and safe work environments that engage those primal human desires. It's how you get people to feel confident in speaking up and sharing their ideas and truths, turning innovation and initiative into everyday cultural outcomes. It's how you develop and maintain trust. ⟵ *Something this digital world is fast becoming short on* It fosters vulnerability, integrity, curiosity, and, above all, genuine advocacy. You can't buy it. You have to earn it, so let's start practising now.

TL;CBF

- In an AI world, brands that have human experiences as their unique value proposition will be few and far between, and competitors won't be in a position to copy them.

- The unique human experience you develop for your customers and employees removes you from the commodity game.

- Developing your own personal emotional intelligence is the first step in successfully developing a team of emotionally intelligent employees who want to help create a trusted and value-driven brand.

- Emotional intelligence, or EQ, involves practising:
  - Self-awareness
  - Self-regulation
  - Motivation
  - Empathy
  - Social skills

- Being nice is a red flag. Choose to be kind instead. Kindness doesn't diminish your capacity to uphold your boundaries and communicate with candour.

- You only have control over yourself. Practise developing your EQ so others can feel the change and either mirror you or remove themselves.

Love it when the trash ← takes itself out

ACTIVITY: GET IN TOUCH WITH YOUR EMOTIONS

- Visit **aileenday.com.au/tjocehx-tools** and download your printable pocket version of the 'Feelings Wheel'.

- Consider the feelings you recall expressing in your everyday life, either at work or at home. In the space provided, document the three most common feelings and break them down via further investigation. For example, if you wrote 'anger', you might ask: Is your anger masking humiliation? Upon deep and honest reflection, is the humiliation due to ridicule or disrespect?

- Once you've documented your three most common emotions, take a moment to reflect on the perception you create when you express them. After sitting in the emotion and considering its deeper cause, reflect on whether or not your responses are surprising.

- Consider if anything in your expression or EQ needs to shift to create a more positive perception and emotionally intelligent culture. Dig deep into understanding how your emotions show up and how they affect you.

Three Common Feelings	Underlying Cause

Perception Created	What (if Anything) Needs to Change?

If this is all new to you or you want to learn more, I highly recommend Brené Brown's book *Atlas of the Heart*.

CHAPTER 14:
CHANGE IS AS GOOD
AS A HOLIDAY

DISCOMFORT IS THE KEY TO GROWTH

If you've been in business for any half-decent amount of time, you've likely come across the beast known as 'change management'. Seriously, it's in the skills of change management that innovation either goes to thrive or is left to shrivel and die. In my years, I've seen change managed in many ways, mostly badly. Fear is one ineffective change model that comes to mind. But let me tell you, when change is managed well, it's worth paying close attention. I mean, change is so hard largely because its main component for success is ... humans. We've already had a whole discussion on how fickle humans are. *We're not finished either*

Whether you want to change your eating habits, change the colour of your walls, implement a new system where team members now need to sign on digitally rather than just rock up when they feel like it, upgrade your accounting system – the list could go on and on – the thing about change management in any part of life is you're ultimately asking humans to opt in or forcibly move themselves out of their comfy zone. This is where change comes unstuck very quickly.

In case you're reading this wondering what the 'comfy zone' is, it's a psychological framework that explains a person's willingness to adopt change based on their current state. Let's have a little look-see at the different states and discuss how they play a role in not just whether your business can be agile and innovative but also the overall quality of the human experience.

1. **Comfort zone:** The individual lives in a relatively neutral state, free from anxiety, stressors, and expansive pressure but upholds a sense of control. In the comfort zone, they can essentially fulfil much of their life on autopilot. It's essentially low-risk and low-reward. Innovation- and agility-free.

2. **Fear zone:** In *Look into the Yerkes-Dodson Law* this zone, fear isn't necessarily bad. For example, let's say you're expanding, and you have a new role opening up. You have a team member who's the right fit, and you want to put them on a development plan, but they need to upskill. They *want* this role, but the new skills aren't for the weak. The fear of losing this opportunity could just well be enough to spur them into action. They might start at the bottom, feeling inadequate, but soon enough they start to reflect on their gains, and, in doing so, they can see that *Which we do now, along with succession plans and performance appraisals* *Impostor syndrome can affect anyone at any level* they're moving through to the learning zone. The flip side to this is, your team member lets others get in their

head, and they turn down the offer, believing they don't deserve it, aren't good enough, could disappoint you, and so on. This is the Pygmalion effect. We'll touch on this in a little bit.

3. **Learning zone:** Let's say your team member takes a chance and gets uncomfy. They recognise that to be good at something, you first have to give yourself permission to suck. Heck, they have you as their leader, so I don't doubt you're being strategically supportive. Conducting WIP (work in progress) meetings, taking a keen interest in any challenges they're facing, and giving them space to find solutions rather than being a helicopter dropping all the answers, not allowing them to stretch themselves. You know, all that helpful leadership stuff ... ⟵ *Humans must break that precipice of frustration to unlock answers*

4. **Growth zone:** When you're doing your job, it helps your team members do theirs. You see their growth as they start sharing with you and their colleagues what they've learnt. They apply their learnings, and they come to you with more considered questions that make you think deeply. They now seem more comfortable in their skin. They have, in essence, reached a 'new comfort zone', but this one doesn't produce as much apathy as the last one. However, keep them stagnant, and it won't be long until the apathy returns in full force. Most humans thrive on being coerced out of their comfort zone, but it generally

has to come with some facet of strategy and framework. If it's all carrots and sticks, or just sticks, you'll find yourself working against the next zone. ← *Bad news, very bad news*

5. **Panic zone:** Not commonly displayed on 'comfort zone' frameworks, the panic zone is another where the Yerkes-Dodson Law applies. Essentially, the law dictates that an optimal level of stress benefits performance. However, too much stress or pushing too hard without the right support and quality leadership can cause your new little buddy to go from 'great success' to 'pissed off and burnt out'. ← *Did I just hear you say, "Join the crew"?*

When it comes to personal and professional development, whether your own or an employee's, be mindful of each state – from growth to potential panic – and take steps to effectively navigate each one.

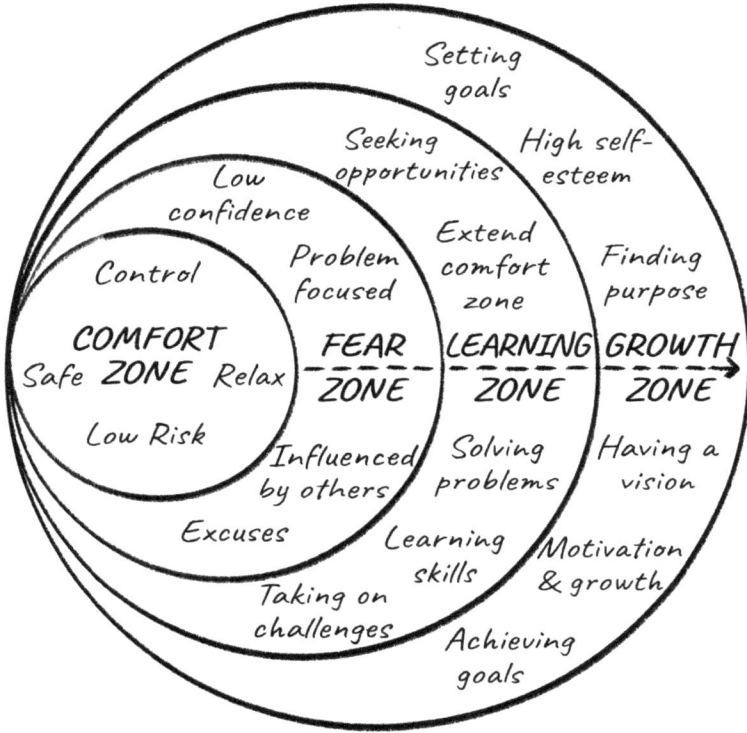

Comfort zone framework.

FEELING THE PINCH

Understandably, when you run a business, especially if you've gone through a growth phase and a lot has changed, you could certainly be excused for feeling the pinch of exhaustion, anxiety on a not-great day, and perhaps even panic on an exceptionally shit day. However, if you don't start to work out the root causes of these emotional responses, they'll soon become physical

If they haven't already ↗

responses. Then everything you've worked to create could be up shit creek without a paddle. No one wants that!

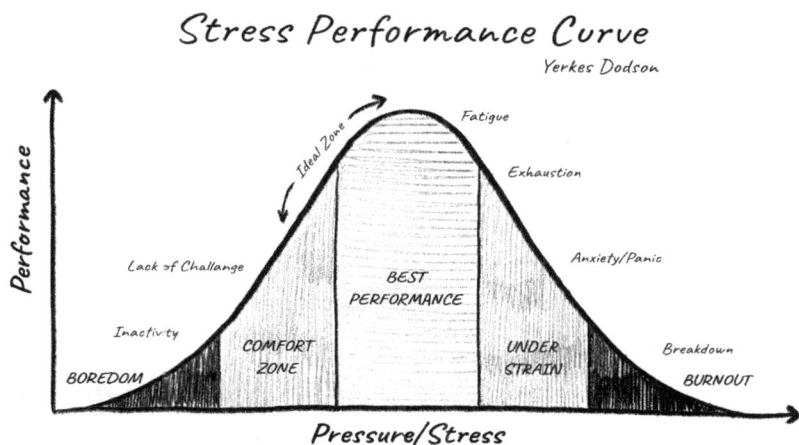

The Yerkes-Dodson Law for stress and anxiety.

Looking at the comfort zone framework, you may remember a time when you went from being the novice to the expert. And it's great to be the expert. However, even expert status becomes comfortable eventually. That's why so many professional associations have continuous professional development (CPD) points to ensure you're 'encouraged' to keep learning and not become stagnant in your skills. ← AKA forced

When we get too comfortable in our expertise, mistakes tend to happen, as we're excellent at running on autopilot. Our brains love routine. Routine keeps us underwhelmed in an ever-overwhelming world. Hands up if you've ever driven somewhere and

legitimately couldn't remember doing it? It's a crazy phenom-
enon called 'highway hypnosis'. You're aware of the road, and
you can react, albeit possibly slower than normal, but you can't
consciously recall the journey. This happens predominantly on
familiar routes and roads. We become too comfy. Imagine what
that looks like at work. Just a bunch of unam- *Who else is thinking*
bitious zombies, there to tap buttons, get paid, *of The Flintstones*
and leave on the whistle. ← *intro?*

Now, in saying that, not all people need to be bursting with
ambition. I know some very fine humans who are happy in their
comfort zone. They're still engaging; they occasionally enjoy
small stints in the growth zone, but never anything that will
lead them to the panic zone. These are hopefully your workers.
We all need them because, again, not everyone *And honestly,*
wants to climb the organisational ladder, and *there aren't*
certainly not everyone is cut out for it. ← *enough*
Find your workers, understand what they value *positions to go*
around
and how they like to show up with their curiosity to learn, and
support them. Then attract your leaders and innovators. Give
them activities that push them to think differently and try new
things while supporting them with great mentorship and leadership from you and your team. Teach them not to fear change
or treat it like an exhaustive trap. Teach them to embrace
change, as it's the path to innovation and new opportunities.

A little pinch is a healthy stimulation for *If my life didn't*
continuous improvement. More than that, *change, I doubt*
I'd be here
we have some work to do to mitigate the *writing this book*
future punch.

" Innovation is the ability to see change as an opportunity – not a threat."

– Steve Jobs

THE PYGMALION EFFECT

Many years ago, I learnt about the 'Pygmalion effect'. As soon as I understood it, I could instantly apply the effect to dozens of personal situations and business situations I've experienced in my life, from childhood to adulthood. You may already know about the effect, but in case you don't, let's review.

The Pygmalion effect originates from a Greek myth. Pygmalion, a sculptor, created a statue so beautiful he fell in love with it. His desire for the statue to come to life was fulfilled by the goddess Aphrodite. The myth of Pygmalion illustrates the power of belief and expectation in bringing about desired outcomes. In the 1960s, researchers Robert Rosenthal and Lenore Jacobson studied the effect on students. They discovered that students whose teachers expected them to excel academically showed significant improvements in performance. The researchers concluded that setting positive expectations on humans could indeed create a self-fulfilling prophecy, helping individuals *You've heard* succeed despite any perceived or actual barri- *you're the sum of* ers.[65] The downside? The opposite is also true. *the five people you spend the most*

Throughout our lives, we'll almost certainly *time with, right?* experience elements of the Pygmalion effect. Perhaps as a teen, it was a component of you doing drugs or, if you were in a different crowd, not doing drugs. Perhaps it was a component of you not working that hard in school because, well, your mates weren't, and if your parents were like mine, you probably heard, "If your friends jumped off a cliff, would you do it too?" The other good zinger they had was asking me if I was a 'lemming' whenever they thought I was being negatively influenced by other people. I used to hate it so much, but upon reflection, *Sometimes* for the most part, I did stay out of trouble, *later rather* *than sooner,* avoiding people who could bring me down. ← *but always* Actually, I became so acutely aware of being *eventually* influenced that I decided to move to a new state at age 16. I began to realise that staying in my comfort zone was leaning me too close to boredom, and there ain't nothing positive about a bored 17-year-old with easy access to nothing good. So, I made the very hard choice to move states, start anew, challenge myself to leave my comfort zone behind, and use the Pygmalion effect for good and not evil.

Let's now take the Pygmalion effect and apply it to your brand. How can you ensure it works *for* you and not against you? Let's keep practising those human-centred design principles and apply the Pygmalion effect to getting your brand closer to successful change management.

1. EMPATHISE: SET CLEAR, HIGH EXPECTATIONS WITH EMPATHY

HCD (human-centred design) principle: *Empathy with employees*

Action: Begin by understanding your employees' current experiences, fears, and aspirations during change events. Use surveys, one-on-one interviews, or informal check-ins to gauge what 'high expectations' mean from their perspective.

Design tip: Co-create goals with employees. ← *Get them seeing the big picture* Instead of imposing targets, involve them in shaping expectations. This builds trust and ownership, making the goals feel realistic and motivating. One of the best things one of my department leaders did was walk me and another team lead around our department and have us point out what needed remedying rather than telling us what she thought or wanted. It taught us to have an eye for detail, a sense of initiative, and feel engaged in the change process. Often, we would set higher expectations on ourselves than she would have, as we were wanting to go above and beyond.

2. DEFINE: PROVIDE ADEQUATE TRAINING AND RESOURCES ALIGNED TO REAL NEEDS

HCD principle: *Design for real-world contexts*

Action: Understand the specific challenges employees face in meeting expectations. Is it a skill gap, lack of clarity, or insufficient tools? Tailor support to these needs, or get ready to battle resistance.

Design tip: Map the employee journey during the change. Identify 'pain points' where confidence or capability drops, and design targeted training or toolkits to fill those gaps. ← *If you fail to plan, you plan to fail*

3. IDEATE: OFFER FEEDBACK AND SUPPORT AS COLLABORATIVE EXPERIENCES

HCD principle: *Co-creation and collaboration*

Don't forget the outward mindset

Action: Make feedback a two-way, collaborative experience rather than a top-down review. Encourage reflection and candid communication.

Design tip: Use lightweight, frequent feedback loops (like weekly check-ins or peer-to-peer reviews) that feel supportive, not evaluative. Design these catch-ups to promote trust and psychological safety and encourage personal growth.

4. PROTOTYPE: RECOGNISE AND CELEBRATE AMPLIFYING THE HUMAN EXPERIENCE

HCD principle: *Iterative and inclusive design*

Action: Test different recognition methods – for example, public praise, gamification, small team celebrations – and ask your team what feels most meaningful to them.

Intrinsic and extrinsic

We'll talk more about this in chapter 16

Design tip: Design rituals for celebration that everyone can be a part of, being considerate of any cultural or religious nuances. Not everyone values recognition the same way, so build flexible, human, and values-centred systems of appreciation.

None of these need to break the bank either

5. TEST: DEVELOP A POSITIVE WORK ENVIRONMENT THROUGH SMALL, CONTINUOUS IMPROVEMENTS

HCD principle: *Continuous testing and iteration*

Action: Use small experiments to improve workplace culture, like redesigning team meetings to be more collaborative or setting up informal support networks or mentoring.

Design tip: Regularly test and fine-tune your cultural practices based on employee feedback and your own observations. What works for a large team may not work for a startup. Keep the environment human, adaptable, and psychologically safe.

Remember to ask open-ended questions

6. REFINE: MONITOR AND ADJUST EXPECTATIONS WITH EMPLOYEE INPUT

HCD principle: *Adaptability and responsiveness*

Action: Don't just track outcomes, track sentiment. Anonymous suggestion boxes can help gauge if expectations are *too* high or not inspiring enough. However, you're building a culture of candour, so have those outward mindset conversations regularly and tune in to how the team is adjusting.

Design tip: Involve the team in adjusting goals, share performance data transparently, and ask, "What do you need from us to succeed?" To drive their personal engagement, ← *They need skin in the game* let them help shape the road map forward.

The key to much of the Pygmalion effect's success is collaboration. If you take over and do the hard stuff for your team, they learn nothing, and they won't be invested in pushing through the fear zone to get to the learning and growth zones. They have no skin in the game.

The point is, rather than being a hovering helicopter parent-like figure, encourage your team to fail fast, and learn fast. It's one of the core principles of being agile, but they have to know, despite your high expectations, you're supporting them to achieve, which means making space for them to, at one point or another, fail, learn, and iterate their next attempt. As step five (test) discusses, give them small experiments in safe, learning zone spaces. In IT, for example, most new platforms are built and functionality tested in what's known as a 'sandbox'. So, what could your change management 'sandbox' look like for your business?

HIGH PERFORMERS BEGET HIGH PERFORMERS

As you develop your next rising star using the Pygmalion effect, coupled with human-centred design, you might start to notice something interesting. The Pygmalion effect really comes into its own when you have a cohort of individuals who have experienced moving from comfort to growth. As new rising stars join your brand, they see the level of performance expected, and because humans evolved as a herd species, ← *Why we love communities* meaning we feel an ingrained desire to be accepted, your new starters will quickly assimilate to those high expectations. Give these people strategic support, something they can sink their teeth into to show you they're worthy, and with a cohort living high-performance practices on the daily, you, my friend, are building a culture and *Not to mention* brand of high-performing humans. ← *high EQ*

Now, all of this isn't foolproof. Thankfully, this hasn't happened much on my watch, because we've had systems in place to mitigate it, but every now and then you'll have an employee who has no interest in being a part of the herd. These people very cleverly manipulate the system to gain entry to a job they don't actually value. As you read this, I don't doubt that you can think of several examples of people like this in your lived experience. You find that, once they get *Hopefully not your current one* in, they have no real determination to move out of their comfort zone, often using tactics such as gaslighting, weaponised incompetence, or narcissism to get through their day with minimal effort applied.

These are the 'dialling it in' employees

The problem with these types of people is that they create ripples of toxicity in your culture. Your high performers start to feel resentful of their co-worker's blasé behaviour, and, sadly, I've seen many organisations lose high performers due to the lack of action taken regarding low performers. Often, the issue isn't addressed because – and we've talked about this before – having those hard conversations can feel confronting. Most of us aren't in business to be confronting; we're in business because we love doing whatever it is that drove us to start a business in the first place.

Apart from the need for therapy

Unless you're Dog the Bounty Hunter

But the reality is, as soon as you enter the arena of business where your business relies on selling to humans and working with humans, it's time to start upskilling in communication. Don't let a fear of hard conversations sink your business. At the same time, ensure you're fulfilling your legal and ethical obligations and following the appropriate performance management process. Is it really worth losing your high performers to avoid a difficult conversation? If the thought of it really is too much, you either might need to question whether you're cut out for all of this, or be in a position where you can employ or engage the services of a HR or people and culture professional or agency.

When it comes to creating successful change in your business, effective strategy makes all the difference. So look around – who is your next rising star? Who will support you to take the team through times of change? How will you use the Pygmalion effect, coupled with human-centred design and your natural curiosities in the human experience, to get them and your brand to MVP?

TL;CBF

- To experience the joy of CEHX, you must sustainably create a culture that's not afraid to be agile and innovative.

- Moving yourself and your team out of your comfort zones to create lasting change and high performance takes consistent communication of expectations, support to fail and learn, and regular feedback opportunities.

- The Pygmalion effect is a psychological effect by which people tend to upskill and improve based on well-defined expectations.

- Letting poor performers keep doing only what serves them will quickly erode your company culture and the employee satisfaction of your high performers.

- Challenge yourself to utilise the Pygmalion effect to create a cohort of high performers who are unwavering in the face of change management.

CEHX SELLS – DESIGN THE HUMAN EXPERIENCE FOR DESIRE

The thing about change and your ability to effectively create, manage, and sustain it is – it's highly situational. The reason for the change largely determines how you go about managing it. There are many frameworks that can help you better understand the steps required to achieve successful change management. Depending on the basis of the change – what you're changing and *why* ← *Always start with the why* – you may need to lean into one or several.

Now, I personally like to start with the change model ADKAR, created by Jeff Hiatt and his company Prosci. The reason being, we're creating change with and for humans, right? Well, ADKAR is one of the few, if not the only, change management model that specifi- *A very animalistic motivator* cally calls out the need to design for desire. ← ADKAR stands for:

- **A**wareness: Understand the reason for the change.

- **D**esire: Ensure being part of the change and the change itself are desirable.

- **K**nowledge: Equip your stakeholders with the education and knowledge they need to understand and navigate the change.

- **A**bility: Support your stakeholders to implement their new skills and behaviours.

- **Reinforcement:** Commit to the new change, using feedback loops and consistent anchoring.[66]

In my experience working with many different types of businesses at different stages in their growth cycles, where change tends to go awry is generally in the awareness *Consent* stage, causing the desire stage to feel forced. ← *matters* Yes, often there's plenty of knowledge thrown around and, if you're lucky, some training. But when it comes time to reinforce the new and say goodbye to the old, so many organisations who haven't followed the correct process see their stakeholders quickly find little back doors, sneaky ways to reverse the change and return to that elusive comfort zone. Ultimately, there's no genuine desire for change, and their human experience triggers their fight, flight, or freeze response. Within no time, you find yourself arguing with people over the change (fight), frustrated that they're not actively participating in creating the change (freeze), or in the worst-case scenario, they leave because they don't feel valued in the change process (flight).

As you transition from the old way to the new, it's so important to understand that not only are you creating momentum for change and innovation for a segment of your business, but you're also expecting the human experience to come and play along nicely, and I don't doubt you already know that isn't a guarantee. The thing with humans, even adults, is, they can quickly revert to toddlers if they deem something as not adding value to *The good* their lives. This can affect change implementation *ol' WIIFM* and prevent its adoption by all of your stakeholders. When people experience bad change management over and over again, they reach a point where they're done. Their hippo-campus (the memory part of the brain) tells their amygdala (the emotion part of the brain), *Nope, we ain't having a bar of that. Retreat!*

So, let's discuss some activities you can do to alleviate the stress and trauma of bad change management experiences while adequately supporting not just the change but also the human experience. Change isn't just a strategic pivot or a project deliv-erable. It's often a disruption to people's routines, confidence, and sense of control, whether they're employees or customers. So instead of treating change like a tick box, let's humanise it with some good old-fashioned empathy paired with bold practical action. ← *Remember, Practice makes possible*

FOR YOUR EMPLOYEES – FROM "UGH" TO "OKAY, I CAN WORK WITH THIS"

1. TELL YOUR THEM WHAT'S CHANGING AND WHY THEY SHOULD CARE

People don't need a 40-page slide deck. They need a compelling 'why' that makes sense in their world.

How to deliver:

- Story-driven town halls ← *Ditch the jargon and use plain language*

- Candid briefings from real leaders

- Visuals that speak their language (not a maze of arrows and boxes)

2. INVITE THEM TO WANT IT

Change sticks better when it feels co-owned. Don't push change at employees. Instead build it with them.

How to spark desire:

Collaboration is king, as they'll have skin in the game

- Co-design sessions

- Involve early adopters as micro-influencers

- Connect changes to what matters to your employees both personally and professionally

3. SHOW THEM HOW TO DO IT (WITHOUT MAKING THEM FEEL DUMB)

Knowledge isn't just dumping info; it's giving people a clear, contextual 'how to'.

How to transfer smarts:

- Role-specific training, not generic webinars or learning manuals collecting dust

- Learning hubs supported by peer sessions

- Walkthroughs, simulations, and real-life scenarios

4. HELP THEM NAIL IT WITHOUT ANXIETY

Knowing what to do is one thing. Feeling confident doing it? Whole different ball game.

How to build ability:

- Micro-coaching (bite-sized, real-time help)

- Job aids co-created with the team (not from a silo comms team)
- Safe-to-fail practice zones, buddy systems

5. KEEP THE MOMENTUM WITHOUT NAGGING

Once they're doing it, help them keep doing it, not out of obligation, but belief.

How to reinforce naturally:

- Recognition that doesn't feel like HR tokenism
- Ongoing feedback loops ⟵ Make it two-way!
- Culture rituals that embed the change

FOR YOUR CUSTOMERS – FROM "WHY ARE YOU DOING THIS TO ME?" TO "OOH, THIS IS SO MUCH BETTER!"

1. BE LOUD, CLEAR, AND HUMAN ABOUT THE CHANGE

Don't surprise them. Don't spin it. Just be straight-up about what's changing and why it benefits them.

How to create clarity:

- Multichannel messaging (email + in-product + social = triple threat)
- Real-world examples that show benefits, not just features

- Simple language – if you wouldn't say it out loud, don't write it

2. GIVE THEM A REASON TO WANT IN

They won't care just because you care. Make it matter to them.

How to build intrigue and desire:

- Exclusive previews or betas ← *Because in being agile, you can't be perfect*
- Opt-in early access ← *Make them feel like VIPs*
- Social proof – customer stories, emotional hooks

3. HELP THEM NAVIGATE LIKE A PRO

They need guidance, not a 60-page PDF left to rot in a dusty drawer.

How to get them confident fast:

Onboarding workflows that actually work.

- Gamified how-tos ← *Yes, even B2B people like a little fun*
- Short videos, FAQs that answer real questions, not legalese

4. DON'T LET THEM STRUGGLE SILENTLY

Support needs to reduce friction, not add to it.

How to create capability:

- Seamless user interface ← *Make it easy for everyone to do what needs to be done*
- Inclusive, accessible design
- Real, quality, human support – live chat or call

← And advocacy for that matter

5. MAKE LOYALTY A NO-BRAINER

Keep the trust tank full with follow-ups that feel thoughtful, not automated.

How to lock it in:

- Feedback requests that actually create change

- Progress updates ("Look how far you've come!")

- Thank you notes, social recognition, loyalty treats ← *Look for intrinsic and extrinsic options*

CHANGE IMPLEMENTATION – THE RIGHT WAY, AND THE WRONG WAY

As a practising psychotherapist, I work with many humans who want to change something in their lives. For example, they might want to be more outgoing, move through a bad break-up, or minimise the hurt and negative emotions associated with a traumatic upbringing. Whatever it is, to be successful, they must lean into the fact that they, and only they, can control what changes. No one else can do the work for them. Hopefully, they have great humans around them to support them through their healing and change journey, helping them see the benefits of getting out of their comfort zone. But even if that's the case, if I, as the therapist, don't set up that launch to change strategically, with deep consideration for my client's strengths and weaknesses, I run the very high risk of setting them back even further.

Change shouldn't be introduced without clear awareness of

the issue. It shouldn't be launched without a consensus on the desired change and overall outcome. It shouldn't be invested in if all aspects of said change haven't been strategically mapped and committed to. No change should occur where you haphazardly, or even purposefully, apply it solely for your benefit and to the detriment of your stakeholders – because it will be your business that pays the price in the end.

> Progress is impossible without change; and those who cannot change their minds cannot change anything."
>
> – *George Bernard Shaw*

TL;CBF

+ Finding the right type of change management framework to strategically support your transition from one state to another in your brand can mean the difference between chaos and success.

+ ADKAR is a great framework to start with, as it supports you in checking:

    + Awareness

    + Desire

    + Knowledge

    + Ability

    + Reinforcement

- Launch into change management prepared and on the same page as your stakeholders to mitigate expensive resistance.

- Commit to the change by observing, understanding, and acting upon any feedback that indicates the change won't be sustained.

- Don't create change for change's sake. As you implement the pillars of the customer, employee, and human experience, innovation and agility will develop within your culture.

ACTIVITY: KNOW YOUR ZONE

1. In the space provided, write down where you are currently in the 'comfort zone' model (comfort, fear, learning, growth, or panic).

2. List five reasons that tell you you're in that zone. ← *Don't forget to use the Yerkes-Dodson Law model*

3. Take your feelings wheel you downloaded in chapter 13 and list five emotions that come up when you reflect on your spot in the comfort zone.

4. Using the ADKAR framework, note your change management plan to further improve your position in the comfort zone model, and find a trusted person to hold you accountable.

Zone

Five Reasons

Five Related Emotions

Change Management Plan

CHAPTER 15:
COMMUNICATION –
THE BANE OF HUMAN
EXISTENCE

THE CONFLICT OF COMMUNICATION

Now, this is the *casual* hook-up to understanding the customer, employee, and human experience, but that can't really be achieved without combating the elephant in the room. Which elephant? you may ask. ← *There's never only one*

It's the fact that no matter where you go, what you do, how much you try, how skilled you think you are ... wherever there are humans, there's the opportunity for shithouse communication to rear its sorry head. In the era where taking offense is an elite sport that just about everybody can get a PB in, a lack of effective communication has long been the bane of human existence.

There are so many facets that can create stress and conflict in our communication, such as:

- **Misunderstandings and misinterpretations:** Your human experience thus far can determine your ability to effectively translate another person's intended communication.

- **Cultural and religious differences:** Another huge issue. Should women be allowed to speak? *[Literally a thing in some parts]* The meaning of words can differ, and mannerisms can be the same but have different meanings. Tonality can differ – for example, aggressive in one culture could be passionate in the next. These challenges and many more often lead to communication breakdowns and conflict, as we tune in more deeply to *how* things are said rather than *what* is said. *[Also, context matters, but this rage-bait-filled world often denies us the privilege]*

- **Lack of feedback or clarity:** This is a huge issue. What you think you articulated, if indeed you articulated anything, may not be understood in the same vein, leading to frustrations, confusion, and usually errors.

- **Power dynamics:** Those in power may ignore or demean those not in power, causing the relatively powerless to avoid speaking up. *[Check out Japan Air Lines flight 123]*

- **Emotional intelligence:** Our emotions may override our rational comprehension and lead to overwhelm, causing defensive or emotionally charged reactions.

With all those headaches, it's no wonder we have generations of humans comforting and shielding themselves behind digital devices. Some, with anonymity behind the keyboard, finding the courage to say what they truly believe. *[Factual or not]* Some just quietly observe the world, shaking their heads. Many are afraid of being the target of words-hurt-me witch hunts, thus wielding no words, just a lot of head nodding.

So why do we bother? Why not just fuck it all off and leave it to the bots?

COMMUNICATION CHOOSE YOUR OWN ADVENTURE

Communication, despite what many believe, exists in many forms. The predominant thinking is that communication can be:

- **Verbal:** The speaking of words, using your vocabulary to articulate your needs, wants, and desires to your communication recipient. Using the correct tone, word choices, and having the ability to listen can make verbal communication an effective method for obtaining your desires.

- **Non-verbal:** The language of the body. ← *I have the movie Dirty Dancing in my head* So many humans are clueless when it comes to body language – how to use it, how to read it. Generally, however, we're better at reading facial cues. A raised eyebrow, indicating scepticism. ← *Thanks to the Rock* A frown vs. a smile. A scrunched face vs. a relaxed face. For pretty much my whole life, my parents and bosses have said I don't need to say a word for them to know what I'm thinking. I have a very expressive face, they insist.

- **Written:** In this day in age, written communication usually means emails and text messages, rarely handwritten letters. Due to digital dominance, the art of handwriting is in sure decline. In around 2015, Australia Post (the Australian government-owned postal service) began reducing their

The excellent humans who deliver the mail

posties due to the massive downturn in things to deliver.[67] Well, thank goodness for Amazon expanding past Kindles and books, hey? I reckon Amazon is a large reason Australia Post has actually innovated the way they do business. Also, tell me that during the spicy cough era, postal delivery wasn't one of the single most essential services next to couriers!

- **Visual:** Research continues to enforce that a picture is worth a thousand words. Why is that? Well, largely because our brains can decipher a visual 6 to 600 times faster than it can comprehend text.[68] The brain loves shortcuts. Remember how overstimulated we all are – so who could blame it?

Australia Post innovating their delivery vehicles to keep up with customer needs, where letters are out and bulky packages are in.

Considering that, as humans, we implement every single one of those communication types every single day, it's interesting to reflect on how little we consciously consider which communication method is the most effective for our intended audience. For example, many years ago, I had to take my son to an optometrist to get his eyes checked. He was too young to read, and I wondered what in the universe technology they had to understand his sight issues. Well, thankfully, this industry had considered communication and their intended audience. On the wall were recognisable shapes – a boat, a teddy bear, a duck – items a non-verbal toddler could still somewhat articulate rather than the text only an older patient would understand. The optometrist used *visual* communication to help with diagnosis. Now imagine if they hadn't thought about it. What kind of customer experience would that create? What effect would that have on part of the population that ended up misdiagnosed simply because the communication method wasn't right for that audience?

The same goes in your business. Communication matters so much that it can be the maker or breaker of any component in your business. It could change the culture; it could be full of perceived power dynamics; it could be untimely or untransparent, causing people to feel unsafe being candid, honest, and open about their working experiences and needs. Get communication wrong, and big errors occur. It could be that you have such a diverse mix of team members that there's a difference in beliefs, in opinions, in understanding, in previous experiences that now define their future experiences. How you then create communication systems to deal with this can be the difference between favourable outcomes and harassment claims. I mean, the latter would be such a headache!

The next question is ... do you know what *your* preferred communication style is? Do you know how it impacts your environment? Do you know if what you mean to communicate is indeed what's actually being received and comprehended?

> The single biggest problem in communication is the illusion that it has taken place."
>
> – *George Bernard Shaw*

In therapy, we discuss learning style preferences such as kinaesthetic, auditory, visual, and logical as being the modes in which our brains can best sort through information and communications. Although we can't say one style or another works best for learning and communication, we can say that, as humans, we use all these modes in combination to decipher *Influenced by the communicator, of course* communication as best we can. ←──────

Additionally, we all have a dominant communication style. We're either predominantly:

- **Passive:** Passive communicators can be indecisive and prefer to avoid conflict. They tend to be resentful, and their communication can lead to misunderstanding, as what they say isn't always what they want to say.

- **Aggressive:** Aggressive communicators express what they need and want to the detriment of others. If anyone speaks up to or challenges them, they can be defensive and hostile. They often believe they're 'in charge' and may look down on those around them. *Generally a tell-tale sign they need a hug and therapy*

- **Passive aggressive:** Passive aggressive communicators are indirectly aggressive and can be somewhat annoying. They tend to avoid conflict but then deliver the silent treatment. They're known to be sarcastic and snide, rather than candidly open and transparent, when *← AKA assertive* situations displease them.

- **Assertive:** Sometimes confused for aggressive, assertive communicators choose to be confident in communication and are aware and in control of their emotions. They tend to be interested in others' needs and capable of displaying empathy. Out of all of the communication styles, this style is more likely to achieve positive outcomes, as assertive communicators practise active listening and check for clarity in their message.[69] ← *Assertiveness is the gold standard of communicating*

Coming up next, you'll find an activity I highly recommend you, your team, and even your family complete to help you understand a little bit more about your own communication styles and how we can all practise becoming the gold standard in communication.

ACTIVITY: KNOW THYSELF

1. Head over to **aileenday.com.au/tjocehx-tools** and download your Communication Style Quiz.

2. Complete the quiz and discuss the results with your family and team.

3. Have your team and family also complete the quiz.

Thus candid

The purpose of this quiz is to help you, your team, and your family become confident in your communication and practise an assertive communication style. To help build a robust discussion, download the Family and Team Communication Style Discussion Guide to help you learn from one another and practise effective communication in your brand and in your home.

CLOSED FEEDBACK LOOPS AND COMMUNICATION STRATEGIES

As your business becomes a brand, creating a systemised feedback loop will become more and more of a priority. Now, I know I've mentioned feedback loops previously and not gone into too much detail, so let me do it here as we discuss the human experience – because communication and, in turn, feedback are a necessary part of humanity.

Achieving quality communication depends on so many human aspects, and often when we go into business, no one teaches us these things. Often, trial and error, or error and error, seems like the only way forward. Well, not on my watch. We're going to work together to get you and your people – be it your team, your family, the weirdo across the street – on the same page to communicate smarter, better, faster, stronger. ⟵ *See what I did there? IYKYK*

Just like when it comes to change management frameworks, there are plenty of feedback loop frameworks to overwhelm you. So I like to consider feedback loops based on the areas of my world I'm applying them to.

Let's start with the one you would use predominantly for your team and your customers, without getting too deep in the weeds or working on advanced frameworks that really won't serve much purpose. ⟵ *There's no need to reinvent the wheel* Every business needs a solid closed feedback loop framework that forms a strong foundation in their communication strategy not only for their customers, but also for their employees. The one I like to start with is known as the 'ACAF closed feedback loop'. Simply, it stands for:

- **Ask:** Proactively seek feedback in intentional, accessible ways.

- **Consider:** Evaluate feedback with a fair, analytical, and empathetic lens.

- **Act:** Make meaningful, visible changes based on that feedback.

- **Follow up:** *Close* the feedback loop by telling people what you did with their input. ← The part so many organisations suck at

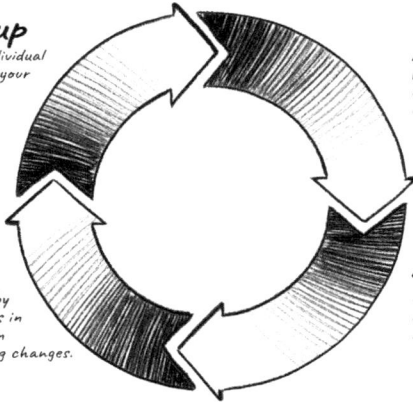

4. Follow-up
Follow-up with the individual who gave feedback on your business so they know you're truly listening.

1. Ask
Ask your customers/employees for feedback on their experienc inc feedback on your product or service.

3. Act
Act on the feedback by sharing it with others in your company who can implement value adding changes.

2. Categorise
Categorise the feedback into different buckets that are meaningful to your business.

ACAF closed feedback loop framework.

Let's break this down into some pragmatic thoughts. As the insights manager for Bunnings and service leader for Officeworks in charge of customer insights for the whole country, I can tell you this little nugget of human psychology for free. Even if we say we don't expect to hear from someone after giving an organisation our feedback, we're 100 percent delightfully surprised when we do. Now, I know you're likely thinking, *Well, of course they're surprised. They said they didn't expect to hear from anyone.* Now, while that *is* true, they were, and continue to be, delighted when they do hear back. But why? you ask.

Well, in my role, I quickly learnt that even if someone doesn't check the *Do you want a reply?* box, they often do provide their contact details. Subconsciously, they don't even know why they've done it, but after experiencing these customers, being one of these customers, and now having 'therapist' on my resume, I can tell you that every human loves two things: *one*, closure, and *two*, recognition. When you apply the ACAF framework, you give your feedback provider the opportunity to subconsciously acquire both closure *and* recognition. Closure creates homeostasis. We can file away any questions our subconscious mind might bring to our conscious awareness like, *Did they tell Mary I loved her service?* or, *Did they get my feedback about the crack in their dressing room mirror?* While we like to pretend these things are unimportant to the running of our daily lives and we just need to 'let someone know', it's funny that at 2 am when your brain is overstimulated and you can't sleep, it starts forming questions. Left long enough, they develop into concerns that prompt your body to pump cortisol through your veins at the least opportune moments. ⌐—— *Stress hormone*

Now, whether you recognise or acknowledge it, you left your contact details because, subconsciously, you want closure. What might be an even harder pill to swallow, and I've had nearly hundreds of these conversations, is that you also, quite

subconsciously, were looking for recognition. Now, I tell you, this fires people up so hard. They rebuke it. Till they truly sit in what I'm saying and consider the possibility that we can make conscious actions based on subconscious motivations. ← *Literally minds fucking blown at the concept*
More times than I can care to keep score of, in my experience, when customers do hear from you after providing feedback, even when they say they don't need to, they're delightfully surprised for a multitude of reasons, including:

1. They legitimately didn't expect to hear from you. ← *But they're glad they did – homeostasis restored*
2. The filing cabinet in their brain gets to file the event under 'closed', appeasing the nervous system and allowing it to pull some other bullshit out of the filing cabinet for them to unnecessarily grow concern over. *If it's not one thing, it's something else*
3. The big reason people get pissed off is: the subconscious mind has set them up for a dopamine hit, and they don't quite know why they feel delight, but they do. All the while, the conscious mind doesn't want to believe it's being manipulated by the subconscious. ← *because we all want to believe we are in control*

Generally, in these circumstances, your brain wants recognition because, well, you took time out of your day to communicate to a business that should be grateful you care enough to share what you think, because, well, you could shop anywhere – but you don't. So you get the call, and your subconscious mind is in a happy little tizz, amplified by the caller thanking you, closing the loop, letting you know that your feedback was not only received but also appreciated. I mean, what epic main character energy is that, right?

The brain loves that little dopamine love stroke, but if it doesn't get it, guess what can happen? Cognitive dissonance. It's a bitch of a thing that essentially shows up as feelings of confusion and frustration when our actions don't match our beliefs – for example, our action of providing our contact details vs. our belief that we don't want anyone to close the loop.

> When cognitive dissonance kicks in, the brain starts fizzing over like a Coke bottle with a Mentos dropped in it.

We say, "I know I said not to get in touch, but it would have been nice to know everything went okay" or, "I know I said not to get in touch, but I still see that crack in the mirror. Don't they care that someone could get hurt?"

So ... what's my point? Well, wherever you have the option to follow up, make it an *Whenever customers leave contact details of any kind* imperative focus in your feedback strategy to close the feedback loop. Whether we acknowledge the fuckwittery of our subconscious mind or not, it does what it does for a purpose. So, put your feedback provider's mind at ease and delightfully surprise them by genuinely showing gratitude for saying what they felt needed to be said. Let them feel heard.

Let them feel valued, even if you don't totally agree with the feedback. It was their perception at the time. You don't have to apologise for everything, but you can still be genuine in your concern for their perception. *←They have it for a reason* Even if you have to create clarity around that perception, you can still do it respectfully and in a way that satisfies their subconscious mind, showing that you care and they are still valued.

APPLYING THE ACAF FRAMEWORK – MODERN TACTICS, CLEAR ROLES, AND CULTURE-DRIVEN METRICS

At its heart, the ACAF loop builds a communication culture where feedback isn't a form; it's a function. Like any function, when it comes to understanding the 'how', it's imperative that, as mentioned earlier, where communication is used (essentially everywhere), the 'why' must precede everything else. Without clarity, we can't expect others to translate our message and uphold our boundaries and expectations, let alone effectively reciprocate with further effective communication. We're dead in the water before we even set off. Having a systemised feedback loop also helps:

1. BUILD TRUST

- Internally (employees, suppliers, contractors) and externally (customers, potential customers, general public).

- Customers see their feedback being taken seriously, which increases brand loyalty, and when done effectively, it can reduce customer and employee churn. ⟵

Imperative in this economic landscape

- Employees feel empowered and valued, leading to higher morale and retention.

2. CREATE CONSISTENCY IN COMMUNICATION

- A standardised method ensures no feedback is dropped or mishandled. ↙

Remember the CX core principles – accountability matters

- Helps scale feedback management as the business grows.

3. FUEL CONTINUOUS IMPROVEMENT

- Repeated feedback on the same topic often signals a deeper issue.

- The ACAF feedback loop becomes a cycle of ongoing brand improvement.

Clear is kind. Unclear is unkind."

– Brené Brown

When you're systemising your business *Because that's what brands do* and developing and evolving your ream of strategies, one of the most important is your communication strategy. Among the other little feathers in my cap, I have a bachelor's degree in public relations and marketing and communication, and when studying, a lesson that impressed upon me most was the importance of effective two-way communication. Now, I see the irony as you read this book, an example of a one-way communication strategy ... however, knowing this, I've worked to make the content engaging and full of activities and takeaways to minimise the sensation of just being spoken at.

In your business, your communication strategy can thrive when you create the capacity for your customers to communicate *with you,* not just you communicating to them. So, keeping that two-way communication model as your priority strategy, let's look at our closed feedback loop framework, ACAF, and couple that with actual tactics *The whats, whos, and hows* to help you create and sustain brand trust through transparency, accountability, and continuous improvement. Now that sounds CEHX-y!

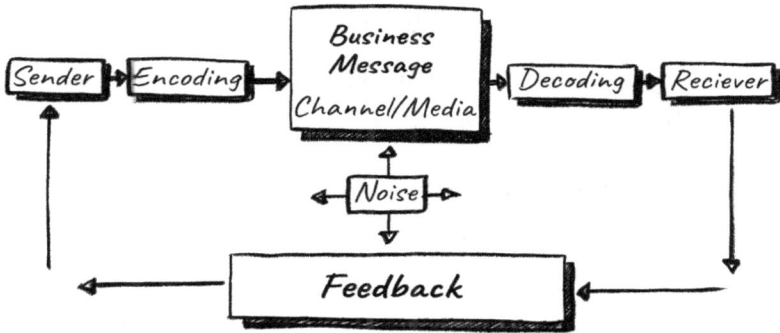

Two-way communication process between sender and receiver.

APPLYING ACAF TO YOUR CUSTOMER COMMUNICATION STRATEGY

1. ASK – PROACTIVELY AND INTENTIONALLY GATHER FEEDBACK (SOLICITED AND UNSOLICITED)

Why: Because customers want to feel invited into the conversation, not like they're shouting into the void. We proactively ask for feedback to show we *value their voice* ← Thus it's called 'voice of the customer' (or VoC) and are intentionally designing a business that listens.

Tactics

- Use multichannel, contextual prompts. ← the type of questions and the part of the journey = context

- Post-purchase SMS: *How did the check-out experience feel? Tap to shar*e (solicited).

- QR codes on packaging for instant feedback (unsolicited).

- In-app micro polls during usage moments – for example, *Was this tool helpful?* (solicited).

- Launch periodic 'customer voice weeks' with live interviews, forums, or Ask Management Anything (AMAs) with leadership. ← *Use storytelling to affect emotions when sharing customer insights*

- Integrate AI chatbots to collect general feedback 24/7, but flag complex cases for human review. ← *Yes, we still need humans*

Stakeholders

- Marketing: Own survey timing, tone, and visibility, and support the storytelling of 'customer voice weeks'.

- Customer experience (CX)/insights team: Analyse initial responses and triage any urgent feedback.

- Cross-functional leadership teams: Through unsolicited and solicited feedback, define which areas of the business either require deeper insights or customers are engaging with. ← *Because remember, everyone affects CEHX*

Smart Metrics

- Feedback completion rate by channel (optimise feedback forms for accessibility, not volume). ←

  We need quality feedback over quantity

- Percent of feedback tied to specific moments. ←

  For example, after delivery or onboarding

- Qualitative signal strength: Ratio of actionable vs. vague responses.

2. CONSIDER – ANALYSE WITH EMPATHY AND STRATEGIC CONTEXT

Why: Because customers deserve to know their input is being treated with care, not just filed away and dismissed. We considerately analyse feedback to find patterns, pain points, and opportunities to make their experience worthy of their loyalty.

Tactics

- Tag feedback by emotional tone using AI sentiment analysis tools. ←

  Or humans if you haven't yet got to this level of automation

- Cross-reference with behaviour data – for example, are complaints about the app's UX linked to drop-offs at the check-out? ↖ *User experience*

- Weekly 'voice of the customer' sessions with cross-functional teams reviewing trends.

  ↖ *Get your teams thirsty to better serve customers*

315

- Use customer journey mapping to align feedback themes to lifecycle stages.

Stakeholders

- CX analyst/voice of customer lead: Syntheses insights into dashboards. ← *Use the data and create actions*

- Department heads: Evaluate feasibility of taking action based on operational capacity. ← *Create business cases that detail the effect of doing something vs. nothing*

- Executive sponsor: Champions CEHX needs at a leadership level. As the business owner or leader, this should be you. The executive sponsor should grow the brand's CEHX alongside the growth of the business.

Smart Metrics

- Time to insight: How fast is raw feedback turned into usable insights? ← *As an act of great governance, this should be agreed upon*

- Feedback density by theme: Spot clustering for strategic action.

- Employee sentiment on feedback quality: Do teams feel feedback is helping them improve? ← *Help teams report on quantifiable impacts*

3. ACT – IMPLEMENT VISIBLE, HUMAN-CENTRED CHANGE

Why: Because without visible change, feedback becomes meaningless, and trust erodes. ← *Without trust, we're dead in the water* We act on what matters most so customers can *see* and *feel* that their input shapes our products, services, and decisions.

Tactics

- Use customer feedback to *co-create solutions*. Invite VIP customers into product design sprints or beta groups.

- Run *micro-pilots* with compulsory feedback loops included (for example, a 2-week test of a revised policy).

- Publish 'you said, we did' updates across channels – social, newsletters, help centre banners. *Show customers their time was well spent and valued*

Stakeholders

- Product/operations managers: Own the change process. ← *Remember ADKAR?*

- Customer advocacy lead: Communicates the narrative of change back to customers.

- Marketing: Helps make change stories feel celebratory, not transactional.

Smart Metrics

- Actionable feedback to implementation rate: Measures actual responsiveness.

- Pilot adoption and feedback cycle time: How fast you can close the experiment loop.

- Customer trust index: Recurring questions on surveys, for example, *I feel this brand listens to me.* ←————

Please make sure you do before asking this

4. FOLLOW UP – SHOW IMPACT AND SPARK ONGOING COMMUNICATION

Why: Because closing the feedback loop builds loyalty and makes customers feel like partners, not transactions. We follow up to share what's changed or what's coming so customers feel seen, heard, and *respected*.

The HX is about relationships ←

Tactics

- Create a public *customer feedback impact tracker*: road map updates, resolved bugs, FAQs.

- Send personal thank you notes or perks to feedback contributors.

- Use video or voice messages from leaders: "Hi Alex, here's what we learnt from you, and what we're doing next."

Stakeholders

- Customer success team: Manages personal and high-touch follow-up. Effective and genuine customer recovery can't be the sole responsibility of just one person or team. Get used to you and your leaders getting comfortable with customer recovery and dealing with high-touch feedback. ← *Some feedback needs that human touch*

- Marketing: Crafts public storytelling around feed-back-driven improvements.

- Leadership: Builds trust through direct involvement in communications. ← *Keep them targeted*

Smart Metrics

- Follow-up completion rate (how often contributors are updated).

- Customer-perceived transparency: Ask, "Do you feel informed about how your feedback is used?"

- Repeat participation rate: Are people willing to give feedback again?

APPLYING ACAF TO YOUR EMPLOYEE COMMUNICATION STRATEGY

1. ASK – MAKE FEEDBACK COLLECTION A HABIT, NOT A HELP DESK

Why: Because employees thrive when their perspective is actively sought out, not passively tolerated. We ask employees for their feedback to build a culture of trust, transparency, inclusion, and shared growth.

Tactics

- Launch always-on, anonymous feedback channels.

- Run 'pulse weeklies' – two-question, mobile-friendly check-ins. ← *Encourage opt-in and opt-out options*

- Hold 'ask me anything' sessions with senior leadership monthly.

- Peer-to-peer feedback circles every quarter to build lateral insight. ← *And that Pygmalion effect*

Stakeholders

- People and culture team: Design and manage employee insight collection systems.

- Team leaders: Reinforce safe spaces for open input. ← *We want teams to feel safe being vulnerable with their ideas*

- HR business partners: Spot patterns that require escalation or coaching. ← *For the betterment of the employee experience*

Smart Metrics

- Psychological safety index: "I feel safe offering honest feedback to my manager."

- Feedback frequency and participation rate: Measured across teams, not just overall. I find it best not to dangle any carrots or sticks with this. Silence can also tell you many things.

- Behavioural follow-through: Percentage of managers who ask for feedback regularly.

2. CONSIDER – TRANSLATE SIGNALS INTO STRATEGIC ACTION PLANS

Why: Because listening without understanding is just noise. We take employee feedback seriously, interpreting it with empathy, data, and context, not just compliance.

Also an epic waste of time

Tactics

- Host 'feedback forums' quarterly to unpack and interpret trends, with cross-departmental input.

- Compare employee feedback with performance or attrition data to detect risk signals. ← *Read that again for clarity*

- Use feedback as a compass for internal innovation, for example, new training modules or workflow changes.

Stakeholders

- HR/people analytics lead: Interprets patterns.

- Department heads: Decide what's addressable vs. what's contextual.

- CEO/founders: Set tone for transparency and credibility.

Smart Metrics

- Signal-to-noise ratio: Percentage of feedback that leads to a recommended action or insight.

- Sentiment shifts over time: Track the emotional trend post action.

- Employee confidence in feedback Loop: Ask directly, "Do you believe your feedback leads to action?" ← *If not, why not*

3. ACT – DEMONSTRATE CHANGE IN WAYS THAT ARE FELT, NOT JUST ANNOUNCED

Why: Because real culture is shaped by what we do, not what we say. We act visibly and intentionally so employees feel their input is *worth more than a tick box.* ← *You are the guardian of employee experience*

Tactics

- Pilot new policies with opt-in teams, gather live feedback, then scale.

- Make visible changes fast: Fix the coffee machine before you talk about DEI policy.

- Launch 'change diaries': Brief, internal updates showing what's been done and who drove it.

Stakeholders

- Line managers: Often first line of behavioural change.

- Ops: Project manage initiatives.

- Internal comms: Tell the story of evolution internally.

Smart Metrics

- Feedback-to-change velocity: How soon are you actively and authentically resolving feedback and any root causes?

- Change recognition score: "Have you noticed changes based on employee input?"

- Employee net promoter score (eNPS): Pre and post initiative. ← *Don't forget to follow the quantifiable up with the qualitative – ask the why*

4. FOLLOW UP – RECOGNISE CONTRIBUTORS, REINFORCE PROGRESS

Why: Because transparency earns trust, and trust fuels engagement. We follow up so employees know what changed, why it changed, and how their voice made a difference.

Tactics

- Acknowledge not just results, but *contributors*, for example, "This idea came from Alex in logistics."

  Recognition where recognition is due ←

- Use internal newsletters, town halls or toolbox meetings, and team shout-outs to report outcomes. I used to stick copies of the one-page daily team meeting notes in each toilet cubicle. If they're going to sit, let them get informed.

- Set up a digital 'feedback loop wall' in your employee portal with a backlog of resolved suggestions.

Stakeholders

- Internal comms team: Owns storytelling.
- Team leaders: Lead team-level reflections and recognition.
- Executives: Publicly thank contributors and show personal investment.

Smart Metrics

- Recognition ratio: Percentage of contributors publicly thanked.

- Loop closure rate: Feedback threads that include visible response and acknowledgment.

- Team trust score: "I believe leadership values our input." ←

  Make it absolutely anonymous

TRUST IS EARNED IN LOOPS, NOT LEAPS

The ACAF framework is more than a process; it's a philosophy. When people know they're being heard and they see action taken, loyalty follows. Whether it's your next employee engagement survey or product feature request, the ACAF method is your secret weapon for sustained trust and growth. ←

I put money on it that your competitors aren't doing this

TL;CBF

- Continuous development in your communication skills for you and your team is an imperative strategy for developing a culture of candidness, clarity, consciousness, and consistency. ← *Aileen's 4Cs*

- Feedback loops aren't a form; they're a function that, to be a trusted and value-driven brand, you must strategically implement, including cross functions of stakeholders.

- Communication works best when it's two-way, where the contributor and the recipient each have an accessible interface. In this day and age, that might look like social media DMs, encrypted messaging apps (such as WhatsApp), SMS, email, support telephone lines, chatbots, and so on.

- ACAF is a simple closed feedback loop framework for business owners to start with, ensuring customers and employees alike feel heard, seen, and valued.

- **Ask**: Proactively seek feedback in intentional, accessible ways. ← *Meet them where they're at*

- **Consider**: Evaluate feedback with a fair, analytical, and empathetic lens.

- **Act**: Make meaningful, visible changes based on that feedback.

- **Follow up**: Close the feedback loop by telling people what you did with their input. ← *Making it timely and transparent*

- Communication is one of the most difficult skills to master in business and in life. Where delegation is required, practise improving your quality of communication by checking in with the message recipient so they can explain what they understand of your needs.

- Encourage questions. Put your ego aside. Questions can open up lateral thinking, gaps in understanding, or needs to improve communication quality.

- Look to communicate in ways that suit the recipient and the situation. As humans, we consume communication as:

  - Written

  - Visual

  - Verbal

  - Non-verbal

ACTIVITY: PERFORM A COMMUNICATION AUDIT

Head over to **aileenday.com.au/tjocehx-tools** and download the 4C Internal Communication Audit Tool. This tool will help you take stock of your status in achieving the 4Cs (candid, clear, concise, consistent).

Taking a structured approach to evaluating and improving communication helps establish accountability while providing specific, actionable feedback. Quantitative scoring also gives you measurable data to track your improvement over time.

In the space provided, audit the platforms and communication types within your business:

1. List the communication platforms you currently use.

2. Note whether they utilise written, verbal, non-verbal, or visual communication.

3. List whether each platform is used for external or internal communication or both.

4. Note whether each communication type is one- or two-way.

Platform	Communication Type	Internal/ External/Both	One-Way/ Two-Way

Once you've audited your communication situation, reflect on where, if necessary, you could amend or add any communication outlets to enhance the provision and quality of incoming feedback. ← *Don't rush over to more surveys*

If you don't already have a scalable, high-accountability closed feedback loop, head over to **aileenday.com.au/tjocehx-tools** to obtain your ACAF Closed Feedback Loop Communication Strategy Template. Regardless of the size of your business, you can utilise this template to ensure a closed loop is actioned, measurable, and meaningful, not just to you as a business leader but also to your most important assets in business – your employees and your customers.

As you develop your 4C communication culture, here are a few additional tips for success:

1. To work out any implementation challenges, start with a pilot group *If you're a bigger biz* ← before rolling out company wide.

2. Consider creating a brief training session to ensure everyone understands the why and how of using the audit tool consistently.

3. Celebrate early wins and improvements to build momentum and enthusiasm for a shifting culture. ← *We're becoming CEHX centric*

4. Pair the audit process with your other communication activities for a comprehensive and holistic approach.

5. After a few months, gather feedback on the audit process itself and refine as needed. ← *Stay agile*

CHAPTER 16:
IT'S IN THE GAME –
GAMIFYING FOR GOOD

WHO DOESN'T LOVE A GOOD GAME?

In 1991 when EA Sports was a relative *Don't tell me you have to be big to make an impact* unknown with seven employees, ← they came out with a new ad campaign, and I tell you, they had it right when they said, "It's in the game."

In the digital era, humans for the most part love games. Now I'm not suggesting you turn your business into a video game. What I am saying is ... as you move through your (*unless the shoe fits* business growth phases, applying a bit of fun and some tactics to gamify how customers, and even employees, engage with your business will step you up a level on *Feels so* the CX Pyramid, as discussed in chapter four. ← *long ago* Let's not forget that our goal is to climb the pyramid from wherever we currently are, aiming for the tippy top to become an 'enjoyable' brand. Gamification is just one of the many CEHX-y strategies that will support these goals.

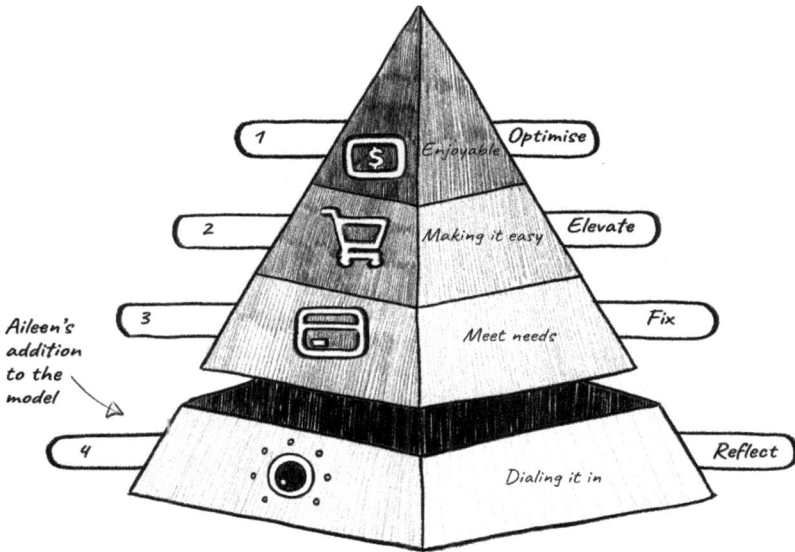

The CX Pyramid, where being enjoyable wins.

Let's back up the carriage and be clear on what gamification in business is, telling it like it is, how it was, how it could be, and of course how it should be. ← Just me, amusing me (IYKYK)

But in all seriousness, it's time to talk about CEHX and gamification.

In 2024, gamification was a US$9.93 billion industry, with a 12.14 percent growth rate expected over the coming 10 years.[70] Nothing to sneeze at, is it?

GAMIFICATION: THE SECRET WEAPON FOR ENJOYABLE CEHX

As a business owner, you're constantly looking for ways to gain an edge. We've discussed customer experience (CX) and employee

↖ If you're not, let's start

experience (EX), but have you considered how gamification can transform these into truly enjoyable human experiences? ← *That elusive HX*

Let me walk you through what gamification really means for your business and how you can start implementing it right away, no matter the size or budget of your organisation.

Gamification is about taking the elements that make games engaging, such as challenges, rewards, progress tracking, and friendly competition, and applying them to your business processes.

Think about the last time you:

- Collected loyalty points at your coffee shop
- Earned a badge on your fitness app after hitting a goal
- Received a 'streak' notification for consistent activity
- Saw your name climb up a leaderboard

That feeling of satisfaction ... ← *That dopamine hit* that's gamification at work, and, as a consumer, you've already experienced it.

WHY GAMIFICATION WORKS IN BUSINESS

Gamification taps into fundamental human psychology. We're naturally motivated by:

- Achievement and recognition.

- Progress visualisation.

- Friendly competition.

- Immediate feedback loops.

- Clear goals and rewards.[71]

Whether you're a micro or even a large business, gamification translates to higher engagement, better retention, and ultimately an improved bottom line – if you do it right! While there are plenty of opportunities to introduce gamification throughout your customer and employee journey, it's imperative *Don't go overboard though* to understand a few things:

- What's the ultimate business goal (for example, increase reach, increase CLTV [customer lifetime value], improve brand reputation, drive team connection)?

- Who are your audience (how will you ethically target them and drive further value to their experience)?

- How do you know what success looks like (what metrics will be in place to know you're winning)?

Once you've established these factors, gamifying tactics can be implemented in real-world applications, for example ...

For Your Customers

- **Loyalty programs with tiers:** Rather than a simple points system, create bronze, silver, and gold levels that customers can progress through, unlocking new perks at each level.

  Make them tangible, value-adding perks ⟋

- **Challenge-based rewards:** "Visit three times this week to unlock a special offer" works better than generic discounts.

- **Progress visualisation:** Show customers how close they are to earning their next reward or reaching a new tier.

For Your Employees

- **Skills development pathways:** Create clear 'levelling up' opportunities with training modules that earn badges or certifications.

- **Performance dashboards:** Visual displays that track individual and team progress towards goals.

- **Recognition systems:** Allow team members to award each other points for help or exceptional work, redeemable for small rewards. *(handwritten: ← Excellent for breaking down silo activity)*

The thing about *good* gamification is it provides accessible (not necessarily easy) and achievable rewards. Far too many organisations get you to 'sign up' to their loyalty programs for absolutely no return to you as the recipient. *(handwritten: These are just shit tactics to get your contact details)* Why would anyone sign up in the first place?

My personal favourite loyalty program – and I don't doubt there are plenty of others doing it well – is Red Rooster's. The rewards are tangible, achievable, and valuable. *(handwritten: ← Well, to me, anyway)* Customers receive *actual dollars* off their orders without having to visit the restaurant an obscene number of times. Red Rooster, owned by Craveable Brands, also gamifies its program by offering challenge-based rewards and loyalty tiers. Hungry Jacks is another company that has harnessed the human need for dopamine hits. If you download their app on your mobile device and shake the device while in the app, free or discounted food vouchers appear for you to redeem. How enjoyable is that?! My teenage son even tore himself away from his beloved KFC to test it out. Now that's a drawcard for new business if I've ever seen one.

ETHICS OF GAMIFICATION: GETTING IT RIGHT

When implementing gamification in your business, the line between motivation and manipulation can become blurred. I keep talking about being ethical, and in gamification, it's no different. Let's examine the ethical considerations and learn from others' mistakes to make sure your gamification strategy strengthens rather than damages your business relationships. Remember, you don't get to the top of the CX Pyramid by doing this badly.

ETHICAL GAMIFICATION: CORE PRINCIPLES

Ethical gamification should:

- Create genuine value for participants, not just extract value from them ← *Give more than you take*

- Respect autonomy and avoid exploitative psychological triggers

- Maintain transparency about how the system works

- Protect privacy and handle data responsibly
- Promote healthy behaviours rather than addiction or burnout ← *Please don't break people*

WHEN GAMIFICATION GOES WRONG: CAUTIONARY TALES

Uber's Driver Manipulation

Uber's early driver app included psychological tricks that pushed drivers to work longer hours in specific locations. The app would show drivers they were close to hitting arbitrary earnings goals right when they tried to log off. This 'one more ride' manipulation led to driver exhaustion, regulatory scrutiny, and damage to Uber's reputation with its workforce.[72] ← *How to undo destination employer status*

The lesson: Gamification should empower users, not exploit them. Respect their decision-making autonomy. ← *And don't potentially kill humans*

Wells Fargo's Sales Metrics Disaster

Wells Fargo, a bank in the US, implemented an aggressive gamified sales system that rewarded employees for opening new accounts. The pressure to climb leaderboards and hit targets was so intense that employees opened millions of fraudulent accounts *without* customer consent. This led to a $3 billion settlement and massive reputational damage.[73]

Bad, bad, bad news

The lesson: When gamification creates too much pressure without ethical guardrails, it can incentivise harmful behaviour.

Facebook's Addiction-Driven Metrics

Facebook (now Meta) employed gamification techniques like variable rewards, notifications, and social validation specifically designed to maximise user engagement and time spent on the platform. This led to

So "Black Mirror"

widespread criticism about fostering addiction and harming mental health, particularly among young users.[74]

The lesson: Prioritising engagement metrics above user wellbeing ultimately backfires and can attract regulatory intervention.

Fitness App Burnout

Several fitness apps have faced backlash for gamification that pushed users towards unsustainable or even unhealthy exercise habits. Leaderboards and streak features caused some users to overtrain, leading to injuries and, ironically, app abandonment.[75]

Not healthy competition after all

The lesson: Sustainable engagement beats short-term intensity. Design systems that encourage healthy, long-term behaviours.

CREATING ETHICAL GAMIFICATION FOR YOUR BUSINESS

FOR CUSTOMERS:

- Opt-in participation: Make gamified elements optional and easy to understand.

- Balance intrinsic and extrinsic motivation: Focus on improving the customer's experience, not just offering rewards. ← *Make it a value-add to their life*

- Value-first design: Ensure the core experience is valuable even without gamification.

FOR EMPLOYEES:

- Fair and attainable goals: Set benchmarks that are challenging but achievable for everyone. Don't make it so hard no one can achieve it or so easy it doesn't feel like it was earned.

- Multiple success pathways: Reward different types of contributions, not just one metric.

- Wellbeing safeguards: Monitor for signs of stress or unhealthy competition. ← *Be agile and adjust in a timely manner*

THE ETHICAL GAMIFICATION CHECKLIST

Before implementing any gamification element into your brand, ask yourself:

1. Does this truly benefit the participant, or just my business?
2. Could this incentivise harmful behaviours?
3. Is this transparent or manipulative?
4. Am I measuring the right things?
5. Does this respect participants' safety, boundaries, and time?
6. Does this help me achieve sustainable and enjoyable CEHX?

Be very candid, ask others if unsure ←

BALANCING BUSINESS GOALS AND HUMAN NEEDS

Remember that ethical gamification creates sustainable enjoyment and engagement. Short-term metric gains achieved through manipulative techniques will ultimately cost you more in damaged relationships and reputation, and regulatory risk, and ain't nobody got time for that.

The most successful gamification strategies align business objectives with genuine human needs. Creating experiences that are engaging because they're inherently valuable, not because they exploit psychological vulnerabilities. Now as much as there is the risk to mess this up, there's also the chance you could create something special. Like these folks:

BUNNINGS POWERPASS

Bunnings has successfully gamified their trade customer program with:

- Project-based tracking that shows savings per job
- Trade-specific challenges and rewards
- A PowerPass app that makes tracking progress intuitive
- Special events and early access opportunities for active members

What makes it enjoyable: Focuses on the professional identity of trades people and offers benefits that support their business success.

STARBUCKS REWARDS

Starbucks created an industry-leading program that:

- Offers 'star challenges' tailored to individual purchase patterns
- Creates limited-time games within their app
- Provides surprise rewards and bonus opportunities
- Uses gamification to drive up off-peak visits

What makes it enjoyable: The program creates moments of surprise and delight while making regular coffee purchases feel like progress towards meaningful rewards.

More impactful than just "the sixth cup is free"

NIKE+ RUN CLUB

Nike transformed running from a solitary activity to a gamified community experience:

- Achievements and badges for personal bests and milestones
- Coached running programs with progress tracking
- Community challenges and friendly competition
- Virtual races and special events

What makes it enjoyable: The app celebrates personal improvement rather than just competition, making fitness accessible and rewarding regardless of ability.

DUOLINGO

Language learning becomes addictive through:

- Streak maintenance with visual cues and reminders *Took Snapchat's feature and bettered it*
- Character-based narratives that unfold as you progress

- League competitions that create social motivation

- 'Health' systems that encourage consistent practice

What makes it enjoyable: Transforms the challenging process of language learning into rewarding, bite-sized interactions that build confidence and competence.

Now that's a human experience

MICROSOFT'S WORKPLACE ANALYTICS

For employee experience, ← *One for the teams* Microsoft has gamified workplace productivity with:

- Focus time challenges that reward deep work ← *Providing environments that encourage flow*

- Meeting efficiency scores and improvements

- Collaboration balance indicators

- Wellbeing metrics and suggestions

What makes it enjoyable: Turns potentially invasive productivity tracking into a personal development tool that employees willingly engage with.

MAKING THE GAME ENJOYABLE FOR EVERYONE

To be the brand that succeeds with gamification and uses it as part of their strategy to reach the 'enjoyable' level of the CX Pyramid, you'll need to adopt several characteristics:

1. **Make progress visible**: Users can clearly see how their actions lead to advancement. ← *Ethically of course*

2. **Create meaningful rewards**: Benefits that actually matter to the user, not just token prizes or the indefinite collection of valueless points.

3. **Balance challenge and achievement**: Difficult enough to be satisfying, achievable enough to avoid frustration.

4. **Incorporate surprise**: Unexpected bonuses and rewards that create delight.

5. **Connect to identity**: Align with how users see themselves or aspire to be. ← *Don't forget how values can play a part in this*

Gamification is more than just a loyalty card. It's a deeper connection to your customers and your employees, as it encourages you to dive in to understand their intrinsic and extrinsic motivations. There are many brands that do it well; there are many businesses that don't. There are even more that could be deemed barely mediocre. So knowing what you now know, gather

Or yourself, you excellent solo pro ←

your team and get activated on activating the humans in
your brand, setting them up for enjoyable status at their next
experience.

TL;CBF

- Gamification is the strategy of applying games into
  your customer or employee journey to improve areas
  such as engagement, advocacy, retention, profits, and
  more.

- To reach the peak of the CX Pyramid, a brand must
  be considered enjoyable. Gamification, in conjunction
  with other CEHX strategies, done well can be a unique
  driver to achieving this.

- To ethically gamify your brand, be sure to develop
  gamification that's:
  - Value-adding to the recipient and the brand
  - Developed purposefully, with clear success metrics
  - Designed to capture intrinsic and extrinsic
    motivations
  - Providing fair and attainable goals
  - Safeguarding wellbeing and monitoring for signs of
    stress or unhealthy behaviours

ACTIVITY: GAMIFY YOUR CEHX

5. Head over to **aileenday.com.au/tjocehx-tools** and download the Small Business Gamification Toolkit and McDonald's Monopoly: A Gamification Case Study.

6. Check out the toolkit and start to consider what gamification could do for your CEHX.

7. Read the McDonald's Monopoly case study and reflect on what you can apply to your brand and which lessons you should heed before getting in too deep.

CHAPTER 17: COMBATING HUMANITY'S GREATEST LOSS

ONE MAJOR PROBLEM IN A SEA OF PROBLEMS

In the era of gen beta, artificial intelligence like we've never experienced, unquestionable increases in inequality, questionable AF politics, ← *Around the world* the breaking down of communities, the sheer reclusiveness and social awkwardness of so many people born in the last 35 years, there's one more thing that has scientists beyond concerned – the ever-diminishing capacity for humans to stay focused.

Builders	Boomers	Generation X	Generation Y	Generation Z	Gen Alpha	Gen Beta
Born: 1925-1945	Born: 1946-1964	Born: 1965-1979	Born: 1980-1994	Born: 1995-2009	Born: 2010-2024	Born: 2025
Age: 80+	Age: 61-79	Age: 46-60	Age: 31-45	Age: 16-30	Age: 15 and under	

The seven generations.

Now, I know that next to genocides, raging wannabe author-itarians, melting ice caps threatening to sink whole countries, and the widening of the wealth gap, lack of focus might not be the most obvious cause for concern. But when you're in business, it can certainly become a glaring observation that leaves you scratching your head and asking, "How do I get anyone to focus?" These days, the average human attention span is all of 8 seconds.[76] Officially less than a fucking goldfish! *Seriously, a goldfish is more focussed* What an embarrassment for the so-called dominant species ...

When we say attention span, we're talking about the average time a person – adult, teen, child, or anywhere in between – can stay focused and concentrate on a single task, activity, or stimulus. The reasons are numerous as to why we, as humans, struggle in general to stay focused. They can include:

- **Lifestyle factors:** Stress, addiction, fatigue, being sedentary.

- **Mental health factors:** Anxiety, depression, neurodivergence.

- **Environmental factors:** Excessive noise, digital distractions, workplace pressures, attempting to multitask. *Maybe you just hate your job*

- **Emotional factors:** Personal issues, relationship problems, devaluing your priorities. *It'll still be there tomorrow*

ACTIVITY: PERFORM A FOCUS AUDIT

In the space provided, perform a focus audit. In the first column, document the areas of your business where you can see a lack of focus. In the second column, document which pillar is affected – customer, employee, or human if it's both. As you read through this chapter, reflect on your awareness and use it to ascertain how you can strategically tackle this challenge. We'll come back to the third column.

Area with Lack of Focus	Affected Pillar	Tactic

BEATING BOWERBIRD SYNDROME

When I was a child, I did a school project on the western bowerbird, ← *Different species from the blue-loving bowerbird* and I told my grandma about it. She responded with, "Ohhh, well, isn't that fitting?" I asked why, and she told me the bowerbird and I were alike – we were both easily distracted by shiny objects ← *Yes, as are many other animals, I've come to learn*

For the next 25 odd years, that remark didn't make much of a mark on me. Fast-forward to the point where I'm running my own business and I come across the magnetic *G'day, friends across the ditch* Lisa O'Neill from New Zealand. Lisa exudes energy. To be in the same vicinity as her is illuminating. Lisa also leads her own successful speaking practice and is known for her transformative retreats. Okay, so I'll calm down on the fangirling. The point being, one of the first times I heard Lisa speak, she talked about the death of focus. Maybe not in exactly those words, but essentially how we live in a world that's legitimately designed to pull us away from being 'in the moment' or 'in flow' with the work we need to complete in order to achieve our dreams. Lisa mentioned being distracted by shiny things, and considering her extravagant earring collection, I can see how that plays out.

Her words triggered the memory of my grandma recounting how, at an early age, I was easily distracted by the next shiny thing. I mean, I like to justify my distractions, as most of us do. For instance, my love for shiny things now includes collecting a bachelor's degree in public relations, two children, two marriages, qualifications in clinical psychotherapy *Not simultaneously* and hypnotherapy, a multitude of other credentials like a CCXP, an accreditation in advising family businesses, not to mention a great understanding of so many facets of business and life from years of wanting to learn about the next shiny thing. I could go on, but I don't want to brag too much about how successful my attachment to collecting shiny things has been over the years. It's not all good though.

In that moment, as Lisa spoke, it was all the not-so-brag-worthy shiny objects that sprang to mind, and I can tell you in all honesty, there are too many shit shiny things to list. We could start with my very bad habit of doom-scrolling when TikTok came out, ← *My inner 14-yo came out to play* which got so severe I'd lose 4 hours of my life on the regular. To try and curb myself, I found a function on my phone that disabled apps after a set time. I used it. It was great for getting me off TikTok. But I didn't set it for *See the justifying happening?* Instagram because, well, I needed that for business, and sometimes I could legitimately be on Insta for a couple of hours actually working. So colour me shocked when I realise one day that TikTok can now just be reposted to Instagram and, well, "Say hello to my little doomscroll friend."

What about my new love of buying books? Only to get halfway through each one as I come across a new must-read book every few weeks, watching the others *Sorry Stephen* pile up on my bedside table. ← *Covey, I'm trying*

Look, I could keep going, but my ultimate downfall is resistance. I don't have any mental or physical health conditions as a very justifiable excuse, I just have humanerisms. Or as I now refer to it in my speaking engagements, I was a sufferer of 'bowerbird syndrome'. That very day, listening to Lisa O'Neill, it dawned on me that I'd experienced so many instances where I lost focus, allowing myself to get distracted and, as a consequence, never quite achieve all I had set out to achieve. When you're your own boss, this can be a problem. I mean, who's really keeping you accountable? I had deadlines, but I was usually the one to set them, and just like high school – and I'm sure many reading this can relate – the best time to get onto a deadline is when? The last minute of course! During Lisa's talk, I realised I had to do some serious soul-searching and find tactics that could help me claw back my capacity to focus before I, like so many others, became worse than a fucking goldfish.

> Focus is the art of knowing what to ignore."
> – *James Clear*

I began really concentrating on my behaviour. Tuning in to how often I was tuning out, you could say, and I tell you, it was worse than I had already given myself shit for. I know you might be reading this wondering, *Why is she admitting how crap she was?* Well, because in some ways, we all are, and it takes a little bit of vulnerability to sit in that and accept there's likely a reason that explains why we haven't That we're in control of if we're honest achieved all we set out to achieve. with ourselves

Any neurodivergents reading this, I see you too, but even if you're on a spectrum or five, there are many excellent resources available to support and guide you into focus strategies that work specifically for you. I know not everyone is the same and what works for one isn't guaranteed to work for the other. *That's the human experience* Reclaiming your focus is about doing the deep work of reflection, of testing tactics, of holding yourself accountable to finding ways to sustain focus, customisable to your needs. *And being kind to ourselves in the process*

After reflecting and self-assessing my misguided use of the precious resource of time, the first step in beating my so-called 'bowerbird syndrome' was to draw a metaphorical line in the sand. In my brain and in my body, I had to be on the same page, knowing that enough was enough. I was doing myself a disservice, and this might sound like tripe, but I was doing a disservice to all the humans that should have known *This book could have come out in 2019 if I'd stayed focussed* about me but didn't because I was too busy resisting doing the work.

Once my body and mind were on the same page, I took on one of Lisa O'Neill's brilliant suggestions of making myself a 'to-don't' list. I had never heard of it before, but it absolutely made sense. In its basic form, it's a list of the 12 common themes that come up when you ask yourself *why* you're doing this. For me, it was time to *not* do those things that hijacked my focus, and having a to-don't list that hung right beside my laptop shockingly became a simple and effective reminder *Visible from all angles of my desk* to stop being a bowerbird. Stop getting distracted. Stop losing focus. Stop losing sight of your purpose. Stay on track.

Now, by no means was that the end and I was all fixed. I still had other areas of my work and life that needed fresh tactics to mitigate being a bowerbird. I started a business coaching program for SME business owners where they're required to post their week's priorities, and I lead by example by doing the same. I mean, if you can't have a boss, there are other creative ways to hold yourself accountable to stop being a bowerbird. For example, if I expected my members to post their priorities, as a leader I should hold myself to the same expectations. ←———— *Remember how the Pygmalion Effect works*

At home, I would start to look for ideas for dinner and very quickly get dragged back into my old doomscroll habits. I would get so annoyed with myself that I decided to find a new way to mitigate my resistance. I found a meal planning app that allowed me to arrange all my family's meals for the week, create a shopping list, and get me off my device sooner. So far, all of these tactics have allowed me to get back to what I know needs to be done, ←———— *Like finally finishing this book* even the hard stuff that doesn't feel very CEHX-y, but we all know it's the 1%ers that make the difference.

So if you're only human and feel like bowerbird syndrome is a daily challenge preventing you ←———— *Or your team or even your family members* from getting where you know you should be, what will you do to change that?

As I explain to my therapy and business clients, the only person who can commit to change and be in control of that change is you.

I mean sure, you can engage someone else to partner up with you and help keep you accountable, but at the end of the day, you're still the one who has to make the very conscious decision 'to don't' do what you always do. To choose productivity or even choose to relax. ← *Shout-out to my recovering busy bitches* Because on the flip side of not getting shit done is the group of business folk who push so hard that, if they don't tune in to themselves, might find that while they're achieving their lofty goals, they're doing it at the expense of themselves and those around them. I'm not saying success can wait or the grind isn't worth it, I'm just saying that a value-driven brand and a value-driven life go hand in hand.

You can't go back and make a new start, but you can start right now and make a brand new ending."
– *James R Sherman*

So, how do you start where you are to change the ending? The folks at Harvard ← *They know some stuff* have studied areas that can assist us meagre mortals in bouncing back from our bouts of bowerbird syndrome.[77] Even if you just start small, again, it's those 1%ers that really add up. So, what's the treatment plan? you ask ...

- **Track your lack of attention:** Observe situations where you lose focus. Is there a pattern? Are you showing resistance for a particular reason, for example, needing more skills or resources? Or is the task something you don't value as much as you wish you could?

- **Practise mindfulness meditation:** This form of meditation teaches you how to bring your thoughts back to the present when your mind veers off. The practice also helps manage anxiety and stress, which can contribute to a lack of focus. I like to imagine a baseball mitt catching my thoughts, helping me reset my mindfulness.

- **Get organised:** Create a five-point priority list every day and aim to achieve at least three goals, with the other two being bonus activities. Utilise Pomodoro or *I don't call them tasks, as it creates resistance* other timekeeping and productivity tools that help you not just work in blocks but, importantly, also help you take replenishing breaks. Use your business goals to keep you on track. If any new opportunities arise, take them only if they drive those goals to become reality. Keep your eyes firmly peeled and on the road. *Get an accountability buddy if needed*

- **Minimise distractions:** Turn your devices to 'do not disturb', including your email inbox, for a working block and only check them after achieving X amount of working blocks. Unclutter your workspace. Be transparent with your team and communicate what you need from them to achieve your goals, for example, no distractions for 2 hours.

Explain why – it always starts with why and what's in it for them ... WIIFM ←

- **Swap it out:** Turn doomscrolling into something that actually engages your brain, for example, only watch content on becoming an AI whiz or how to develop your brand awareness or anything that drives benefits to your brand or life.

- **Give multitasking the flick:** Modern-day science backs up that effective multitasking is bullshit and our brains can't effectively multitask multiple activities that require effort.[78] It's important to have a level of awareness about what you're doing, staying conscious and not going into autopilot despite how much the brain loves shutting down. If you find yourself multitasking, it's a red flag moment where you need to stop and analyse why you're trying to do so much to the detriment of *everything*. For those of you saying, "Nahhh, I'm really good at multitasking," you might be, but it's now proven to activate the body's stress response, which isn't great for your nervous system or your sanity.[79] Your cognitive ability also suffers, as you actually become *more* distractible, and research shows that chronic multitaskers display lower levels of executive control.[80]

For you and business to develop into a CEHX-centric value-driven brand, we must fight back against bowerbird syndrome. I know there's shiny shit everywhere – that's the universe testing you, tempting you into failure. There's no prize for being too busy, which is just another form of resistance, and there's no prize for being a bowerbird, ⟵ *Or a fucking goldfish* so together let's fight the good fight. A revolution against bullshit algorithms and self-sabotage. Taking control starts today!

TL;CBF

- Humanity's greatest loss is our capacity to focus – we're constantly searching for instant gratification.

- The average human now has an attention span lower than a goldfish.

- I refer to our lack of attention as 'bowerbird syndrome', as we're always distracted by the next shiny thing and unable to control our impulses to stay on the path of getting shit done.

- Bowerbird syndrome is 100 percent within our control, and there are many tactics we can implement to help us fight back and regain our concentration.

- In practising the art of knowing what to ignore, we miraculously start to experience more aligned opportunities that further drive us to achieve a value-driven brand and a value-driven life.

ACTIVITY: COMMIT TO CHANGE TODAY

1. Go back to the previous activity on page 348 and add any new examples that came up while reading.

2. In the third column, draft at least one tactic you could implement that could mitigate bowerbird syndrome in your brand, in your life, or both. If you think that tactic might require a support buddy or accountability partner, note who that might be, but remember, it's your responsibility to draw the line in the sand and make the change you need to make ... the change you **want** to make.

3. Go and make it happen, because that change **starts today**!

CHAPTER 18:
THE JOY OF CEHX

YOU'VE CHANGED

Collectively, we've chewed the fat over so many areas, such as designing your business to become a trusted and value-driven brand through being an organisation that attracts the right humans for your ← *Human-centred* vision. We've established that the right type of employees, living for your brand vision, actively encouraged to be candid and, when necessary, organisational contrarians, are ← *Those who oppose the popular but offer discernment* magnets for customers who love and can't get enough of you. We've dived into how we as *Customer-centric* ⌐ humans process information and whether the communication strategies you have now are serving you to deliver a clear, concise, and consistent message. ← *Not to forget candid inside our brand* We've talked about information overwhelm and the dangers of autopilot in its capacity to stunt innovation and business growth, as well as personal growth. We've discussed strategically getting out of our boxer-short comfy zone.

We've casually hooked you up with insights into designing a customer and employee journey that delivers on the 'jobs to be done' and creates a reliable and safe environment for both cohorts to feel like they *belong* to a community, not an environment they have to shoehorn themselves to fit into.

We've touched on the brand benefits of being accessible and diverse. Not the woke and broke version but the version in which you, as a business leader, comprehend that in building your brand to be accessible and diverse, ← *Equitable shouldn't be passed over either* you open up to markets and profit centres other businesses haven't even conceived. Now, the disclaimer on this is I'm an able-bodied, white woman. I joke that I'm the whitest Greek I know, but then I stand next to my twin sister and realise she is. Anyway, despite the jokes, the point is, I highly recommend finding an expert in diversity who can speak from lived experience. Don't 'do a Trump' and hold a cabinet meeting about women's issues with only men in attendance.[81] This is dead arse the real joke. If you're considering making your brand more accessible, more diverse, and, when done well, more profitable, find an expert in the field and start the conversation. Just like you, they like to be paid for their skills and experience, so please don't get out there expecting them to do the homework for you without being paid. Do some research first, gather some quality questions, and *Again, this HX strategy done right is profit $$* book a consultation. ←

The beauty of CEHX is it really is the whole pie. Everything in your business aligns to it, whether you realise it or not. We know that customer experience is more than just the way ↖ *Hopefully now you do realise it* we show up and service customers. We know that for an employee to stay loyal, they need to feel a sense of autonomy, the capacity for mastery, and intrinsic alignment to a purpose bigger than them. We already knew how fickle humans are, but at least for the next couple of generations, they're our employees and our customers, so understanding what we can do to help them enhance their human experience is part of being of service. Now, that statement can hit differently depending on the individual, but if you're in business, you should already understand that you're in the business of being of service. Not in a submissive, no authority, no boundaries kind of way, but in the way you understand that the human experience is amplified by the simple act of bringing joy to another human. ← *Love those serotonin hits*

The thing about CEHX is, as you implement it into your business, turning yourself into a trusted and value-driven brand, you'll start to take those lessons and apply them to your life. In turn, practising a value-driven life. It's when all the pillars – **C**ustomer, **E**mployee, **H**uman e**X**perience – are strategically designed to align and work together, and not against one another, that you, your team, your customers, your friends, and your family will all feel the shift, the *transformation*. They'll remark, "You've changed."

In response, I want you to knowingly smile and say, "Yes, I have, thank you for noticing."

You've created a community of advocates, and what you're feeling is the effervescent joy of CEHX.

Community is much more than belonging to something; it's about doing something together that makes belonging matter."

– *Brian Solis*

NOW WHAT?
CONTINUE YOUR JOURNEY
TO EXPERIENCE THE
JOY OF CEHX

As a business owner, I know how difficult it can be to break the cycle of the daily grind. Testing out new ways to get things done, achieve your goals, and still find the energy to be an invested and engaged human in everything else outside of your business. Here's what I hope you take away from this book: there are tactics and activities that, while they require a new-found commitment to change, will not only amplify your customer experience but also amplify every other area of your life.

As you well understand by now, the journey to experiencing the joy of CEHX isn't just for business; it's for life. It's the very start to an education that has the potential to exponentially transform you, should you commit.

My vision is to support 10 million business owners, leaders, and entrepreneurs in developing their own trusted and value-driven brands. My vision is to see them change so much that those around them aspire to be like them. My vision is to see them impact others so significantly that humanity is made all the better for it. That's a value-driven life.

If you've read this far, I believe that you have this potential within you. You are the instigator, the change-maker, the sparkler in the dark.

I know all of this can feel overwhelming, ← *Yes, it's a lot to take in* so to help you know where to start, I set you this challenge. For the next 30 days, do nothing discussed in this book. Instead, for the next month, I challenge you to only observe and document the following daily:

- What did we do today that made someone want to tell others about us?

- What was the general sentiment of the team today (positive, neutral, negative) – why?

- Did I fall into traps of distraction, resistance, or excessive problem resolution (yes or no)?

- On a scale of 0–5, how satisfied am I that we all achieved our goals today (0 being not at all – it was a dumpster-fire day – and 5 being absolutely achieved them all)

From this observation set, I want you to come back with a fresh outlook on what areas of your business need immediate attention, remembering that setting your priorities is key to achieving your goals. Like with anything worthwhile, achieving the joy of CEHX can take time, commitment, and energy – but how good is it when it all comes together?!

The steps to great CEHX are here in this book. In saying that, it is the *causal hook-up* to understanding how to design your customer, employee, and human experience for maximum joy. There's so much more to teach, to learn, and to do that's not covered in this book. Areas such as:

- Customer service design and implementation
- Customer recovery and staying trusted in the hearts of the humans you serve
- Applying your marketing efforts to your new-found personas and journey maps
- Developing your own leadership qualities
- Designing products and services using systems thinking
- Setting up your business to utilise grants and tenders
- Recruiting from a difficult talent pool in a difficult economic landscape
- So, so much more!

With that, I encourage you to stay curious. Continuous learning and growing your adaptability quotient (AQ) is all a part of this CEHX-y journey. Develop practices to investigate these topics and design and apply them to fit your brand. CEHX isn't a project. Projects have an end date. Invigorating CEHX is forever.

Should you decide Aileen on the page isn't enough, you can always get in touch to engage my services, no matter where you are in the world. I want you to know I'm in your corner, and together we'll transform your business into the brand you deserve, landing on the right side of the statistics, to the exasperation of your competition and to the advocacy of all who have the good fortune to experience your trusted and value-driven brand.

Here's to having great CEHX.

ACKNOWLEDGEMENTS

First and foremost, I want to acknowledge my husband, NailZ Van Diggele. Without you, this investment wouldn't have been made. You invested in me in a way no one ever has before. Thank you for being my illustrator and my partner in this value-driven life.

To Archer, thank you for getting excited about all of my consequential and even inconsequential milestones whilst writing this book. I adore that my teenage son considers me brag-worthy. To Laife, thank you for justifying a good 2 years of resistance in getting this book published. We got there in the end, with tenacity to spare.

To my amazing and willing publishing team at Dean Publishing, the way you have let me be me in my writing is something I am beyond grateful for. I am not for everyone, and I am so appreciative that you support me in being genuinely me to attract the right audience, helping us all feel authentically valued.

To you, reading and learning from this book, I legitimately thank you. Whether you paid money for this book or somehow bootlegged it, I only care that you do something that benefits you creating a value-driven brand and a value-driven life. The world needs you to stay in business, innovating and passionately designing advocacy-generating CEHX. You having the opportunity to build a legacy is why I wrote this book.

ABOUT THE AUTHOR

Aileen Day is the founder of Aileen Day Advisory. As the Principal CX Advisor, Aileen uses her 20-plus years of experience working throughout some of Australia's most trusted brands to help her clients' organisations become commercially smart by learning to deliver value-driven customer-, employee-, and human-centric experiences. Aileen is also a practising Public Relations Specialist and Clinical Psychotherapist and Hypnotherapist, an unusual combination but one that allows her to support her clients in many facets of business and life.

Aileen's work is industry-agnostic, and she enjoys proliferating the joy of CEHX all over the world, helping business leaders gain the clarity and skills to implement the pillars of the Customer, Employee, and Human eXperience into their business strategies.

Aileen is also on the board of directors for XMGlobal Collaborative, a worldwide association designed to bring together a global community of experience management (XM) professionals, aimed at unifying and educating organisations globally on the importance of XM and its strengths in strategic collaboration.

Aileen uses her warm yet pragmatic and candid personality to cut through the resistance. She is raw and engaging, and thrives on being the solution provider and professional cheerleader to those wanting to make a meaningful difference with their organisation and in their lives.

aileenday.com.au

END NOTES

1   Sinek S (5 May 2010) 'How Great Leaders Inspire Action | Simon Sinek | TED', *TED*, YouTube, accessed 7 April 2025, https://youtu.be/qp0HIF3SfI4.

2   Barney N (2024) 'What Is Customer Experience (CX) and Why Is It Important?', *TechTarget*, accessed 8 April 2025, https://www.techtarget.com/searchcustomerexperience/definition/customer-experience-CX.

3   Norris CJ (2021) 'The Negativity Bias, Revisited: Evidence from Neuroscience Measures and an Individual Differences Approach', *Social Neuroscience*, 16(1):68–82, doi.org/10.1080/17470919.2019.1696225.

4   McClelland B (13 March 2017) 'Let's Talk About CEX, Baby', *LinkedIn*, accessed 9 April 2025, https://www.linkedin.com/pulse/lets-talk-cex-baby-bernadette-mcclelland/.

5   Sato K (30 August 2023) 'Business Failure Rate Reaches 15-Year High, National Retail Association Calls for Government Action', *ABC News*, accessed 9 April 2025, https://www.abc.net.au/news/2023-08-30/business-failure-rate-worsens-calls-for-government-action/102788742; Australian Small Business and Family Enterprise Ombudsman (2023) 'Small Business Matters' *Australian Government*, accessed 9 April 2025, https://www.asbfeo.gov.au/sites/default/files/2023-06/Small%20Business%20Matters_June%202023.pdf.

6   Main K (31 January 2023) 'Top Small Business Statistics', *Forbes*, accessed 9 April 2025, https://www.forbes.com/advisor/business/small-business-statistics/.

7   Espinosa C (2 September 2024) 'One-Year Business Survival Rates in Selected European Countries in 2018, By Country', Statista, accessed 9 April 2025, https://www.statista.com/statistics/1114070/eu-business-survival-rates-by-country.

8   Kotashev K (9 January 2024) 'Startup Failure Rate: How Many Startups Fail and Why in 2024?', *Failory*, accessed 9 April 2025, https://www.failory.com/blog/startup-failure-rate.

9   Passport to Tarde 2.0 (n.d.) 'Business Culture', *Businessculture.org*, https://businessculture.org/business-culture/.

10 Cameron KS and Quinn RE (2006) *Diagnosing and Changing Organizational Culture*, Jossey-Bass, San Francisco.

11   LinkedIn News Europe (18 January 2023) 'LinkedIn Jobs on the Rise
        2023: The Roles That Are Growing in Demand Across Europe', *LinkedIn,*
        accessed 10 April 2025, https://www.linkedin.com/pulse/linkedin-jobs-
        rise-2023-roles-growing-demand-across-/.

12   Bodine K (16 July 2012) 'Strategy: The First Step Towards Creating A
        Great Customer Experience', *Forrester,* accessed 11 April 2025, https://
        www.forrester.com/blogs/12-07-16-strategy_the_first_step_towards_
        creating_a_great_customer_experience/.

13   CXPA (n.d.) 'Core CX Competencies', accessed 11 April 2025, https://
        www.cxpa.org/earn-your-ccxp/competencies.

14   Allen J, Reichheld FF, Hamilton B, and Markey R (2005) 'Closing the
        Delivery Gap', *Bain and Company,* accessed 11 April 2025, https://media.
        bain.com/bainweb/PDFs/cms/hotTopics/closingdeliverygap.pdf.

15   Pine II BJ and Gilmore JH (2011) *The Experience Economy,* Harvard
        Business Review Press, Boston.

16   Userpilot Team (n.d.) 'How to Measure Customer Loyalty In SaaS: 10
        Important Metrics to Track and Improve', *Userpilot,* accessed 11 April
        2025, https://userpilot.com/blog/measure-customer-loyalty/.

17   Ramaswami R (2020) 'Brand Strategies Focused on Dependability Score
        Highest on Customer Trust', *Gartner,* accessed 14 April 2025, https://
        www.gartner.com/en/marketing/insights/articles/brand-strategies-
        focused-dependability-score-highest.

18   Levy HP (2019) 'Effortless Experience Explained', *Gartner,* accessed 14
        April 2025, https://www.gartner.com/smarterwithgartner/effortless-expe-
        rience-explained.

19   McLeod S (14 March 2025) 'Maslow's Hierarchy of Needs', *Simply
        Psychology*, accessed 14 April 2025, https://www.simplypsychology.org/
        maslow.html.

20   CXPA (2024) 'CXPA CX Framework', accessed 15 April 2025, https://
        www.cxpa.org/earn-your-ccxp/cxframework.

21   Wainwright R (2018) *Rocky Road: The Incredible True Story of The
        Fractured Family Behind the Darrell Lea Chocolate Empire*, Allen & Unwin,
        Crows Nest, NSW.

22   IKEA (n.d.) 'Benefits When Working for Us – IKEA', accessed 16 April
        2025, https://www.ikea.com/au/en/this-is-ikea/work-with-us/bene-
        fits-pub8c6da021/;

23   Smith F (17 December 2015) 'IKEA Buys Employee Loyalty with $152
        Million Gift', *Australian Financial Review,* accessed 16 April 2025, https://
        www.afr.com/companies/retail/ikeas-buys-employee-loyalty-with-152-
        million-gift-20151216-glomrc.

24   Deloitte (n.d.) 'Customer Loyalty: A Relationship, Not Just a Scheme', accessed 16 April 2025, https://www2.deloitte.com/tw/en/pages/consumer-business/articles/gx-consumer-review.html.

25   Dunn M (2025) 'Research: Is a Picture Worth 1,000 Words or 60,000 Words in Marketing?', *Email Audience,* accessed 16 April 2025, https://www.emailaudience.com/research-picture-worth-1000-words-marketing/.

26   Murphy N (10 November 2021) 'Types of Bias', *CPD Online College,* accessed 3 July 2025, https://cpdonline.co.uk/knowledge-base/safeguarding/types-of-bias.

27   Bell S (n.d.) 'SMART Goals', *Mindtools,* accessed 22 April 2025, https://www.mindtools.com/a4wo118/smart-goals.

28   Hill N (1937) *Think and Grow Rich,* The Ralston Society.

29   Afshar V (6 December 2017) '50 Important Customer Experience Stats for Business Leaders', *HuffPost,* accessed 3 July 2025, https://www.huffpost.com/entry/50-important-customer-exp_b_8295772.

30   Pink D (2010) *Drive: The Surprising Truth About What Motivates Us,* Canongate Books, Edinburgh.

31   People Insight (2025) 'People Insight Model: PEARL™', accessed 28 April 2025, https://peopleinsight.co.uk/wp-content/uploads/2025/03/PEARL-rebranded-2024.pdf.

32   People Insight (2025) 'People Insight Model: PEARL™', accessed 28 April 2025, https://peopleinsight.co.uk/wp-content/uploads/2025/03/PEARL-rebranded-2024.pdf.

33   Jefferey R (n.d.) 'Where Does HR Come from? A Brief History of the People Profession', *People Management,* accessed 28 April 2025, https://www.peoplemanagement.co.uk/article/1746498/where-hr-come-from-brief-history-people-profession.

34   Woodard A (2017) 'The Best and Worst HR Names', *Australian HR Institute,* accessed 28 April 2025, https://www.hronline.com.au/section/featured/best-worst-hr-names/.

35   Australian Council of Social Service (n.d.) 'Poverty in Australia', accessed 28 April 2025, https://povertyandinequality.acoss.org.au/poverty/.

36   Shrider EA, Kollar M, Chen F, and Semega J (14 September 2021) 'Income and Poverty in the United States: 2020', *United States Census Bureau,* accessed 28 April 2025, https://www.census.gov/library/publications/2021/demo/p60-273.html.

37   Eurostat (2024) 'Living Conditions in Europe - Poverty and Social Exclusion', *European Union,* accessed 28 April 2025, https://ec.europa.eu/eurostat/statistics-explained/index.php?title=Living_conditions_in_Europe_-_poverty_and_social_exclusion.

38   Fair Work Ombudsman (n.d.) 'Minimum Wages', accessed 28 April 2025, https://www.fairwork.gov.au/pay-and-wages/minimum-wages.

39   U.S. Department of Labor (1 January 2025) 'State Minimum Wage Laws', accessed 28 April 2025, https://www.dol.gov/agencies/whd/minimum-wage/state.

40   Pink D (2010) *Drive: The Surprising Truth About What Motivates Us*, Canongate Books, Edinburgh.

41   McLeod S (14 March 2025) 'Maslow's Hierarchy of Needs', *Simply Psychology*, accessed 29 April 2025, https://www.simplypsychology.org/maslow.html.

42   Pabilonia SW and Redmon JJ (2024) 'The Rise in Remote Work Since the Pandemic and Its Impact on Productivity', *Beyond the Numbers: Productivity,* 13(8), https://www.bls.gov/opub/btn/volume-13/remote-work-productivity.htm.

43   Oxford Economics (2014) 'The Cost of Brain Drain: Understanding the Financial Impact of Staff Turnover February 2014', accessed 9 May 2025, https://www.oxfordeconomics.com/wp-content/uploads/2023/05/cost-brain-drain-report.pdf.

44   Scott K (2017) *Radical Candor: How to Get What You Want by Saying What You Mean,* Macmillan, London.

45   Emmett J, Komm A, Moritz S, and Schultz F (30 September 2021) 'This Time It's Personal: Shaping the "New Possible" Through Employee Experience', *McKinsey & Company,* accessed 9 May 2025, https://www.mckinsey.com/capabilities/people-and-organizational-performance/our-insights/this-time-its-personal-shaping-the-new-possible-through-employee-experience.

46   Startup Gnome (2022) 'The State of the Global Startup Economy', accessed 9 May 2025, https://startupgenome.com/article/the-state-of-the-global-startup-economy.

47   Swan M (24 January 2024) 'The Scalable Lifecycle: 4 Phases of Business Growth (or Decay)', *Scalable,* accessed 9 May 2025, https://scalable.co/library/the-scalable-lifecycle-4-phases-of-business-growth-or-decay/.

48   Alchemer (n.d.) 'Unlocking CX Excellence: Use Gartner's Maturity Model to Evolve Your Customer Experience', accessed 9 May 2025, https://www.alchemer.com/resources/blog/unlocking-cx-excellence-use-gartners-maturity-model-to-evolve-your-customer-experience/.

49   Moran A (8 February 2021) '15 In-Demand Jobs that Didn't Exist 10 Years Ago', *CareerAddict,* accessed 19 May 2025, https://www.careeraddict.com/12-jobs-that-didn-t-exist-10-years-ago.

50   Eads A (27 March 2025) 'Leadership vs. Management: When to Manage and When to Lead', *Indeed,* accessed 19 May 2025, https://www.indeed.com/career-advice/career-development/when-to-manage-vs-when-to-lead.

51   Merriam-Webster (n.d.) 'Culture', accessed 20 May 2025, https://www.merriam-webster.com/dictionary/culture.

52   Comparably (2024) 'Best Company Culture 2024', accessed 20 May 2025, https://www.comparably.com/awards/winners/best-company-culture-2024-large.

53   Education and Health Standing Committee (2015) 'The Impact of FIFO Work Practices on Mental Health', *Legislative Assembly Parliament of Western Australia*, accessed 20 May 2025, https://www.parliament.wa.gov.au/Parliament/commit.nsf/(Report+Lookup+by+Com+ID)/2E970A7A4934026448257E67002BF9D1/$file/20150617%20-%20Final%20Report%20w%20signature%20for%20website.pdf; King T, Humaira M, Taouk Y, and LaMontagne AD (2023) 'Suicide in the Australian Mining Industry: A National Study', *Mates in Mining,* accessed 20 May 2025, https://mates.org.au/media/documents/Suicide-in-the-Australian-Mining-Industry-Report-2023-%C6%92.pdf.

54   Pink D (2010) *Drive: The Surprising Truth About What Motivates Us,* Canongate Books, Edinburgh.

55   Rushe D (2 June 2022) 'Elon Musk Tells Employees to Return to Office or "Pretend to Work" Elsewhere', *The Guardian,* accessed 20 May 2025, https://www.theguardian.com/technology/2022/jun/01/elon-musk-return-to-office-pretend-to-work-somewhere-else.

56   Maurer R (14 February 2022) 'Recruiters Respond to the Great Resignation in 2022', *SHRM,* accessed 20 May 2025, https://www.shrm.org/topics-tools/news/talent-acquisition/recruiters-respond-to-great-resignation-2022.

57   Atlassian (n.d.) 'ShipIt', accessed 20 May 2025, https://www.atlassian.com/company/shipit.

58   Intercom (31 August 2017) 'Atlassian's Dom Price on Scaling Team Culture', *The Ticket,* podcast, accessed 20 May 2025, https://www.intercom.com/blog/podcasts/atlassian-dom-price-team-culture/.

59   Governance Institute of Australia (n.d.) 'A Behaviour Science Approach to Organisational Culture', accessed 20 May 2025, https://www.governanceinstitute.com.au/news_media/a-behaviour-science-approach-to-organisational-culture/.

60   Natoli S (2020) 'Eating Together White Paper - January 2020 PDF', *Scribd,* accessed 20 May 2025, https://www.scribd.com/document/468878169/Eating-Together-White-Paper-January-2020-pdf.

61   Strijbosch W, Mitas O, Gisbergen MV, Doicaru M, Gelissen J, and Bastiaansen M (2019), 'From Experience to Memory: On the Robustness of the Peak-and-End-Rule for Complex, Heterogeneous Experiences', *Frontiers in Psychology,* 10, doi.org/10.3389/fpsyg.2019.01705.

62   Bohn RE and Short JE (2009) 'HMI? How Much Information?', *Global Information Industry Center,* accessed 23 May 2025, https://group47.com/HMI_2009_ConsumerReport_Dec9_2009.pdf.

63   Kolb B and Gibb R (2011) 'Brain Plasticity and Behaviour in the Developing Brain', *Journal of the Canadian Academy of Child and Adolescent Psychiatry*, 20(4):265–276, https://pubmed.ncbi.nlm.nih.gov/22114608/.

64   Millas C (n.d.) 'The Brain's 3 Main Filters – Distortion, Deletion & Generalisation', *ChrisMillas.com*, accessed 27 May 2025, https://chrismillas.com/distort-delete-generalise/.

65   Rosenthal R and Jacobson L (1968) 'Pygmalion in the Classroom', *The Urban Review*:16–20, *https://sites.tufts.edu/tuftsliteracycorps/files/2017/02/Pygmalion-in-the-Classroom.pdf.*

66   Prosci (n.d.) 'The Prosci ADKAR Model', accessed 30 May 2025, https://www.prosci.com/methodology/adkar.

67   Ryan P (26 June 2015) 'Australia Post to Slash 1,900 Jobs Amid $500m Mail Losses; Boss Warns of "Tipping Point" as Letters Business Plunges', *ABC News*, accessed 2 June 2025, https://www.abc.net.au/news/2015-06-26/australia-post-to-slash-1900-jobs-amid-mail-losses/6574752.

68   Dunn M (2025) 'Research: Is a Picture Worth 1,000 Words or 60,000 Words in Marketing?', *Email Audience*, accessed 16 April 2025, https://www.emailaudience.com/research-picture-worth-1000-words-marketing/.

69   UMatter (n.d.) 'Understanding Your Communication Style', *Princeton University*, accessed 3 July 2025, https://umatter.princeton.edu/respect/tools/communication-styles.

70   Market Research Future (June 2025) 'Global Gamification Market Research Report', accessed 6 June 2025, https://www.marketresearchfuture.com/reports/gamification-market-11313.

71   Smartico (10 January 2025) 'Psychology of Gamification', accessed 10 June 2025, https://www.smartico.ai/blog-post/psychology-gamification.

72   Scheiber N (2 April 2017) 'How Uber Uses Psychological Tricks to Push Its Drivers' Buttons', *New York Times*, accessed 11 June 2025, https://www.nytimes.com/interactive/2017/04/02/technology/uber-drivers-psychological-tricks.html.

73   US Department of Justice (21 February 2020) 'Wells Fargo Agrees to Pay $3 Billion to Resolve Criminal and Civil Investigations into Sales Practices Involving the Opening of Millions of Accounts Without Customer Authorization', accessed 11 June 2025, https://www.justice.gov/archives/opa/pr/wells-fargo-agrees-pay-3-billion-resolve-criminal-and-civil-investigations-sales-practices.

74   Solon O (10 November 2017) 'Ex-Facebook President Sean Parker: Site Made to Exploit human "Vulnerability"', *The Guardian*, accessed 11 June 2025, https://www.theguardian.com/technology/2017/nov/09/facebook-sean-parker-vulnerability-brain-psychology.

75   Arora C and Razavian M (2021) 'Ethics of Gamification in Health and Fitness-Tracking', *International Journal of Environmental Research and Public Health*, 18(21), doi.org/10.3390/ijerph182111052.

76   McSpadden K (14 May 2015) 'You Now Have a Shorter Attention Span Than a Goldfish', *Time Magazine,* accessed 11 June 2025, https://time.com/3858309/attention-spans-goldfish/.

77   Harvard Health Publishing (1 February 2020) 'Focus on Concentration', *Harvard Medical School,* accessed 12 June 2025, https://www.health.harvard.edu/mind-and-mood/focus-on-concentration.

78   Rubinstein JS, Meyer DE, and Evans JE (2001) 'Executive Control of Cognitive Processes in Task Switching', *Journal of Experimental Psychology: Human Perception and Performance,* 27(4):763–797, doi.org/10.1037//0096-1523.27.4.763.

79   Becker L, Kaltenegger HC, Nowak D, Weigl M, and Rohleder N (2023) 'Biological Stress Responses to Multitasking and Work Interruptions: A Randomized Controlled Trial', *Psychoneuroendocrinology,* 156, doi.org/10.1016/j.psyneuen.2023.106358.

80   Rubinstein JS, Meyer DE, and Evans JE (2001) 'Executive Control of Cognitive Processes in Task Switching', *Journal of Experimental Psychology: Human Perception and Performance,* 27(4):763–797, doi.org/10.1037//0096-1523.27.4.763.

81   BBC News (24 March 2017) 'All-Male White House Health Bill Photo Sparks Anger', *BBC,* accessed 12 June 2025, https://www.bbc.com/news/world-us-canada-39375228